W9-BWI-730

MORALITY AND THE MYSTICAL BODY

MORALITY AND THE MYSTICAL BODY

By
EMILE MERSCH, S.J.

Translated by
DANIEL F. RYAN, S.J.

P. J. KENEDY & SONS
PUBLISHERS NEW YORK

IMPRIMI POTEST

JAMES H. DOLAN, S.J.
Praepositus Prov. Novae Angliae
July 31, 1939.

NIHIL OBSTAT

ARTHUR J. SCANLAN, S.T.D.
Censor Librorum

IMPRIMATUR

✠ FRANCIS J. SPELLMAN
Archbishop New York

October 20, 1939

Printed in U. S. A.

Translator's Preface

An ever-increasing interest is observable among the faithful in the doctrine of the Mystical Body of Christ. Numerous books, including the author's "The Whole Christ," have explained the doctrine and established its truth from Scripture and Tradition. Father Mersch's "Morale et Corps Mystique" applies this beautiful doctrine to the everyday problems of individuals and of nations.

An effort has been made to preserve the meaning of the original as exactly as possible. Some may, however, take exception to the translation of the important word "démarche". It has been variously translated in the pages which follow as "Way of Life", "procedure", "action", etc. No one of these is adequate and as the word is entering rather largely into English usage, it might have been better to keep the word itself.

Approximately seven pages of the original have been omitted in the interest of conciseness.

Scriptural texts wherever used are cited according to the Douay version.

I gratefully acknowledge my indebtedness to Rev. Walter van de Putte, C.S.Sp., LL.D., for helpful advice and to a number of my brothers in the Society for their customary eagerness to help in gracious and little ways. Quam bonum et quam jucundum. . . .

In the year 1940 the Society of Jesus will celebrate the four hundredth anniversary of the approval of the first formula of her Institute by Pope Paul III. One of her sons, in loving return for love received, offers her this translation Ad Majorem Dei Gloriam.

Author's Preface

This volume is not a treatise, but a series of studies. The studies are a rather thorough revision of articles which have appeared in different reviews, especially in the Nouvelle Revue Théologique.

They have been arranged as far as possible in a logical order: first those which treat especially of the general principles, then those which deal with certain particular applications.

The grouping has involved some modifications: the omission of repetitions, the transposition of developments. These changes, together with a number of corrections and increased detail, give a desired cohesion to the group.

We have not been able to avoid some repetition for the subjects treated are so neighborly that their development could scarcely help passing twice by the same place.

We could wish that the changes were more radical. It is an entire Moral Science which we would like to have constructed, a Moral Science specifically Christian and theological, a Moral Science whose principles would be the great Christian dogmas of the Trinity, of the Incarnation and of the Incorporation through Grace in the Incarnate Word, a Moral Science which would address itself to the members of Christ inasmuch as they are members of Christ and to the children of adoption inasmuch as they are children of adoption.

But the work would have been too vast, and, as we had already been delayed for a long time by studies on the speculative theology of the same subject, the Mystical Body, we could foresee its realization only in a distant and uncertain future.

We have then decided to retouch to some extent the studies which have already appeared and to publish them. We are, therefore, happy to give this response to requests which have come from many quarters. This series of studies is incomplete, certainly, but our desire is to suggest at least the spirit of supernatural ethics, the spirit of the precept of Charity.

The unifying idea is that the Christian law is essentially positive even and especially in its demands of sacrifice and of mortification: its purpose is that the divine seed may increase at whatever cost. Optimism then, but optimism which, far from denying suffering, illumines it, the optimism of redeemed and risen men.

Just as incorporation in Christ and union with the entire Trinity through Christ are the most magnificent gift which man could receive in the order of being, so the power and the blessed obligation of detaching oneself from oneself in order to act as a member of Christ and as God's son of adoption is the most splendid grace which could fall to man in the order of the will.

Such is the goodness of God that His orders are in the first place benefits: He claims complete possession of our soul only to fill it totally, and if He requires the offering of all our being, it is not to annihilate it, but to divinise it quite entirely.

"The Way of the Lord is mercy and goodness," sang the Psalms in the Old Testament. What must be said now that Christ Himself has become our Way? Ego sum via . . . nemo vadit ad Patrem nisi per Me.

Contents

		PAGE
	Translator's Preface	v
	Author's Preface	vii
CHAPTER		
I	Religion, Christianity, Catholicism	3
II	Christianity	19
III	Catholicism	38
	General Principles	
IV	The Incarnation and Spiritual Doctrine	61
V	Holiness of Christians, Holiness of Members	97
VI	Prayers of Christians, Prayers of Members	115
VII	All Priest in the Unique Priest	138
VIII	The Mystical Body and Contemporary Humanity	161
	Some Applications	
IX	Christian Poverty	179
X	Love, Marriage, Chastity	206
XI	Authority, Obedience	237
XII	The Obedience of Children and of Citizens	257
XIII	Religious Obedience	270
	Remarks and Bibliography	287

MORALITY AND THE MYSTICAL BODY

CHAPTER I

Religion, Christianity, Catholicism

THE PAGES which follow have an apologetic bearing. But they do not constitute, nor do they pretend to constitute, a complete Apologetic. There is no question of mapping out an itinerary which will lead from incredulity to faith; we are addressing the faithful who already believe and who wish to establish for themselves a fuller justification for the hope which is in them. Our object is to show progressively that the Catholic attitude, as the Church defines it, is the most perfect religious attitude, and that its acceptance is enjoined upon all. We are convinced that such an exposition has a considerable persuasive power even for non-believers. But that will be only an additional happy result.

They have besides and especially a religious and moral bearing. For their purpose is to show what religion is and what Christianity and Catholicism are, precisely inasmuch as they are religions. Perhaps, they will assist us in assuming before God the attitude which He demands of us and the attitude demanded of us also by the life which He placed in us at our Creation and for which He has made such marvelous amends in our Redemption.

Here then, to begin by mapping out the road, is the sequence of thoughts to be run through; a series of theses, if you wish:

I. *Religion is not an attitude or a group of procedures alongside other attitudes or other procedures: it is pre-eminently The Way of Life, which gives value to all the others and which is man in his entirety.*

II. *Christianity is not a religion alongside other religions: it is pre-eminently The Religion, supernaturally and absolutely perfect.*

III. *Catholicism is not a Christian confession alongside other Christian confessions: it is Christianity, the only integral Chrstianity.*

I

Religion has been defined as the relation of man to God; or again, the union of man with God; or again, the sum of our duties before God. These definitions are perfectly exact. It is important to show their entire meaning.

The relation which unites us to God is not an ordinary relation.

Ordinary relations are the most unsubstantial things in the world. As Philosophy explains, these *esse ad* are only accidents, and the most superficial of accidents. One might say that they reside between the substances which they unite rather than in the substances themselves; for they add nothing intrinsic to them. Whether they come or go, these latter are so little affected, that no one, considering them only, will perceive any difference.

There are most assuredly certain relations which are not so unpretentious as others. For example: the relations which attach one to another all the parts of the universe and which set up between them a thousand intercrossing series of reciprocal dependence, so multiple that each thing, closely pressed on every side, finds itself determined by all the others. Or again: the relations which unite the members of an organism among themselves and give them coherence; i.e. relations which follow of necessity from them. But, let us remark: if the chain becomes more solid, the distance between the objects which it joins tends to disappear, and, consequently, the chain also. Between the parts of a whole, and still more between the organs of a body, the distinction is less radical than one between separate objects: it even tends towards unity, and, the two terms of the relation ceasing to that extent to be two, the relation itself loses in reality what it gains in intensity.

Not so with our relation to God.

It is a real relation by supreme right: it expresses, in us, that which makes us be.

It is an indestructible relation: God will always be another, and, before Him, our being will always remain an *esse ad*.

It is a total relation also, in this sense, that it affects not merely some modality of our being, but absolutely all that we are.

In brief, it is a relation so essential and it is so incorporated with our reality, that one scarcely dares to call it an accident. It is in us, that is true; but we are by it, or rather by that which places it in us. One would falsify all perspectives by likening it to a kind of adventitious quality or quantity, which would have in relation to our substance only a secondary reality. Assuredly, suppressing our being would be enough to suppress it by the same stroke: *accessorium sequitur principale*. But, on the contrary, without this relation to God our being would be non-existent, impossible and absurd.

Do not imagine then a sort of hook fastened into a rock already cut and trimmed to hoist it onto a coping. Think rather of that other, hidden bond, which draws the entire rock in each one of its particles towards the centre of the earth; or again, rather, of the very solidity which holds together the block of rock; or still better, of the reality itself of the rock, of its being. But no: it is still too little. Think of the very thing which brings it about that the being of the rock, this miserable being, limited and on all sides penetrated with nothingness, is nevertheless an existing being.

It is a constituting relation and not an adventitious one.

It is a Substantial relation even, in this sense, that it is our substance itself, considered, not in itself certainly, but—what is still stronger—in that which makes it be and be itself.

Esse ad, for us as for every finite being, is to be.

Such is religion considered in the very substance of things. We may now watch it rise from this interior depth and shape activities. From the point of view at which we have arrived, we can even discern, welling up from all the universe, that which, when it emanates from a human heart, is called religion in the language of men.

To make this transition from the ontological aspect of the problem to its moral aspect, let us take up again the last formula at which we arrived. To be, it is to be by God, and it is to be pure relation towards God.

What an immense view and how transparent the air is! All the universe is there before us and it is only an act of obedience. All things and in all their depths are only a conformity to a divine will. The eye sees the heavens tumbling their clouds, the earth covering itself with vegetation, the stars in their spaces, and, on the wisps of straw, the climbing insects. But all this has reality only in virtue of a divine will. Without it all would collapse into empty semblance, or rather, into nothingness, for the solidity of the world is effected in its entirety, since the first beginning of the ages, by the word of command.

Every being in itself and through all its structure, is a limitless submission. It is created; that is to say, its very existence, being a relation, is a dependence and a homage. The universe is only cult and religion.

This homage, in every case, is blended with the being itself. Besides, it varies from being to being according to the function of the being. In beings deprived of reason it is a simple ontological relation. In man, who is endowed with intelligence and will, it should be conscious and free. And further, because man is not a pure spirit, this reference to God should incarnate itself in certain external acts. These acts also, since man is a social being, must have a collective element.

In this way does religion, in the ordinary sense of the word, affirm itself in us: an attitude of soul with external and public demonstrations. But, it must be carefully noted, this ordinary sense runs the risk of dwarfing the real meaning. Religion is not merely a human phenomenon; it is but the new and infinitely more elevated expression taken in us by a manner of being which is necessarily the manner of being of all things. So, the different aspects which it assumes in us are in continuity with the constitution of the universe.

II

We shall first consider things from the static point of view.

To exist is an act of obedience. We are only a submission which has taken body. The kind of action which our manner of being dictates to us, is then a limitless obedience.

Without doubt there must be certain acts which express more particularly and more clearly our ontological dependence. But religion is not limited to these few procedures; one would wound it mortally by cutting it up in that way. Its essence is conformed both to the immensity of need from which it sets out and to the immensity of existence to which it brings us back, and throughout, it implores that no bounds be set to it.

Let no one then take it for a procedure similar to others, or a little better, but still of the same order. It is a thing apart; it is, we can say, *the* procedure, the pre-eminent act, and in it alone the essence of our being expresses itself.

So it, and it alone, can be the inspiration and the support of all the other procedures, so true is it that what makes it the one thing necessary, makes it also natural: natural religion in all the magnificent import of the term. Since in its origin it is identified with our being, its unfolding ought to coincide entirely with every expansion of the activity of our being. Nothing is as simple as serving God. Let us only be what we are, all that we are, and nothing except what we are; but let us be that joyously, greatheartedly, ardently, because so it has pleased the Lord, and, in performing as a holy mandate our prosaic role of rational animals, we shall serve the Lord with all our heart and all our soul, just as, willingly or unwillingly, we obey Him with all our being.

To exist is our first cult. Thereafter our entire existence can be a religion. The mountains honor God just by being mountains, by the mighty thrusting of their summits; the oceans celebrate Him, just by being oceans, by the plane infinity of their interminable docility. We also can praise Him with all our substance, with our muscles and our bones, in accepting our being, in wishing it, in loving it, because it is from God, and because God has made it ours.

Acceptance then and also gratitude. We and the entire universe are but a gift.

A sense of belonging and respect. The land which Moses trod was holy because of the presence of Jahveh in the bush. The same is true, with due proportion, of the universe. Everything belongs to God and everything is sacred in virtue of that relation. Everything exists through God, and the shape of things is only the imprint of the creative contact. Respect then, and universal respect, for the immense sanctuary. In the presence of everything that exists, our attitude can be a religious attention. *Revereri quantulamcumque rationem entis*. Veneration even for the infinitely small. All is august, not merely because of the magnificences which the eye discovers even on the wings of flies and in the drops of dew; all is august because of the marvels of structure which, after ages, the mind is just beginning to guess at in organisms and even in minerals; but especially, all is august, because all is the unconditional service which creatures render to the Creator.

But respect especially for ourselves. And this, not in the first place because we are closer to ourselves; but especially because, possessing being in a more perfect manner, we are, when we consider ourselves, in the presence of a more complete belonging to God.

Religion is the whole of man. But this static point of view does not suffice. The religious attitude, if it wishes to take possession of us quite entirely, and of the universe besides, does not confine itself within itself; it asserts itself as a tendency, and it is this dynamic element, which we would like to consider now. Like obedience and respect, it takes possession of us quite entirely, and of the universe besides.

We are often deceived by our imaginations, when we form an idea of finite beings. We readily represent them as little princes in their little manors; as realities, limited certainly, but limited only on the outside; as masters and absolute lords within their tiny selves. Illusion. It is within especially that they are incomplete. Lacking of themselves that which renders them possible and thinkable, they are constituted by an indigence; an indigence so radical that there is nothing like it: they have need, not of external nourishment or of extrinsic complement, but of themselves, of a principle which differentiates them absolutely from nothing.

To exist, for those things which are not necessary, is only a borrowing. To hold to their reality is then for them, in the first place, to hold to the cause of their reality. Also, with all the weight of their being, they are drawn towards the First Cause; and all their activity, tending only and being able only to tend to finite being pushes them without their knowledge toward Him Who is. *Omnia tendunt Deo assimilari.*

To exist is an appeal for help. The universe is but a field of grain pointing straight towards heaven. And man traverses the field, destined to translate into a voluntary hymn that which in things is only a relativity of nature.

For man himself is a borrowing; to exist, for him, is to receive; to act, then, should be a cry for assistance. *Irrequietum est cor nostrum;* the substance of our being is a lack of equilibrium. He who is the soul of our soul and the reason for the existence of our being is also absolutely superior to us. It is then, in a total reference of all our being to this transcendent, in a radical aspiration towards this unique principle of our entire selves, that our adherence to our being should express itself.

Our Ego, that most interior element of our being which expresses our personality, does not escape the common law. If it knows itself, if it possesses itself when it reflects on itself, what it holds in thus seizing upon itself, is a tensely coiled spring ready to unbend towards the infinite.

There are many ways in which we might set about showing in the consciousness of men an indigence more complete and a tendency more living than is found in the rest of things. In order better to continue in one line of research, and not to prolong our exposition endlessly, we shall make our examination bear here on the act of knowing and on it alone.

To know, is to be in search of a last explanation, absolutely valid. That is the reason why, driven from finite being to finite being, the faculty of knowing is forced to turn towards the infinite Being. But, this last explanation remains beyond our power to grasp. The pure intelligible, by the splendor of its light, blinds these eyes of ours accustomed to the night, and, powerless to fix the sun, we perceive only its reflections on things.

Let us pursue our way for the present. It remains to be seen in what manner the supreme act of intelligence is produced in relation to the supreme intelligible itself. From the beginning, the act of intelligence is composed of aspiration: released by an aspiration towards the intelligible, it develops, from intellection to intellection, from insufficiency to insufficiency, in a perpetual aspiration towards the intelligible. But, in proportion as it advances and as it disengages itself from the too easy satisfactions of sensibility and of material contingencies, the aspiration purifies and vivifies itself. In its last stage it is only the trembling of desire.

How can we know God? How can we know that which renders everything else and the mind itself knowable? To this question, as we might expect, the answer is double and antinomic: the opposition of which our finite being is composed is evident in the relation of our intelligence to the first light, just as it is clear in our other relations towards God. Immanent and transcendent to our being, God is immanent and transcendent to our knowledge also.

Let us see first the positive aspect: in what measure is God in our knowledge? God, because He is the only necessary being, the only *A Se,* is also the only one who is intelligible *de Se,* and who has no need of further explanation. It is necessary then, that every intellection bear, ultimately, on the first intelligible (first *Quoad se, absolute*), just as, finally, every act of the will should be referred to this unique last end. The rest, having no sense or value except by Him who is necessary, it follows that this inevitable is necessarily understood, in some way, in every intellection, just as He is willed in some manner in every volition.

Besides, what can we know except His image? All the things which surround us and even the activity of the mind, are participated being, and nothing but participated being. On the other hand, He is pure Being, Being without restriction. To be, then, to exist, is to resemble Him. Resemblance as imperfect as you wish, more imperfect even than one can say. But resemblance just the same, and, in a certain sense, resemblance more complete than any other. By all that they are, by all their substance, by all their aspects, by all their movements, finite beings are only participated being; it is, then, by all that they are that they resemble the Being, and this resemblance is not less indispensable to them than their existence, because it constitutes the reason for their existence.

Our intelligence then, is surrounded only by indices, and each one of its acts, in a certain manner, teaches it something about God. We can say, then, that the Infinite, immense in us according to our poor resources, as in Itself it is immense absolutely, occupies, in its transcendent fashion, the entire field of knowledge, in such a way that it is, to that extent, the most known of known objects. Finite beings are known in a manner altogether finite: their limits exclude them one from another and we think of one only by forgetting in proportion the rest. But, whatever we think of and through everything that we think of, God is, in some manner, always present to our mind.

But the counterpart must be added at once. In the presence of the supreme intelligible, we can make many a stammering statement, but we ought also to keep silent; for, in truth, what we know is equivalent to nothing. The most known of beings is also the least known; and always for the same reason: the infinite purity of His Being which makes of every act of existence an image of His essence, brings it about also that this image has no trait truly common to Him. We attain only the finite, and He is the Infinite, in all limpidity and simplicity.

Shall we try, then, for what it is worth, to represent Him by traits borrowed from finite beings? Impossible. Such a process can be defended, when there is question only of finite beings. A blind man, for example, can form some idea of colors by making use of his other sensations: he will put together the notion of sensible impression, of straight line, of propagation, etc., and he will make for himself a substitute for vision which is incomplete, to be sure, but, after all, perfectly objective. But, to represent God, what traits shall we choose in that which is only finite?

There are, certainly, among our concepts many which are more ethereal than the others. Certain of them even, the most elevated, do not include of themselves any essential imperfection: those, for example, of will, of intelligence, of being especially. But it suffices to examine them only a little closely to learn that, as they figure in our knowledge, they represent only the human fashion of thinking and of existing, that is to say, the human and finite level of these perfections, in themselves unlimited.

Very well then! We shall correct them! We shall purify them of every imperfection! It is still impossible. They would no longer retain their proper signification. Language, here, can deceive: we have made up certain expressions to designate these concepts inasmuch as they are applied to God; we say: Being Itself, Subsistent Goodness, and so on. But, mark it well, the concept is not thereby elevated to the necessary level. The operation is indicated, even commenced, but not effectuated, and never shall we be able to conceive perfectly what a being can be which is only being, and a goodness which is so totally identified with itself that it is, at the same time, intelligence, necessity, justice, and all the divine attributes.

What shall we do then before this inconceivable? Ignore it? Untenable attitude: the act of knowing is only a relation to Him and it attains only images of Him; how could it be uninterested in Him? Shall we be so bold then as to treat Him as a known object? Useless to try it: we would thus place Him in the order of finite things which are measured by our yardsticks, and this anthropomorphism as fully contradicts His essence, as does agnosticism, which is the other horn of the dilemma, and which is repugnant to the nature of the mind. Neither in abstention nor in activity is there rest for the intelligence. *Irrequietum. . . .*

It remains for us then, to pass from repose and to know without knowing. We wish to say that, when we consider God, the only valid attitude is to affirm the highest perfections we can conceive, but adding at once that He is not that, or rather, that He is that, but otherwise—better, infinitely better, in a manner purer and more splendid, in a manner veiled from us by shadows, which, even in our noblest notions, we do not succeed in dissipating. We shall accumulate then, all possible grandeurs, we shall intensify them with all our power, and at the same time we shall declare them too slight. Before God, these victims crowned with flowers will be led forth only to be sacrificed, and the intelligence will think only to avow itself insufficient, itself and all its notions.

But this renunciation of knowing, the last term of intellection, is also supreme intellection. Witness rendered to the grandeur of God, it makes us surpass ourselves in some sort and gives us the least inexact concept possible of the infinity of the Infinite.

So with a swimmer lost in the wide sea. As long as he struggles with the waves, he knows not what the sea is. But when at last, broken by fatigue, he ceases swimming, when, weary of war, he yields himself up to the immense rhythm of the surging swell, then only does he know the grandeur of the ocean. The same for God: as long as we try by means of positive notions to form an idea of Him, we approach true knowledge; but we do not attain it. His transcendence claims another homage. It is necessary, after having done all, after having accumulated perfections, that, from the summit of heaped-up grandeurs, ever more immense and more ethereal, we renounce attaining the sky, and, without ceasing to tend, think no more of arriving. At this moment, while attempting a flight which it can never complete, the finite mind recognizes the infinite. Homage of dependence and of inferiority: it knows the infinite, not by classifying it within itself among other known objects—how should the unlimited reduce itself to an idea comprised in our science?—but in subsuming itself under it.

In this consists the supreme act of the human mind on the subject of the supreme intelligible, the act in which the spiritual nature of our being and its close relation to God best expresses itself. This is an act of radical humility, a total homage of thought, which without comprehending, knows that it is comprehended, a religion of the finite intelligence as finite intelligence, a silent adoration of the spirit. It is also an act of tending and one which resembles an act of love, so much, at these heights, is our being unified and so much do our faculties approach and accompany one another. From aspiration to aspiration, the act of knowing ends in an aspiration, an aspiration already realized from the first step of the mind, but which does not manifest itself at the maximum of clearness until the moment when the mind, at its maximum of awareness, perceives itself as a pure relation towards the Absolute and actuates itself in a pure *esse ad.*

To know is then, to tend, and we can conclude these considerations by saying that, in the mind of man, as in his other acts, as in his being, religious activity is not a portion merely: it is everything.

There is a cult of the mind—and the critique of knowledge, like everything else, terminates in religion.

But all this ends in a tendency; that is to say, without ending entirely.

Our aspiration, in fact, like all our activities, is finite;

it can never embrace the infinite. Though we are all relative to it, it is in no way relative to us.

The Infinite is free without doubt to come and take, to elevate even to His grandeur these beings which tend towards His goodness. We shall speak in the following paragraph of this great mercy of our God. But such a condescension surpasses our power and our merits and our concepts. We are capable only of human things.

But, it will be asked, what is this tendency towards God, which springs from our entire being, going to do? Are we then dedicated to the impossible and created unhappy to the point of being projected by all our being towards the inaccessible, yet always destined to fall back upon ourselves?

Not at all. This tendency was not made to attain God: its reason for existence is to perfect man. Law of all our being, it is destined to confer on all our being the moral elevation which it requires of us. It should give us (but as interior, as desired, as affecting our Ego at its freest and most personal), that bond with God by which our being subsists. This result attained, all that our nature claims in this mortal life is accomplished. In our fashion we possess to the maximum the supreme Good. *Summi boni summa possessio.* Nothing within us takes a step further.

Strictly speaking, this is unconsummated beatitude; incomplete perfection. But our being is imperfect, hence our natural perfection and natural beatitude should be so too, and this incompletion is necessary in order that they may adapt themselves perfectly to our being.

As finite beings, we are, by essence, a relation and a tendency. And this attitude is not intended to be content with a few manifestations: some acts lost in the midst of others; still less is it intended to surge upward for a moment and then to rest satisfied. The religious aspiration, law of our being as being, relation of all our reality with the only Necessary, should subtend all our other aspirations. It is the aspiration, the unique and perpetual tendency. Religion in man is all of him.

But in his religion man is not all.

CHAPTER II

Christianity

RELIGION is all of man, as we saw in the preceding study. Let us add now: and Christianity is all of religion.

This proposition, evidently, would demand for its demonstration an entire apologetic. We cannot dream of that within the limits of this study. Besides, this immense work has been done many times and the reader who desires it can betake himself to a number of excellent treatises. We recognize here then a deliberate lacuna in our exposition. From natural religion we transport ourselves to the completely supernatural without showing the road which leads thither; our purpose is rather to see in an inverse sense how *the religion of Christ takes up in itself, but with a supernatural perfection, all the religion of men.*

I

The religion of Christ, we say. The Christian religion in fact, as we shall see more and more clearly, has Christ for an essential, and, so to speak, a unique element.

And so, the first requisite is to recall what Christ is. Let us begin then by doing that.

Christ is, in the unique Person of the Word, perfectly God and perfectly man.

This point must be developed a little; otherwise Christianity will not appear in all its beauty.

Let us consult then Scripture and Tradition.

Scripture first. And, to abridge, let us content ourselves with the gospels. Certainly they do not give a definition properly so called of what the Saviour is; still less do they give a collection of theses. Their authors, and those whose recollections the authors report, and still more the unique principle author, who is the very Spirit of Christ, desired only to outline the image of Jesus as the first witnesses saw Him; Mary, Peter, John, Matthew and the others. The recitals follow one another, often without apparent order, but the group of them, like so many features, makes to live again a unique physiognomy, very human, very divine, and always very living and very one. That is what we must explain.

"Alas," St. Francis DeSales used to say, "I am so much a man." Yes: But Jesus was that too. *Apparuit humanitas et benignitas*. It was even a revelation: without this sweet vision of humanity and of goodness we would never have known all that the human heart, the work of God, can be.

He was so human, so marvelously in accord with what is most profound in us, so accessible and so open that the little children ran to Him; instinctive reaction of our humanity at its most candid before the perfection of the Son of man. He commanded respect, however, and the Sanhedrites did not always have the courage to withstand His glance.

But especially He captivated men. The mothers harassed Him to compel Him to touch their little ones. The lame, the blind and the leprous, those whose miseries had habituated them to rebuffs; poor men, beggars, publicans, those whose condition had accustomed them to contempt; sinners, thieves and condemned persons, those whose falls had embittered them against themselves; all, far from being frightened by His entire purity, pressed towards Him, as flights of birds, lost in the night, rush towards a beacon-light. Ὥστε ἐπιπίπτειν αὐτῷ so much so, says St. Mark, that they fell upon Him, a needy and tumultuous crowd swarming about His Goodness.

In His presence everyone was at ease, and without pretense. Peter at once took possession of Him; the sick, the crowds, His own, felt Him so near to them that they considered Him their own property. And He allowed Himself to be taken. That was why He came: to engage Himself in the gear of our events and of our psychology. Like us He was hungry and thirsty and He said so; like us He had His mother and He loved her; like us He admired the splendor of the fields in flower and the settings of the sun, and He willed to show it. His soul trembled to the rhythm of the universe as ours does. And, when His hour of suffering was come, He suffered as we suffer. No theatrical attitude, nothing false, no pretense; He did not deny sorrow, He did not defy it; but He accepted it; He allowed Himself to be overcome by it; He even allowed Himself to be overwhelmed by shame and disgust. He, who could have been of stone, wished to be only man, and His point of honor and the magnificence of His goodness lay in being simply that.

Like all men He had His familiar gestures, His ordinary expressions and His own manner of looking at His interlocutors. Like everyone else He was of His own time and of His own country. There was nothing hazily abstract or vaguely extratemporal in His attitude. His procedures are frankly stamped and dated: today we would conduct ourselves differently. Even His manner of teaching religion is the one which was suited to the Palestine of that time. Soon Paul will speak in a different manner on the Areopagus, and Thomas of Aquin, His humble disciple, will build his expositions in another style.

Still, despite this local and temporal color, He remains a contemporary of all the ages. What this Jew said in Aramaic to the laborers of Galilee reveals to the intellectuals and to the workers of today, the mystery that their souls are their own.

If He enters into our forms, He surpasses them. If He is man, and in the fullest sense of the word, the very fullness of His manhood causes Him to be a man in a way that is astonishing and full of contrasts.

Contrast, one might say, is His proper element. He can comfort all the afflicted; but He Himself in His agony stays near His own and begs their moral support. He reads souls; but He asks them questions. He forgets Himself, He effaces Himself; but He declares that He is Master and Lord. He is nothing; and He is all. Last end of our tendencies, He affirms that He came only to be a means, to give His life for His brothers. His miracles are His own and they are the sign of His power; but He did not perform them for His own advantage; and He who multiplied the loaves of bread for others, Himself suffered from hunger.

This perpetual servant has limitless exigencies. As God He wishes our hearts without reserve, and one cannot glance backward once one has set himself to follow Him. The key of consciences and the key of Heaven are in His hands, and He gives them to whom He pleases. But He does not allow it even to be said that He is good; God alone is good, He replies, and the places which are nearest His own are not His to give, but the Father's.

He is man, and He continues to be man. But to His grandeur neither He nor the Gospel set any limits. The word alone is lacking and it seems to have been rarely on His lips and on those of the Twelve. But the word is a secondary thing. The difficulty is not to affirm that one is God; it is to make it believed by the companions of one's daily life.

So Jesus did. *Coepit facere.* He dared to take the rôle of God, to act all His days according to the last rule of all perfection, as a model of all virtue, without ever ceasing to conduct Himself as a man and to wish to be like His brothers. And He did not sunder Himself with the effort; and He was not overwhelmed in ridicule. All took Him seriously; and after twenty centuries no defect has been found in His claim.

There is something more marvelous still: He has maintained this overwhelming rôle without stiffness. The terrible contrasts of which His conduct is composed, far from destroying His personality, make it stand out in perfect unity.

The synthesis is so complete, it is so well incarnated in Him that by a sort of communion between two extremes, He makes His grandeur shine forth in the very marks of His weakness.

It is after having fallen from fatigue upon the pillow of the pilot, that He lifts Himself up to make the sea lie down and to silence the tempest with a word. He was so simply man in His sleep that the Twelve did not hesitate to shake Him to wake Him up. And in the miracle itself, which filled them with terror, He remains still so human that soon they are again familiar and indiscreet. The most prosaic comparisons serve Him in speaking of divine realities. Scorpions, eggs and pebbles become in His discourses messengers of Providence. The birds of heaven, when He speaks of them, form a part of His teaching about our adoptive sonship. A glass of water, provided that one gives it in His name, demands an eternal recompense; and even His body, yes, His flesh and His blood, that of a condemned man, are made to give to the world the divine life.

The unity of divine and human is in Him so total that it leads like a living way from one to the other. Merely by seeing this man, the Apostles ended by believing in His divinity. The vision of their eyes of flesh became faith in their souls; Peter finally one day understood and, perhaps before Jesus stated it, he confessed who Jesus was.

The attitude of Jesus before God resembles His attitude before men: the same contrasts and in the same unity. Only here there is no longer equality and superiority, it is equality and inferiority; but the unity of divine and human is still total: before His Father Jesus unites perfect ease to adoration.

He prays, He drags Himself along the ground, He obeys even to death, and, when it shall be necessary, He will go Himself with a step anguished but decided, towards the whips and towards the Cross.

And still He, the sweet and humble of heart, installs Himself in the place of God. He lifts Himself up above the Law and the Temple and the Sabbath, above everything. And these divine prerogatives He exercises without excuse or oratorical precautions, in His own name and as something that belongs to Him.

Rigorously equal, infinitely inferior, He remains tranquilly from one part to the other identical with Himself. He prays, yes; but He knows that He is all-powerful. He obeys and He sacrifices Himself; but on His gibbet He gives paradise to the good thief.

Such is Christ always: a perfect synthesis of a perfect dualism. As natural as it is to us rational animals to be at once spirit and matter, so simple and easy is it, in a certain sense, for Him to be man and God both together. And just as we, since we are a unit, can give a spiritual sense to our bodily gestures, He can, in the supernatural perfection of His humanity, make plain His divinity to those whose souls are pure.

It was reserved for Tradition to express in formulas this unity of the two natures, which Christ has realised in His person and in His actions. It was a long and delicate work, often crossed by heresies, always taken up again by Christian thought. Generations have brought their efforts to it. So, when the Council of Chalcedon defined the dogma, it merely summed up a great Christian activity.

The point of departure of these researches, the base of the argumentations, is the contrast in the Saviour's manner of acting.

Let us hear Saint Leo, for example, describe Christ for us:

> The very same one who is true God, writes the Pope, is also true man, and this unity is not an artifice, since the humility of the man and the grandeur of God exist, the one in the other.
>
> No more than God is altered by this condescension, is man absorbed in the glory. Each of the natures operates, in communion with the other, that which is proper to it: the Word does that which is proper to the Word, and the flesh receives that which is proper to the flesh. The one is radiant with prodigies, the other succumbs under injuries. And, just as the Word does not remove itself from its equality with the glory of the Father, neither does the flesh lose the nature of our race. One only and the same one, it must be often repeated, is truly Son of God and son of man. . . . The nativity according to the flesh witnesses to His human nature, but the virginal birth is the indication of the divine power. His human infancy appeared in the

humility of the manger; but the grandeur of the Most High is declared by the voices of the angels. . . . To be hungry and thirsty, to be tired and to sleep, these are evidently human. But to nourish with five loaves of bread five thousand men, and to give to the Samaritan the living water . . . this, beyond possible doubt, is divine.[1]

And the saint, after having piled up examples of contrast, ends with this phrase, of which all the words are weighty.

Although, in our Lord Jesus Christ, God and man are only one person, yet, it is one thing which gives access in the two to common humiliations and another thing from which a common glory comes. From us He holds a humanity inferior to the Father; from the Father He has a divinity equal to the Father.[2]

That is what the Council of Chalcedon will define, after having canonized the *Tomus ad Flavianum* which we have just quoted. Here is this important definition:

Following the holy Fathers, we confess one only and the same Son, He who is our Lord Jesus Christ. He it is whom, with only one voice, all of us, we preach. He is, the same one, perfect (complete) in divinity and, the same one, complete in humanity; God veritably and man veritably, the same one, composed of a rational soul and of a body; consubstantial to the Father according to the divinity and consubstantial to us, the same one, in His humanity, in all things like to us, sin excepted; born of the Father before the ages according to divinity, and, in these latter times, the same one, for us and for our salvation, born of the Virgin Mary, Mother of God, according to humanity; one only and the same Christ, Son, Lord, Only-Begotten, in two natures, without confusion and without change, without division and without separation, the differences of the natures being in no way removed by the union, but much

[1] S. Leo, *Epist.* XXVIII, P.L. LIV, 767-769.
[2] Ibid. 769-771.

rather the particularities of each one being preserved, and both uniting themselves in one only person and in one only hypostasis; not to form one (Christ) divided or distinguished into two persons, but one only and the same Son and Only-Begotten, God, Word, Lord, Jesus Christ; as once the prophets said on this subject, and as He Himself, the Lord Jesus Christ, has taught it to us, and as the Symbol of the Fathers has transmitted it to us.[3]

A capital text in which Christianity gives the formula of its Christ, a sacred witness which one should often meditate upon. Urgent affirmation also, almost anguished. The Church cannot often enough repeat the great truth: the Saviour is truly God, truly man, truly one; He is "one only and the same," and perfectly like to the Father, and perfectly like to us.

At first sight, these distinctions between natures and person, these controversies against the heresies with abstract names, Gnosticism, Apollinarism, Monophysitism, can seem like the minutiae of theologians. Error. From the beginning the great bishops of that time have declared that here the least iota cannot fall without its being a catastrophe for humanity.

The fact is that *the formula which defines Christ defines at the same time Christianity.*

Let one attenuate, as little as may be, either the perfection of one of the two natures, or the perfection of their unity in the Word, and it is all over: the divine plan is deflected, and the supernatural life flows alongside the human race, as close as you wish, but not within it.

If the body of Christ is not very exactly of our flesh and of our blood, if His soul is not in all points what ours

[3] Denz. 148.

is, He has then assumed another than the human nature, and it is not we who, in Him, have access to the Father.

And if He differs from God, by the most delicate nuance, if He is not of the very substance of the Father, it is not then truly to the Divinity that we are united in Him.

Finally, if He Himself is not one with the real unity of only one person, the tie which should attach us to heaven is broken at the moment of its binding and we are still in our first abjection.

One with God, One with us, One in Himself, Christ has a function which is no other than His very essence. And this function is to be our union with God, our sanctity, our redemption, our Christianity, merely by being what He is.

That is the mediation of the Saviour.

It signifies that Jesus is not merely an intermediary who places Himself between us and God, a sort of intercessor whose good offices assure, by a sort of going and coming, frequent relations between two different points. He is rather a bridge which establishes continuity between two banks of a stream, or rather, a marvel which would place the two banks in full contact. His rôle is Himself; merely by existing He brings it about that in Him humanity touches divinity directly.

Likewise, the formula which expresses His mediation with relation to humanity forms a unit with the dogma which defines Him, Himself. The two have developed from the same movement, and we might say even, that it is through reflecting on what the Saviour is for Christians, that the Church has come to say so well what He is in Himself.

He is then Everything in the religion of which He forms

the centre, and, if He were not all that He is, Christianity would be nothing.

But He is all that He is, and, in Him, Christianity is everything.

II

Christianity, the religion of the Man-God, is the perfect religion of humanity.

Religion is a relation between man and God. It is an appeal for help, a tendency in which our entire being expresses itself.

In Christ, this relation becomes the hypostatic union; the appeal is heard and granted beyond all merit and all desire, and the tendency arrives at possession.

Towards this summit tended, by their essence itself, all the aspirations of our being. But its very elevation, which gave it its attractiveness, screened it from our efforts and from our vision.

As a general takes possession of the unique defile which joins two countries, Christ came to occupy the precise point where all the appeals of our being would converge, if our natural weakness did not arrest their flight, the point where every man must pass to go to the Father. Or rather, He has not had to take this position; He constitutes it by His substance.

In the midst of us an Individual has arisen, who, man and God at the same time, is the perfect priest. Let our religion be organized about this Emmanuel and in this Emmanuel, let it pass through Him, and it will pierce the skies and will penetrate into the Holy of Holies. God Himself, if we dare say it, could not resist this pontiff taken from our midst.

And, in order to pass through Him, our religion need

not impose any mutilation on itself. Christ has assumed all our nature. There is then, nothing human which cannot be integrated into His religion.

The required manner of thinking is our own manner of thinking.

Not because it is ours, but because God has taken it in Christ.

Had not Christ assumed all our nature, evidently, it would have remained lamentably insufficient. Have we not said that natural religion, in our intelligence, consists in a perpetual effort to purify our most elevated concepts from an ineradicable anthropomorphism?

But the Word itself has become flesh. To the incurable ill, the truth has brought a remedy by accommodating itself to it, and to our native weakness has become a light.

The Man-God is there, let us look at Him: to know God, the best thing henceforth is to have eyes of flesh and the heart of a man. We shall learn much more about the Ineffable by seeing the Son of Mary act and by hearing Him speak, than the proudest geniuses have been able to perceive in subtile speculations on the Pure Act.

The required manner of suffering is our own manner of suffering.

It must be so: God has come here below to take it.

But how simple, and human, suffering has become, in Him!

By implanting it in His soul and in His flesh, He has made something expiatory and divinising of what before was merely terrible. We can then, even in the embrace of suffering, even in death, be joyous, and love and open our souls to it, and receive it, and will it. And even while suffering—for nothing of the human in us is suppressed—

we shall be happy because of the life which enters into us like a sword; for suffering, as suffering—that is the miracle—makes us like to the Word of God.

The Incarnate Word does not ask that we should be made of bronze in order to suffer well. He Himself suffered as a man suffers. The human manner of suffering, with its numbness, its revolts of the flesh and its powerlessness in prayer, is the one which is necessary for us; humble, confident, and drawing its virtue, not so much from our courage, as from the resemblance to the Crucified, which it implants in us.

Even in its most rigorous requirements Christianity remains human, and its restrictions and retrenchments should overturn only our narrowness, and open us wide to the Infinite.

"God was made man": this is our religion and the formula for the ennobling and divinising of our race.

Our little human values have received a divine worth. God has come down to the roads we tread. He has walked by our side under the same sun and under the same rain which the Father sends down equally upon the just and the unjust. Our trifling earthly events have from now on an interest for Him: He has taken part in them. We may speak to Him then in prayer of harvests and of storms, of thorns and of gall, even of silver and of hammers; all this, in Him, has taken on a religious meaning.

The required manner of praying is our own manner of praying.

Why should we treat God as a grandiose abstraction, or as a superhuman entity, or even as a simple Pure Act? Of what advantage is a complicated etiquette and a laborious approach, when there is no longer any distance between us?

God expects of us something other than remote homage. The supreme value for man, after God, is it not man? And is God not man in Jesus Christ? Sociable by nature, sociable even with all the supernatural perfection of His nature, He has need of those who are like Him.

We can go to Him then as we are. When we speak to Him with sincerity, we shall never find that we were of no interest to Him or that we were importunate. We shall open our hearts to the heart of another man; we shall speak of our sufferings to One who has had experience of sorrow; we shall confide our faults to One who has willed to feel in His soul the shame of being covered with all crimes, and we shall have adored God, as God, since the Incarnation, wishes to be adored. Henceforth, to believe in God, we shall need to have the immense simplicity, or rather the imperturbable assurance, that we are precious in the eyes of the Infinite.

The required manner of loving is our own manner of loving.

God, through the Incarnation, wishes to be loved with a human love, in the Man-God, in the neighbor.

We may note especially this last point: charity towards the neighbor.

No cult goes so straight to the heart of God as the love of man for man, when it is given in the name of Christ. Man, in fact, is united with God through the Incarnation; it is in a man that God places Himself within our reach; it is the Incarnate Word which every human creature resembles. So, in every man, we must venerate God; and God will treat us, Jesus assures us, as we shall have treated others.

These are some of the features of the religion of the Man-God. In Christ, men can go to God on the same level with God; that which, without Christ, would always have forced our cult to be merely human, becomes the means required for rendering it divine.

Christianity then, is human, as human as anything can be; just as Christ is fully man.

It is then, in perfection, the religion of men.

But, we must add at once, it is not merely human. The very perfection of its humanity is due to a character of divinity. Its features are composed of the same contrasts as those of Christ, and are resolved in the same unity.

It exalts human nature, yes, but in humility, and to give to it a divine importance, it insists in the first place that it cease to belong to itself.

It respects in human nature all its resources; but it is to hand over all of them to God. It opens up humanity to the Infinite, but requires of it a total abnegation.

Opposites and paradoxes. But no collisions. Total humility and religious great-heartedness; exaltation and abnegation join in a unique adoration and in a limitless confidence in the God who, by becoming man, has made us like to Him.

God remains then, whole, and man remains also quite entire; Christianity can be totally human and truly divine, and still one, as Jesus is human and divine and one, and all this through Jesus.

Seductor ille. This seducer of the crowds, the enviou
Pharisees called Jesus. And, in fact, Jesus had a way o
His own of being man, so integral, so perfect, that what i
best in us should go to Him to find itself. Human grandeur
created grandeur, but an effect of personal unity wit
divinity.

So with Christianity. It is human. But with such perfec
tion that its divinity shines through it. Thus, it is not neces
sary that long syllogisms should precede, before it ca
impose itself on upright souls. *Ostende mihi faciem tuam*
Let it only show itself as it is. Religion of the Man-God
reflection of Christ, it is powerful over us with all the virtu
of the Saviour, and with all the need of God with whic
men are filled.

III

*Christianity, when compared with other religions, is no
just one religion, even a better one, among others less good
it is "The Religion," unique, total, absolute.*

The difference here is not a matter of nuance or of de
gree, but of nature. It is religion "differently"; it unite
to God, not by our efforts alone and in human fashion, bu
by all the power of God in Christ. *Differt in ipsa ration
religionis.*

Suppose it has some points in common with other reli
gions: what is astonishing in that? Did not Jesus wish t
resemble His brothers?

That it has, like these religions, some secondary parts
some practices, some devotions, attributable to the circum
stances of its origin or to the particularities of its history
is most certainly true. Did not the Saviour, in order to b
totally human, take similar individuating notes? So wit
Christianity. It has particularities which could have bee

different and which it could change. These or others it must have had to be truly a human religion.

But it is not for that reason less unique and absolute. And even its accessory or common elements assume, in it as in Christ, a dignity beyond comparison. They become, in it, supernatural means of going to God, and so, while being themselves divinised, they help to render it perfectly human, with an unequalled excellence.

So, in spite of these common traits, it can claim in the presence of all the other religions, an absolute superiority.

And its supereminence is so incontestable that it can even unite, like Christ, a total intransigeance to a totally receptive sweetness. Always the same contrasts, and in the same unity.

What attitude then does it demand of us with regard to purely natural religion? Hostility? Contempt? Not at all. The soul of natural religion, if we may so express it, is the tendency towards God. That is the very thing which the religion of the Man-God realises, but in a manner supernaturally perfect. And this perfecting of natural religion is not a sort of crowning superadded to it, but much rather an internal consummation which intensifies in transcendent fashion what was most essential in it. Between it and the Christian religion there is no division; it is natural religion which was assumed and elevated in Christianity, as it is our nature which was assumed in Christ. To despise this natural religion then would be to blaspheme Christ. But to be content with it, when Christ is there, would be a crime against it. Being the call of man to God, it insists with all its energies, once the Man-God is born, that we go towards Him.

And what must we think of the other religions, those which, in fact, exist, or have existed?

The problem is complex, but it can be simplified. These religions, we think, are the concrete manners in which men have conceived and practiced natural religion. On the common foundation of an aspiration towards God they have built their diverse interpretations; a manner, sometimes elevated enough, sometimes unworthy and gross, of representing God to themselves, and an ensemble of procedures intended to honor Him, procedures sometimes touching, but, often also, fantastic or abominable.

Must we, to be Christian, condemn all this *in toto,* as an immense diabolical deception, as a long fermentation of our evil leaven?

To us, so summary an execution appears neither just nor Christian. Alas! It is only too evident that, in the religious history of our fallen humanity, sin has not stood idly by. But has it labored alone? Was our nature vitiated to the point of producing only iniquity, even in those procedures through which, according to the formula of Saint Paul, human souls sought to lay hold on God? Together with elements of obscure and equivocal origin, would nothing remain of that religious tendency which pertains to the very substance of our being? Who knows? Did God never elevate by any grace of His those appeals to Him which were made in good faith? Are not sinners precisely those whom the divine mercy takes pity on? Is it not to the sick that the physician should come? And should we not say that, since the Incarnation was decided on, that is to say from the first origins of the world, God wishes seriously the salvation of all souls? We know that the profane history of the world is all orientated towards Christ. Why not the religious history also?

Whatever may be the fact about these divine secrets, one thing is certain: Christ is the point of contact, unique and perfect, between God and men; everything in natural religion, everything good in every possible religion, is found again in Him, in plenitude.

A Christian can, then, and ought then, to respect all the religious attitudes which he meets, and this without taking away anything from the exclusive devotion he owes to the perfect religion, which is his own. In all of them he will venerate the very same thing which Christianity alone realises fully; and, in a universal esteem for the good which his fellow-men have attained, he will express an absolute preference for the unique excellence of his own religion.

Such an attitude gives to the Christian apostolate an inimitable virtue. To attach himself to the unique mediation, no man need renounce anything truly religious. Between the authentically religious elements of all the cults and the religion of the Man-God there is no opposition. There is no continuity either, save in the measure that supernatural grace, outside Christianity, works on souls to lead them to the unique Saviour. The Man-God and His religion is not the culmination of any possible natural process: it comes from heaven.

But He comes from there so divinely man that nothing human, thereafter, can remain stranger to Him: He is the religion of men even before men accept Him: because, whether they wish it or not, God has become man in Christ.

We must always come back to that. The grandeur of Christianity is only the grandeur of Christ. The formula of Chalcedon—two natures, one person; Christ truly God, truly man, truly one—is what gives to our religion its transcendent qualities and its expansive force. It is, at the same time, the essence of Christianity and the religious charter of humanity.

CHAPTER III

Catholicism

BETWEEN natural religion and Christianity there is an abyss, which grace alone has filled up. Between Christianity and Catholicism there is none.

Never, even by perfecting itself without cessation, would the simple cult of men have attained God, as it attains Him in the Man-God. But, unless one stops it halfway, the religion of Christ can only be the Catholic religion.

Christ, in fact, is not complete without the Church, which prolongs Him, and the Church which prolongs Christ is the Roman Church. We must briefly consider these two truths one after the other.

I

The Man-God is not complete without the Church, which is His prolongation.

To know what the complete Christ is, we must consult Scripture and Tradition, as we did in order to know what Christ is as an isolated individual.

But such a study would demand a long development, which may be found in other works.[1] Here some indications will suffice.

[1] The Whole Christ, Mersch.

In Scripture we shall consider only some of the principal books. In the first place the Synoptic Gospels. They furnish only some isolated traits, but they are extremely clear. The Kingdom of God, which Jesus came to establish, is presented to us as closely united to the Saviour; it implies the perpetual presence of Jesus in the midst of His own; still more, a unity between Him and the faithful. So, when the Judge on the last day shall pronounce the definitive sentence on our race, He will sum up all our history and all the history of the Kingdom in an affirmation of identity: "I was hungry," He will say, "and you gave Me to eat; thirsty and you gave Me to drink; I was naked and you clothed Me." He alone then, in some sort, will have truly existed on the earth, and to Him alone will have been done all that has been done.

Then, continues Saint Paul, Christ and his own form not two, but one; one organism, one body, one man, one only Christ. He is the Head, they the members, and He the whole. Jesus Himself came down from Heaven to teach this doctrine to Paul: "I am Jesus whom thou persecutest," He said to him; and thereafter Paul wished to know nothing else. Everywhere he announces that Christ is in the faithful and the faithful in Christ; that the life, the death, and above all the resurrection and the glorification of the Saviour are continued in men, and that they are even their only hope and their only justice here below. God does not see nor bless them except in His well-beloved Son; thenceforth, all, Jews, Gentiles, Greeks and barbarians, are equally called to the same supernatural dignity in the one Body of Christ.

So, Saint John adds, pushing the same doctrine to its last consequences, Christians, united in Christ, are, in Him, something at once divine and human, as He Himself is at the same time man and God. The Incarnation is continued in the grace which divinises, and the fourth Gospel was written only to give this total view of the plan of God: that Christians might believe that Jesus is the Son of God, and that, believing, they might have life in Him. Between the eternal generation of the Son and our justification in the Man-God, there is no division: as Christ lives of the Father, Christians live of Christ; He is the Vine, they are the branches; He is the Light and they see in Him; they dwell in Him and He in them.

We can conceive of nothing stronger than the last words of Jesus in the last of His discourses. Jesus asks of His Father that, as He is one with the Father, so His own, among themselves, may be one. The unity of Christians, the unity of the Mystical Body, has its beginning and its exemplar in the unity of the divine Persons. A participated unity; a very imperfect participation, and one which comes to us only in the measure in which all is common between the head and the members. But a real participation, and one which even forces the love of the Father to descend to the last of the faithful, because thus far Christ extends: *ut dilectio, qua dilexisti Me, in ipsis sit, et ego in ipsis.* The Mystical Body is theandric, through the Man-God and in imitation of the Man-God.

On this inspired theme Christian thought has meditated through the ages.

And just as Christ assumes His fulness in the Church, this truth has found its full expression in ecclesiastical dogma.

Little by little, a doctrine has been elaborated, which, in formulating the Incarnation, has formulated at the same time the vivification of men in the Incarnate Word. It was the work of ages, as we have already said in speaking of Christological dogma; it was an ecclesiastical work also, in which, one after the other, all the great theological authorities have co-operated. It comes to an end in the fifth century in the teaching of Saint Cyril of Alexandria.

For the doctor of the Incarnation, as for the evangelist of the Incarnation there is continuity between the Incarnation and the vivification of Christians in the Incarnate Word. The Word has assumed humanity, he says; but, He is life; it must then follow that His humanity too is life, in its own way. It must then have in it that wherewith to vivify before God the entire Church. The entire Church, and each Christian in the Church, will live then with a life which shall be the prolongation of the life of Christ, and Ecclesiology, in consequence, will be only a continuation of Christology.

The Scholastics, for their part, though they considered things from a completely different point of view and with a very different method, have arrived at a similar system. The humanity of Christ, they teach, since it constitutes only one person with God, has in plenitude that intrinsic divinisation, which is grace. It must then, have it in sufficient abundance to effect, in the Church, the intrinsic divinisation of all Christians. So, with them too, Christology, without ceasing to be Christology, becomes an Ecclesiology.

This harmony is instructive, as it shows how truly Christian doctrine lives, in Christ, a life which is one.

II

But, the Church which truly is the plenitude of the Man-God, is the Catholic Church.

The doctrine of Chalcedon, we shall now see, is, unless

one halts it half-way, the doctrine of Trent and of the Vatican: the teaching is the same with the same tone and the same sense, but articulated to the end.

Let us take then, some truths particularly essential to Christianity; let us compare the Catholic teaching on these points with that of the dissident sects, especially with the teaching of Protestantism, of which we are thinking especially here, and let us see on which side one is faithful to Christological dogma and, hence, to Jesus Christ.[2]

In the first place, what is the Christian life, the religion which is in us?

It is not a product of our nature, reply all Christians: it comes from Christ, and, like Christ, it comes from God.

And likewise, the Protestants will continue, it is only for Christ: He alone is holy, even in us, and we, we are nothing before Him. Only, His holiness is so vast that it covers our miseries, and God sees, in those who have the faith, only the splendid veil of the merits under which Christ hides them.

But in that case, says the Catholic Church, Christ is not truly the life of souls, since He does not make them live.

And if He is not holy enough to cause in them a real and intrinsic holiness, can we still say that He constitutes only one Person with the Holy of Holies? In the Saviour, the union between the divine nature and the human nature is perfect. Why then hold as separate, in them who are His members, the divine and the human, grace and nature?

Why then still speak, in the Christian, of a humanity corrupted and powerless to do good? In Christ, the two natures are most intimately united and His humanity neither subsists nor acts outside the divinity. How then,

[2] Cf. *la Symbolique,* F. Lachat and *la Robe Sans Couture,* P. P. Charles.

in Christians, could nature exist apart and act apart, escaping totally the grasp of the Word, which was made flesh?

But nature, of itself alone, is nothing from the supernatural point of view, the Protestants will say. Yes, without doubt; but such a contention is quite beside the point for, in fact, nature alone is so slight a thing apart from grace that it does not even have to be considered. It is merely that which grace lays hold on, sanctifies and divinises.

Christ is everything, they will say.—Yes, without doubt; but annihilation is not the object of His coming. He is all in us.—Yes; but there will be nothing there, if His entry into our soul consists only in driving us out. In order that He may be all, in order that our justification may neither add nor suppress anything in the mystery of the Incarnation, it must be the Incarnation mystically prolonged. But then our supernatural life, derived from that of Christ, must be analogous in us to what it is in Him. But in our Chief, the humanity is holy in itself, though not of itself. We must then say that in us also, who are His Body, it is holy in itself, though not of itself.

This then, is the Catholic doctrine of justification. It alone, as we see, is not ashamed of the Incarnation.

The same thing appears, and almost in the same manner, in the doctrine of good works.

We must do good, we must try to resemble the Incarnate Word in His acts and His dispositions of soul: all Christians declare this.

But, continue the Protestants, it must not be imagined that these good works have any efficacy in the work of salvation. *Deo non fit additio.* They are necessary, because

God requires them: but they are useless, because, being finite, they can add nothing to the Infinite.

All this might be true, replies the Catholic Church, if the Word had not become flesh: one adds nothing to God; but God has joined Himself to humanity. Human action is then integrated in Christ in the theandric operation of one sole agent, the Man-God. In us, will it be so different from what it is in our Chief, that it will remain, even when we are incorporated in Him, the mere effect of our resources alone? Perish such a sufficiency and such a dereliction! Natural activity and supernatural activity are united in us—making all the necessary distinctions, for there are distinctions to be made here—as the two operations, human and divine, are united in Christ. No separation, no confusion either: "each form produces, but in communion with the other, what is proper to it," according to the formula of Saint Leo. *"Non ego tamen, sed gratia Dei mecum,"* according to the formula of Saint Paul. What acts in our good works is not ourselves alone, nor grace alone, but we and grace with us. When the work is done, it has a divine value because of grace; it is ours, because of our operation, and it is a unit, because the grace of the Incarnation is the union of the divine and the human. We do then truly perform divine works worthy of eternal reward. To deny it would be to assert that the work of the Incarnation does not proceed to its normal term, that is to say, to the Mystical Body.

In order to make more apparent the continuity between the Catholic doctrine of good works and Christology, let us compare the rôle assigned by the two sides to human effort.

The humanity of Christ has saved us, say the Fathers,

but not by being the first principle of our salvation. In the beginning there was only the Father, the Word, and the Spirit, and it is from Them that everything comes. In Christ, the first principle of everything is the Divinity. Only, in Christ, the Word unites itself to humanity, in order that its action may be more adapted to men and that men, in Him, may approach God. This mediating humanity is then for Him a means, an instrument, and the causality which it exercises is an instrumental causality. As the Scholastics, for the most part at least, have explained it, this instrumental causality is real, physical, and it even holds, among the instrumental causalities, a place apart, so excellent is it.

Coherent with itself and with Christian truth, Catholic Theology, in the doctrine of good works, merely adapts to Christian action this conception of the action of Christ. Our efforts have no value of themselves in the order of salvation; that is true. Nevertheless, God, Who has not disdained our race, makes use of them to sanctify us. They have then a wonderful power. And they have it, not by a kind of occasional causality, as if they were only the signal to which forces superior and altogether separate might respond. No, their virtue is in them, though not through them; they have a real efficacity, though secondary and derived; an instrumental efficacity; it cannot be better expressed, if we thoroughly understand that there is question of a free instrument, which, even when prevented by grace, is the initiator of its own action. Attached to Christ by mystic incorporation, as the humanity of Christ is attached to the Word by hypostatic union, they prolong in themselves, through Christ, the quality of instrument of God, which was in Christ.

Humility, then, and forgetfulness of our interests, attachment, dependence, obedience: for the saving of ourselves, we are only instruments. But great-heartedness also, joy, gladness: in this divine work we have our active, our indispensable part to play.

We find here again, in the Catholic attitude, that same opposition of grandeur and lowliness, which, from Christ, passes into the Christian attitude. Only here, as the Incarnation goes on in us to the end of its mystic effect and as the extremes are completely in contact, it is in us that the difference shines out between divine grace and sinful humanity.

So the Church cries out for works, for human works, because the divinisation of the universe is at stake. Let the faithful mobilise in their entirety: let them use their greatest ingenuity to combine the surest spiritual doctrines; let them deploy, in order to sanctify themselves, all the energy, all the sagacity, all the responsibility of which men are capable in their own affairs. Therefore, in the field of collective missionary and Catholic action, let there be works —studies on methods, associations and discipline, even assessments, propaganda and advertising. The salvation of the world is a human affair, and, save for miracles and the sacraments, we know nothing, if not that men are responsible for the eternal life of men. Let nothing human then, be cruel enough to absent itself.

Integral humanism, therefore—or rather, supernatural humanism. This exaltation of all human resources has neither its beginning nor its end in man. We must respect our efforts, venerate our prayers, lift up esteem of our action to the dignity of a cult. But we must realize at the same time the lamentable insufficiency of all this equipment. If God is not their strength, they labor in vain who build the house. We must, then, have forgetfulness of ourselves, abnegation and humility. And also, as we shall say in another place, the spirit of penance, of sacrifice, of immolation, in union with Jesus Christ.

Humanism, yes, but one in which man must renounce inflating himself with empty importance, so that he may be taken up, as an instrument, in a work which surpasses him and which comprehends him. Our purpose is not to make ourselves robust and clever rational animals: the destiny of a member of the Saviour is to resemble the eternal Father.

Let us consider the same contrast on still another point. We refer to the human aspect which the work of God takes in us.

One of the reasons which prevent Protestants from really uniting our human action to the divine action is the banality, the heaviness of our effort. Our virtues are so tepid, our progress so imperceptible. How believe that God lives in this? If God lives in us, everything in us should march with His step.

Rigorism then: be of iron and impose on men, upon the instant, a perfect sanctity; or contempt: tell them once and for all to dream no more of mixing in the work of God. But, in any case, piety: do not assert that grace is in their heavy gait.

Catholic spiritual doctrine has never admitted these extremes. Deeply impressed by the fact that God shows Himself to us only in the Man-God, she declares that God's views of us are human. Grace does not turn the natural laws upside down any more than divinity has altered the human nature of the Saviour. Miracles, even interior miracles, are rare. The laws of our Psychology, of our action, of our manner of making progress, are the instruments of which God makes use and not obstacles over which He makes us leap. But in all this, hidden like the life of an organism and secret like the God from whom it comes, circulates the grace of God. The proper marvel of Christianity is not God, but the Man-God, and the marvel of the Christian religion, declares Christianity, is not what God has done alone, but what He has succeeded in making us do. Our efforts are lamentable miseries, certainly, if one compares them to God, and if one sees only their human aspect, but magnificences, if one realizes that they have sent out roots in our dust and that a divine sap is slowly working there.

If we pass now from the order of action to the order of knowledge, we shall see that here, too, Catholicism, and it alone, believes completely in the Incarnation.

Let us take, for example, the attitude towards theological science, for nothing is more characteristic.

Protestants, always on guard against infiltrations of the natural element into the supernatural, have branded it with shame as a monstrous mixture of human thoughts with the transcendent truth. The Greeks too have a certain suspicion for new systems and new words.

As if the Word were not united to flesh in Christ.

The Catholic Church on the other hand, from the age of the Fathers, has never hesitated to think about revelation, and never has it ceased nor will it ever cease to seek the most complete understanding of it, to organize it into a system; in brief, to make of it an object of science. She knows, she who prolongs Christ, that ever since, in Christ, the eternal light united itself to a human brain in the unity of a divine Person, the subsistent Truth is bound up with human intelligence. In the same way as Christ, because He is united to life, renders our actions salutary and vivifying, so, because He is one with the light, does He make our eyes luminous. And just as all sanctity, in the Church, is not an addition to the sanctity of Christ, but merely an effect and an efflorescence of that which is in Him in fulness, so too, all that Catholic Theology points out of unity and of beauty in revelation only renders more approachable and more human the plenitude of truth, which is our Chief.

If then, in Theology, we must distinguish carefully between what is a truth of faith and what is a theological explanation, we must not, however, separate the two. The two natures in Christ are united *inconfuse, inseparabiliter;* so too, in Him, our stammerings are, not principles evidently, but still bearers of eternal light.

We have up to this point considered Christians especially in their separate individualities. It remains to see them in their collective life. Here, too, and here especially, the Catholic conception of the Christian life is alone faithful to the Incarnation.

The humanity of Christ, says the dogma of Chalcedon, because it is united to the Word of life, is the life of the world. The entire world then is vivified by one alone.

Consequently, continues the Catholic dogmatic teaching, the life of each of the faithful communicates, in its principle, with the life of all the others. It is then, though it becomes completely personal to each individual, a universal thing at bottom. Just as, by their own virtue, the actions of Christ were salutary for all humanity, so, by the intrinsic virtue which they have from their intrinsic incorporation in Christ, all the meritorious acts of the faithful co-operate in the salvation of the entire world.

This doctrine of the communion of saints, which is only an aspect of the Catholic doctrine on good works, has, like it, aroused the objections of Protestants.

Blasphemy against Christ, they have said. There is an injury to the universal mediation of the Saviour in this multiplication of salutary interventions. Christ, alone, has done enough for all.

The Catholic Church takes a different position. Refusing still and always to separate in us what God has united in Christ, she sees the mediation of Christ as excellent enough to prolong itself (in lower degree but really) as far as the Mystical Body, through grace, extends the Incarnation. Like the Saviour, all Christians and all the acts of Christians are Catholic and universal.

They have then, taken all together, a unity.

And this unity, all the Christian confessions declare, is that of Christ.

Also, continue the Protestants, it is not right to add any other. The Church has only one Chief: the Man-God; no man, were he Peter or the Pope, can without blasphemy declare himself the universal pastor.

On the contrary, affirms the Church, in order that the Man-God may remain always our only Chief, it is necessary that the Popes be always His vicars. The unity of the Church, in the Man-God, should be human, and a human unity is a man; and on the part of the Church, which still struggles on the earth, it ought to be a man living on the earth, visible, real, in flesh and bone, as the prolongation of the Incarnation is, on this earth. Not only the words of the Saviour assure it; but even His person and the rôle played by His visible humanity render it highly admissible: there should be always here below a man whose function, not his person evidently, is that of Jesus. A simple accord, the simple unanimity of a senate of bishops or of patriarchs would not suffice: these tend to exhaustion in the hours of crisis and are not readily discernible in stormy times, precisely when the rallying sign should be most incontestable. These purely spiritual and interior unities are not the ones which God chose when He became incarnate, nor are they the ones which suit our nature, which He has united to Himself.

As it is one in Christ before multiplying itself through deficient participations in the faithful, the Christian life should be one before being multiple and in order to have the power to be multiple.

The Protestants look upon ecclesiastical unity as the result of common aspirations spread abroad among Christians, and as the social aspect of the supernatural. Ecclesiastical authority, in its turn, is for them only the condition of unity and of mutual agreement, a simple function of the collectivity. So, they say, it should not embarrass at all the expansion of private piety nor the liberty of the children of God.

Yes, says the Church, if the Incarnation had not occurred. But, in the supernatural order it is Christ alone who causes life and movement to flow into His own. Unity and authority are then the principle of the multitude of members, and are far from being an emanation of it.

But, the grace of the Incarnation continues to vivify us. God occupies Himself with us, not in a manner altogether interior and spiritual, but in a visible manner. Grace forms a unit with exterior rites, with gestures, with persons. In this consists what we may call the sacramental order, of which the sacraments are the perfect realization, but whose principle rules all the economy of salvation. The entire

Church is like a vast sacrament, in the wide sense of the word: a visible form of invisible grace, an empiric organism which serves as an instrument and as a canal for the divine life.

Also, submission to the magisterium, observance of ecclesiastical precepts—and still more, total obedience, religious obedience—are not constraints, but the necessary bonds which attach the members to the body and the tool to the worker; and the closer the bonds the more beneficent they are. Constraint and complete suffocation result when one is cut off from life and from truth.

The Christian life, once again, is only a prolongation of the life of Christ. Alone among Christian confessions, Catholicism is completely Christian.

III

Catholicism is not then one of the Christian religions, but "The Christian Religion"; just as Christianity is, not one of the human religions, but "The Religion."

In the presence of the other Christian confessions its attitude is at once simple and complex: because its purity and its totality are the criterion for judging what is mixed and incomplete in them.

On the one hand, they possess authentic Christian elements, in variable quantities, certainly, and tending at times, alas! towards zero. But they possess them: they believe in the Incarnation, in our union in Christ with the Father and the Spirit; they recommend the filial attitude towards God, confidence, humility, prayer; they have the Our Father, the Sign of the Cross, apostolic rites, and even veritable sacraments. These gifts of heaven conserve their transcendent value, whatever may be the sins of us Christians, who have broken by our faults the unity of Christ. Wherever they are found they claim from us a veneration full of love, and Protestantism, because of them and in spite of everything, is holy.

But this veneration cannot degenerate into doctrinal indifference. In fact, alongside the Christian elements which it conserves, Protestantism has placed a negation. Following a natural repugnance to admitting that our substance, our acts, our knowledge, our ecclesiastical unity and its authority, are truly united to the divine action and intrinsically divinised, it does not wish to admit, in Christians, that union of the divine and the human, which, realised in fulness, constitutes Christ.

If it limited itself to saying that an elevation like this surpasses our human merits, it would say the very truth. If it brought up only a difficulty of fact, by maintaining that the conferring of this grace is not sufficiently demonstrated, there would be place only for a discussion of facts. But in reality, it seems very clear, the objection is a question of principle. It does not believe our nature capable of such grandeur, and it sees blasphemy—an excessive kenosis—in uniting God so closely with our clay.

But, with due proportion, the blasphemy is exactly the one which was found intolerable on the lips of Jesus, "How dost thou, being a man, make thyself God?" He was asked.

And in fact this repugnance to admitting in Christians the real and intrinsic union of the human and the divine, is aimed directly at the transcendent exemplar of this union, at the Man-God and the Incarnation.

And still, Protestantism wishes to believe in the Incarnation.

It is then constituted by two opposed tendencies, bearing

on the same object: faith in the incarnate God and incredulity towards this same incarnate God, as He is continued in Catholicism.

No stability is possible with such an interior antagonism. Even if it escapes an earlier stagnation and death, Protestantism can develop only by opposing itself more and more to itself, to end, by dint of clashing with itself, in exhaustion.

Of two things, one: either negation will win, or affirmation. If it is negation, if, through respect for God, through contempt for man, or through concern for natural autonomy, Protestants must separate the divine from the human in the Christian, the same reasons will demand the same separation in Christ. No more of the Man-God then, and no more Christianity.

And can they stop even there? If God must be considered far from us, what becomes of religion, which is, by essence, only a tendency towards God? The true God, we shall have to say, is inaccessible and unknowable: for us He is as if He were not. Imprisoned as we are in our finite being, we attain in our aspirations towards the transcendent only poor human fancies; religion is only a dream and a sentiment; some will say even a nightmare; let us call it the most beautiful of dreams and of ideas; in the last analysis, it is a vapor of the brain.

So a rent develops. In this closely woven fabric, which the work of God is, all holds together: to attack the Church is to sin against Christ and against God.

But also, in the inverse sense, to take oneself as one is, to tend to the supreme Good with all one's energies, is to be ready, though on an inferior level, to mount by grace towards the incarnate God. And above all, to be a Christian, even in an incomplete way, is to possess in one's self a Catholic element, which tends towards the Catholic Church.

Such is the second member of the alternative which presents itself at the interior of the Christian confessions. By the grace of God, affirmation can win over negation, faith in the Man-God can win over repugnance to admitting the theandric reality of the Church. As the aspiration towards God renders easy the belief in an incarnate God, attachment to Christ will bring faith in that organism, visible and one, in which Christ continues to be attached to His own.

And, for this return to unity the germ is found in all the Christian religions: it consists in everything Christian which they have retained. There is nothing to take away, consequently, except mutilations; nothing to suppress, except halts: it is a road which ascends, a seed developing, a flower which opens out at last. . . . Let the Christian life be intensified in the separated confessions, let the Christian elements, which are their enduring glory, reach their full unfolding: Christ and His Church have nothing else to ask. On the day when their Christianity shall be integral, they will have done everything necessary for entering into unity.

They will be, finally, themselves; for now they are not themselves. Bearing in their very life the negation of their life, they are in the anguish of death, or of birth.

In attaching themselves to the Catholic Church, they will find themselves, not in strange surroundings, but at home, in the unique family dwelling which God has made for the human race, and in which each nation has its exact place, prepared in advance.

They will have gained everything, and themselves besides. The Church will have acquired nothing, at least nothing essential. For secondary perfections, even important ones, are a different matter.

Made for humanity, Christianity does not attain its full meaning and its complete physiognomy except by informing all humanity. Each race, each people, realizes the human type in a different manner: the Latin genius is one, another the Anglo-Saxon, American or Germanic, another the Japanese, Hindu or Congolian.

There are then certain manners of resembling Christ, of being the divine man in the theandric Church, which only certain peoples can realize. The Catholic Church will not be perfectly Christian until the incorporation of all the nations into the unique body of Christ shall permit her to make explicit all the divinising virtualities of the Saviour. But this will be only an accidental perfecting and not a true addition.

At this moment she presents herself as Catholic and total. And this totality permits her to be as intransigeant as she is sweet and humble; she is infinitely comprehensive, not because she is capable of being distorted, but because she is so complete.

Non est quo a te omni modo recedatur. One does not succeed, when one has been united with Christ, at breaking absolutely with her. So the Church can, and should, consider as her own everything Christian that exists, no matter where. In respecting and in loving what is good in the other confessions, she does not doubt either her own unique love or her exclusive fidelity to the Spouse. What she insists on admiring in the fallen branches is what the tree has put in them, and what, with every vital force within them, cries out to be again attached to the root.

Total exigencies, but no slightest aggression; the Church

wishes to be everything, but not by suppressing anything; on the contrary she wishes to give to the rest its plenitude.

And that is what differentiates her from the other Christian confessions, and establishes in her the centre of attraction of all them: she is distinguished from them, not by a nuance or a particularity, but by her integrality: *differt ipsa ratione quasi generica christianitatis*. The others are constituted by their limits; she by the fulness with which she allows herself to be assimilated by the Man-God.

Toti non fit additio. To such perfection nothing can be added. By the return of the separated churches, the Church will gain nothing, except that she will at last expand in all their fulness her bound energies and her repressed vitality.

It is true that in fact the work of God, in our heavy hands, has scarcely begun and is already lacerated. It makes no difference. The Church stands erect as a demand, a promise, a leaven, of universal unity. The Spirit which is in her makes her solicitous about the human race.

We shall live truly with her life when we are tormented with the same anxiety.

It is not only on the map of the religions of the world that there are frontiers and divisions. Who would dare to say that he is Catholic, universal, in heart and soul, as he is in name? Our interests, our narrowness, our vanities, our incomprehensions, based on persons, caste, race, civilization, prevent us, not merely from being men in all the grandeur of that term, but from knowing and from feeling all the love that God places in our Church for the human race which He wishes to unite in the Man-God.

In our souls then, as on the surface of the earth, the Christian life is in combat against frontiers. A distant mission, and a mission wholly interior; but everywhere the same militant push, the same ocean which hurls itself into the assault against the dikes.

Our egoisms must surely yield at last; we shall become Catholic, and on the face of the Church will shine the immense invitation and the immense goodness of God.

On that day the world will not resist Jesus Christ; Catholicity will be a fact.

For, let us say in closing, Catholicism is "Christianity"; and Christianity is Religion, the Religion supernaturally perfect; and Religion is the whole of man. Humanity is then made for Catholicism, as Catholicism is made for humanity.

GENERAL PRINCIPLES

CHAPTER IV

The Incarnation and Spiritual Doctrine

JESUS CHRIST, according to Saint Thomas, is a first principle in the order of those who have grace. He is the Chief, and all their supernatural life and activity derive from His influx on His members. So this life and this activity have in Him their first norm, as they have their origin in Him. It is then from Him that we must learn what Christians are and how they ought to act, since it is by causes that we may best know effects.

But, in Jesus Christ, what is first is what He is, His person, His reality. What he has done, wished and ordered, comes second and has value only because of His personal dignity. *Operari sequitur esse,* says the Scholastic adage.

This is the logical and supernatural concatenation: the conduct of a Christian should be regulated by the life of grace which is given to him, by the precepts of Christ, and by the life of Christ. And all of this: Christian life, commandments and examples of the Saviour, is derived from what the Saviour is in Himself.

The Christological dogma, that is to say, the doctrine of the Church concerning the person of Jesus, is, consequently, the first foundation of the science which studies Christian actions: Christian morality is essentially theological.

From a principle so primary and so general, we can deduce, as is evident enough, only norms which are themselves altogether general. We have no further purpose in these pages. But such an end does not lack importance. It is the first directives which give spirit and sense to the rules of detail.

The task we are undertaking will occasionally recall the method and the teachings of the "French School" of spirituality. The points of contact are evident enough, as are also the differences, not to require us either to indicate them or to make them the object of discussion. It will suffice to offer our homage of admiration at the very beginning to the masters of the oratory and of Saint Sulpice.

I—CHRISTOLOGY

Let us begin then with the principle. The first truth of Christianity is the definition of Christ. This definition has cost the Church long struggles. It was formulated little by little in the Fathers and in the Councils, and was the more difficult to express as it supposes the doctrine of the Trinity already fixed, and as it must itself make a synthesis of all the different and apparently opposed elements in the Saviour's manner of being and of acting.

It was the Council of Chalcedon which pronounced the dogmatic words: "We all confess, following the Holy Fathers, and we all teach with one only voice: one only and the same Son, our Lord Jesus Christ, perfect, the same one in divinity, and perfect, the same one, in humanity." And the Fathers continue, repeating tirelessly both this unity of person and this duality of natures. Christ is "the same one," they insist, one only and the same Son, and in this unity, He is at the same time both all that God is and all that men are.

In this Christ the aspect which touches us, the one by which He communicates to us, in Him, the divine life, is the human nature, and that is what we shall especially consider here. It is this, according to Catholic doctrine, which constitutes Him mediator, second Adam, supernatural founder of humanity, and, to take up again the formula of Saint Thomas, first principle in the order of grace.

In the very first place, the Christian dogma declares, the humanity of Christ is a complete humanity. It implies a body and a soul, flesh and blood, passions and sentiments, an intelligence and a will. From the beginning, the Church has had to defend against heretical dreamings the concrete reality of "the man Christ Jesus." Her affirmations do no other than continue the protestations of the Saviour: He Himself objected when His disciples took Him for a spirit: He made them touch and see "that He had flesh and bones."

In this total resemblance sin alone is lacking. But, in truth, that is no true difference. For sin, far from adding anything to our nature, only takes away from it its integrity. Exempt from this privation, Christ is for that reason only the more a man, such as God conceived and wished a man to be, such a man as we ought all to be.

This total purity makes Him virginally free of all concupiscence. Pride of the flesh, pride of the spirit, all haughty, hard and distant egoism is absent from His soul, and no narrow introversion places between Him and others the barrier of petty calculations and of incomprehensions.

It is true that the holy humanity of the Saviour differs more from ours in this, that it has no personality of its own. It subsists in the very Person of the Word, and the first act of all its substance and of all its components: soul, body, flesh, blood, all in fine, is, as Thomism explains it, the existence which the Only-Begotten receives in the eternal generation.

But, like the absence of sin, this absence of human personality does no slightest injury to the resemblance of Christ to us, to His consubstantiality with us, as the Fathers say. He Himself has announced it, and the Church proclaims it. He has all the concrete rush of reactions, of habits, of sympathies, of will, which constitute an individual truly living; He has His own tone of voice, His favorite gestures, and, even after His resurrection, He can be recognised by the manner in which He walks by the river bank or in which He breaks bread. Personality, as the dogma understands it, is not, in fact, one of the constituting elements of nature; it is, explains the Thomist theology, the last act of all of them. Everything which constitutes Christ subsists in the Word, in the Infinite, and the humanity of the Saviour, not being in the last analysis hypostatized by a limited act, it follows—we begin at least to be aware of it here—that the very thing which distinguishes it from us and which gives to it in abundance what is most proper, most incommunicable, most "personal" in itself, puts it in the position of being able to contain us all mystically, and of being the life of the human race.

This is the truth which will become more and more clear to us.

It is not only by the moral dispositions of goodness and of kindness that our common Saviour is united to us. It is by function and by reality.

He came, He exists, He suffered for us. All the symbols proclaim it: *Qui propter nos homines et propter nostram salutem descendit de caelis. . . . Crucifixus etiam pro nobis*. Alone amongst men He has not had as the purpose of His life the acquisition of His own personal sanctity. He possessed it from the outset, total, and He has had to live only for others.

His reason for being is to constitute the contact between God and men. His humanity is a means: The Word took it to use it, to sacrifice it, to exalt it too, under the title of first fruits of the human race. In consequence, it has a mysterious union with all the other human natures, a union which is the supernatural exaltation and the divinisation, in some sort, of the union, already so close, which exists by essence among men, on the ground that they all participate in one same form and in a form which has truly, though imperfectly, its act. It is sociable, if we may so put it, with a transcendent perfection; it is magnificently and immensely human, because it subsists in God; it is then, as intimately united to the others as a human nature can be without ceasing to be a human nature, that is to say, without ceasing to be individual and personal. But is it not precisely a human perfection, an exquisite achievement of human nature, to be intimately bound to others and, as it were, interior to all? In intensifying this natural sociability in all possible measure, the hypostatic union, far from diminishing the individual character of the humanity of Christ, renders it, on the contrary, more total. We do not say the personal character, for, in the case of this humanity, the unique personality is that of the Word, and that is not the kind of personality, we have seen, which could prevent it from being united to all the others, merely by being itself.

Its action on others, in consequence, has, at its base, at its first point of departure, an infinity. Also, by itself, it is capable of having a universal efficacity. Because of what and who He is, His effectiveness will permeate its every action. Each of the events of its life has, in itself, the expansive force which renders it salutary for the entire universe.

On this subject the Scholastics propose a doctrine to which we should call attention, because of the application which we shall have to make of it in what follows. We mean the doctrine which attributes to the humanity of the Saviour a causality of the instrumental order in the work of salvation. The Word, they say, has taken human nature in order to apply to us more closely and to adapt to us more perfectly the divine action. The best analogy is that of the instrument which a workman takes hold of to do his work.

Evidently, however, it is an instrument in its own proper fashion, which is only analogous to that of ordinary instruments. This instrument is excellent, unique, without peer, because of the altogether singular relations which bind it to God who employs it, to men whom it works upon, and to the effect which it produces.

Instrumentum conjunctum: The humanity of the Saviour forms only one person with the Word of God; it is more inseparable from It than our organs and our members are from our bodies. Death was able to separate the soul and the body of the Saviour, but not His humanity and His divinity.

The humanity of the Saviour likewise forms a unit, only one mystical person, with the men whom it sanctifies, and it is through their interiors that it works upon them. We must not believe that its virtue is quite limited in itself and that, in order to act upon us, it needs the divinity as intermediary. This would be to overturn the economy of the divine plan. The divinity does not take an instrument in order, later, to have to serve as an intermediary itself, and as an instrument of that instrument. The divinity is and remains the first principle, and, if it does everything, it is in its transcendent manner, that is to say, by choosing its instrument, by giving it the necessary forces, by using it, but not by supplying its place. The instrument should have, through grace assuredly, a certain power to sanctify: it will have it then; it needs, in order to act really upon souls, a contact with them: again, it will have it; otherwise, what would it be in the work of God but a useless excrescence?

Also, by its very constitution, the human nature of the Saviour is capable of such an action. The end sought is precisely to communicate to souls what it itself possesses in plenitude: grace, union with God, the supernatural life. It acts then by its own form, if we may so put it, and produces its own resemblance.

The excellence of such an instrument makes it very close to being a principal cause. It is even, we may say, a principal cause, a first cause, but among the secondary, dependent, and instrumental causes: God being the only veritable First Cause. It is *causa prima in genere habentium gratiam,* but not *causa prima ordinis gratiae.*

To continue logically, we should say now, that the principal action for which the Word took its instrument, the supreme procedure also in which Christ is mediator, is the Sacrifice of the Cross.

But for ease of development, we prefer to reserve for a second part the exposition of Soteriology, and to draw at present the ascetic and spiritual consequences which flow from the Christology, which we have just been recalling.

Now, then, let us see in Christ the exemplar of this Christian life of which He is the Source.

Appareat itaque nobis in nostro capite ipse fons gratiae, unde secundum uniuscujusque mensuram se per cuncta ejus membra diffundit. Ea gratia fit ab initio fidei suae homo quicumque christianus, qua gratia homo ille ab initio suo factus est Christus, de ipso Spiritu est hic renatus, de quo est ille natus.[1]

Already Saint Augustine was proving against the Pelagians the gratuity of grace by the gratuity of the Incarnation. We would like here, following the same road, to deduce, from the different points of doctrine which we have recalled on the subject of the Incarnation, the different aspects which the union of nature and grace presents in us.

God, we were saying, *willed to unite human nature to Himself in the unity of person.*

What are we then, we men, if not those with whom God has sought resemblance and proximity? *Domestici Dei:* we are of His race and He is of ours, and henceforth He and we are bound together.

And forever. *The Incarnate Word has never ceased and will never cease to be a man;* his two natures are united without separation, ἀδιχιρέτως, and His Kingdom will have no end.

We too: no force can snatch us from His hands, and alone, our weakness can carry away for us that which, of its very nature, is life eternal.

God, for us, was made man.

He comes then to treat us in a human fashion.

Everything comes to us from Him in a celestial apparition of humanity and of goodness. His manner of acting will not be the *coup de force,* nor the multiplication of bizarre or unexpected prodigies. He does not act to show His superiority nor His inconceivability, but His union with

[1] St. Augustine, *Liber de Praedestinatione Sanctorum,* 31; P.L. XLIV, 982.

our nature, His humanity, we may say. He will not then upset the order of the world and overturn all the laws of which our nature is in part made and which He has assumed in the body which He has taken. His miracles are human, marvels of benignity and of love, such as that which is best in our souls secretly desires.

The work of God will walk amongst us as God has walked, so adapted to our manner of being that the lovers of pomp and of noise will not wish to recognize it. It will go the slow rhythm of the hours and of the years, by imperceptible progressions, and the increase of eternal life in us will have the patient allure which is suited to our modest powers of ascent.

God was made man; humanity, in Christ, is united to the Word.

A change has occurred, not merely in our relations with God, but within our race itself.

That is the essential thing, and its aspects are so multiple that it is hard to tell where to begin. A happy constraint directs our choice of plan: the order in which the consequences of the Incarnation have appeared to us in the humanity of Christ.

The human nature of Christ has been elevated to the hypostatic union with the Word, and that is the Incarnation.

Then we, the members of Christ, are no longer simply men. An elevation is given to us which changes us into divine men, and that is grace.

It is grace, appearing in our nature—and that in the first place—as an ennobling of our nature.

We must have respect then, for nature and the natural order. Respect even for matter and material goods: the use of the most prosaic creatures, of silver, of gold, of property, can make the matter of a vow; there is in science and in its interest in empirical phenomena something which goes, if one does not stop it half-way, to the Word, which has dwelt amongst us.

Respect for corporal things and, let us be frank, for the animal element too in our organism and in its activities. The origin of man merits a sovereign respect, the love which propagates him demands in the name of God that it be made the object of a sacrament among Christians, and perfect chastity, mounting still higher, is the consecration of all human love to the work of God.

But respect above all for man himself.

Because of the hypostatic union, the humanity of Christ is worthy of adoration.

Respect for man ought then to be elevated to the dignity of a cult. The members of Christ, once they are perfectly united to Him, are worthy of the cult of dulia. And all men, members, in right at least, of the Man-God, claim a supernatural love and veneration; they are the object of theological charity, that is to say, of a love which, in them, is really related to God, so much are they united to God in Jesus Christ. This love will lead a man to sacrifice himself humbly in their service, as, with due proportion, one sacrifices himself to God.

But the Word has assumed our nature in its entirety.

He has taken all our substance and our human manner of acting. *Totum cum toto:* "Nothing of God, in Him, is separated from man, and nothing of man is separated from God." [2]

[2] Council of Florence, Decretum pro Jacobites, Denz. 708.

Important truth, as the greatest of the Fathers have vied with one another to point out. If any part of us had been despised by the Saviour, this part would have remained outside salvation, and the divine life would have been given, not truly to the descendants of Adam, but to some other species like it.

But He has taken all: body, soul, will, intelligence—all.

Nothing human then remains exclusively ours. The total consecration of our being implies total exigencies. Everything human, in our spirit and in our body, is matter for holocaust and God does not wish rapine in the sacrifice.

Certainly, as we must state at once, there is an exception. The Word, in its humanity, wished no sin; so grace cannot admit it in us. We sinners then must pluck out sin from ourselves, if grace is to dwell in our souls. Abnegation, suffering, sacrifice, have a capital rôle in Christian spirituality: did they not fill the life of the Saviour? There is consequently in the supernatural life and in spiritual doctrine, a negative aspect, which is extremely important. But we prefer not to develop it for the moment. It will be more advantageous to reserve the study of it for the second part of this work, which considers Soteriology, that is to say, the attitude taken by the Saviour Himself before sin and the consequences of sin. That then will be the place to state what our dispositions should be, in union with our Chief, before the evil which is in us. Up to that time there will be a lacuna in our pages, which you will please note. The delay will not be inconvenient, however. Evil has no necessary connection with our nature, and we shall be able to continue speaking of it without mentioning evil.

The Word then has despised nothing in our nature.

Then, no more have we, in order to unite ourselves to

Him by grace, anything to despise in ourselves or anything to destroy. Sinners as we are, we ought to go to God with all our poor heart, with all our weak forces, and with all our complicated and obtuse spirit.

Alas! To truly take men, ought we not always to take them as they are, quit of rendering them, as much as we can, better than they are? So God has done. Such as we were, such as we still are, He has taken us and continues to take us every day.

So must we dispose ourselves in order to imitate God and His wisdom. Sanctity, like Christ, is totally human. A Christian spiritual doctrine ought to outline asceticism on the divine method, which does not commence by destroying man in order to redeem him. *Non in commotione Dominus:* God does not fashion us by a series of explosions.

Austerity, yes; mortification, yes, and total; we shall see that later. But in order better to cure and better to conserve. All the delicacies of our sentiments, all the shades of our Psychology ought to be respected. More still: all our resources, each according to its importance evidently, ought to be cultivated and developed. The law of our nature is to grow, and the God Who wished as an infant to increase in age and in wisdom before God and men, demands that we become men in fulness in order to become like to God.

We do not cease to march towards heaven by stopping before the lilies of the field. On the contrary, by allowing our souls to vibrate in unison with things, we make our hearts more human, and reproduce the action of the Incarnate Word, who stopped Himself before these created splendors to contemplate there the traces of an eternal love. It is not necessary to renounce the love of country because of perfection, since Jesus wept over Jerusalem. It is not necessary to extirpate friendship from the soul, since Jesus loved Saint John. It is necessary rather to respect strongly these human affections, and to require that they be limpid as the looks of infants and strong as death, since Jesus loved His own even to the giving of His life for them.

The Christian life is then simple, like the mystery of the Incarnation. Let one only be a man, let one be a man joyously, great-heartedly, and piously, but let one be a man because of God, who was made man for us, and in His manner.

A human ideal, consequently, but human in a supernatural manner.

The entire human nature of Christ subsists by assumption in the Word. The perfection of His humanity is due to the splendor of the divinity.

What interest have we then in the Apollo Belvedere and the moderate maxim of ancient wisdom: a healthy mind in a sound body! It is all over with these low aims since our nature forms only one person with God in Christ. Certainly one must be a man; but not to dream of being more is, henceforth, to refuse to be totally human. Our dust can by grace resemble the Only-Begotten, and the divine goodness can transfigure our smile. It is finished then: the naturalist idea is a profanation.

The material universe itself has received from the Incarnation increase of dignity. What shall we say then of our souls and of our acts? What is done in man surpasses human conceptions; for the divine work a divine master is required; we, we are only children in school.

The science of human actions is not then exclusively human; it is subordinated to the science of God, and our intelligence enters into it in a subordinate capacity. Still more: we are ignorant in large part of the aims of God on the world and on our souls. Only the general directives have been revealed; we know that God wishes to save all men and to give to all of them resemblance to His Son. But how, by what means, under what modalities, God does not tell us; and if he deigns to take us as workmen, he does not appoint us architects.

Christian spiritual doctrine is not then a special part of natural morality: an Ethic with some additions. Like Christ, it constitutes one whole. Its first principle belongs to it entirely, and it is the Man-God, force and light for His own.

Without doubt, natural speculation and philosophical reflection have their place in it, and we shall have to say in a moment what it is. But in any case, although it is not separated from anything human, it constitutes a science independent of the others.

Or rather, more than a science, it is a docility to an ever living master. Everything, for the member, consists in receiving from the chief thought and movement. But it remains to be seen in what this dependence and this docility consists.

Christ is the Son and no one else but the Son.

Members of Him who is the Son, Christians are then sons by adoption, "the adoptive filiation being a certain participation in and resemblance to the eternal filiation." [3]

So, though they are nothing, and though they are completely exterior to God in themselves and in all their qualities, even their supernatural qualities, Christians, in Christ, possess union with the holy Trinity: they are united with it, exclusively in the measure in which they are united to Christ, and exclusively by the union which Christ has.

They live of Him as He lives of the Father, and their

[3] St. Thomas, S.T. IIIª, Qu. XXIV, Art. 3.c.

life in consequence, in Him and in Him alone, has its first principle in the Trinitarian life, whence it comes to them by participation and resemblance, as Saint Thomas says.[4] Does not the Apostle affirm that Christians, in Christ, are seated at the right hand of the Father?[5]

We may surmise then the primordial importance of the Trinitarian dogma for the Christian life: it may be said that it is the great principle for the morality of Christians, inasmuch as they are united to Christ.

We see also how, for Christians, the Pater Noster, the prayer of the children of adoption, is a true moral code: a very simple, but very exacting moral code and one very sweetly adapted to us.[6]

We see too all that the Gospel means, when it demands that the faithful become like children. We see all the meaning of the "little way of spiritual childhood, which, according to the doctrine of the Gospel, Saint Theresa of the Infant Jesus taught,"[7] and which the Pope recommends so earnestly to all Christians.[8]

In Christ, the humanity has no personality of its own. It subsists in the proper being of the Son, Who, Himself, proceeds altogether entirely from the eternal generation.

So also with us. Our nature is no more independent. In the natural order, it makes a complete whole, so finished that all its obligations are determined by its possibilities; in the supernatural order it is no longer worth anything unless supported by grace. *Omnia autem ex Deo.* God must, by His action in us, arouse our acts; He must aid them, elevate

[4] Ibid.
[5] Eph. II, 6; Rom. VIII, 34.
[6] St. Thomas, S.T. IIa, IIae, Qu. LXXXIII, Art. 9.c.
[7] Brev. Rom., Oct. 3, Lesson 6.
[8] Acta Apostolicae Sedis, t. XVII, 1925, p. 213.

them, make them persevere to the end; otherwise, for our salvation, they are useless: the aspect under which they would be exclusively ours, would be that under which they would be without veritable solidity, without subsistence, without value.

In us, the first principle of our acts is no longer ourselves. Assumed by grace, as the humanity of Christ was assumed by the Word, we cease, not to be human persons certainly, but to be human persons in the isolated way and with the narrow completeness which would have been ours without this assumption. *Exclusa est omnis gloriatio.* We have done with all pretended sufficiency. Considered alone, we are incomplete beings.

Or rather, the very supposition which we have just made is what is incomplete. To consider nature in itself alone and without grace is a trick of the mind.

In Christ the humanity is so united to the divinity that, in wishing to study it separate from the Word, we think of it as it is not. In it, the absence of distinct personality is not an intrinsic lacuna, but, exclusively, the hypostatic attachment to the Word.

The same in us. There is not, in the first place, a powerlessness in our nature and in the natural order which grace might afterwards succeed in strengthening. Our insufficiency is only the consequence of the transcendent dignity which has been given to us and of the obligations which flow from it for us. *Dedit eis potestatem filios Dei fieri.* It is by relation to the immense power which is offered to us that, by ourselves alone, we are inept for everything: *sine me nihil potestis facere.*

Dogma of nothingness then, of humility and of absolute weakness: what is a man, Lord, when there is question of becoming perfect, as the heavenly Father is perfect?

But also dogma of omnipotence, of achievement and of plenitude. What can a man not do, Lord, in you, who are his strength?

Let us look at Christ. His two natures, united, act each in its own manner, but also, each in communion with the other. "Agit utraque forma, cum alterius communione, quod proprium est." Subsisting, not in itself, but in the Word, flesh of God, body of the Life, soul of the eternal Light, the humanity of Christ, by all its fibres and by all its acts, becomes a principle of life, of light, and of divinisation.

This elevation, like everything else, flows down from the head into the members, and should rule their conduct. *Non ego tamen, sed gratia Dei mecum.* We alone, we no longer exist, and when we work, we place in action something other than human energies. *Agit utraque forma cum alterius communione.* Our reality and our actions remain of themselves what they were, banal and tiny things; but because of their union with grace, they acquire in themselves, though not by themselves, a value for eternity.

Here one of the essential principles of the spiritual doctrine begins to appear in outline: the one which attributes to our actions and sufferings a causality of the instrumental order in our sanctification. It will help also to put an increase of precision into our formulas.

Instruments, in the ordinary acceptance of the term, are inert things which apply an action to an end, but which do not act by themselves. In the sense in which we understand them here, they are not inert: they are free beings. They will be then, in a real sense, the principle of their act, *causa sui actus*. But, and this is what we wish to say, they will be principles in a dependent, an essentially dependent, manner, and what they shall have to effect, and shall have to wish to effect in every act they initiate, will be the very thing which another, the principal cause, shall wish to make them wish, but shall wish to make them wish in a manner suited to free beings. Precisely because they are free, they cannot be reached, in their depths, by an action which is not theirs. God makes use of them then in order to act on them in the manner which they require. So, at the same time, they apply the divine action to the term which it is working on, and they are essentially dependent on the principal worker in the work undertaken. These are the two reasons which justify the application we have made to them of the term, instrument.

For what concerns the relation between Christ's manner of acting and ours, it must be noted that, between the union of the two natures in Christ and the union of nature and grace in us, there is this great difference, that in Jesus Christ the two natures are complete, while grace in us is not a complete substance. Grace, as we know, while it is an entity *sui generis,* cannot claim to be more than an accident. It is, not God Himself, not a being complete in itself, but a modification and an elevation of our being, a deiform and permanent quality which has no reality except in affecting our substance.

As regards its intrinsic nature, the question is obscure, and it does not seem that theology has said its last word on this subject. Let us say only, for what concerns our study and without wishing to make a methodical exposition, that the grace of Christians, while it is something for them and in them, is connected with the union of their souls with God, that is to say, with the increated grace, and it is inseparable from their incorporation in Christ. It is because they are united with God, inasmuch as they are members of the Saviour, that they are divinised.

Divinisation by grace, being thus a diminished prolongation of the excellences which union with the divinity gives to the humanity of the Saviour, does not differ from this union, except as a participation differs from the archetype. From the moment that one takes account of this essential subordination, all that remains is to grow in knowledge by contemplating their continuity. Let us take up again then the formula which expresses the communication of idiomata in Christ. We shall there see the communion of nature and grace in men.

Each nature in Christ, operates that which is proper to it, in communion with the other, because Christ, in spite of His double operation forms only one operator.

In the same way, in us grace and nature do not have two separate operations which develop their series of acts in two parallel lines and in different planes. So much the more because grace, not being a complete substance, is not an isolated principle of activity. It is "that by which" we are intrinsically divinised in Christ. It is then, for what concerns our manner of acting, "that by which" the activities of our nature have a divine worth. And the worth is as intrinsic to our activities as is the dignity conferred by grace on the very substance of our soul. When the supernatural work is effected, our nature has truly produced it through union with grace.

Union then, yes certainly. But also dependence.

Human nature has been taken by the Word as an instrument for the salvation of the world.

In the same way our own humanity: in the hands of grace it is the instrument of our salvation.

It is even the only instrument which depends on us. For the miracles of sanctification which God can perform when it pleases Him, remain His secret and His privilege. In the sacraments it is Christ who acts, and our rôle is limited to administering them, to accepting them, and to placing no obstacles. We must note, however, to be complete, that the effect of the sacraments depends in its intensity on the dispositions with which they are received.

But, apart from miracles and the sacraments, it is human nature which is the carrier of grace and the agent of divinisation here below. Not of itself, certainly: but inasmuch as, through continuity with Christ, who is the excellent and perfect instrument, it is the instrument of the unique First Cause.

Instrumental causality: the notion, for the subject of our study, appears to us capital, and we shall do no more than draw applications from it.

It will allow us to clear up the indefiniteness that still remains in the spiritual doctrine. The spiritual doctrine is not so much a science as a docility to an everliving master. That is true. But this docility is not a passive attention. The instrument of the Word is humanity, even our humanity. We must then make our divinisation our own affair. It is, to that extent, the object of human sagacity and tactics, the object of human science. We shall, therefore, have to determine exactly what our nature and its Psychology is, what our manner of acting is, and what are its moral laws. The common maxims of human prudence ought here to neighbor with our philosophic theses and the results of even clinical observation. "Sweetness does more than violence; to the small merchant a small basket; it is by hammering that one becomes a blacksmith; a bird must sing according to the shape of its beak," these humble proverbs will have their word to say, and an important one, in the human science of the divinisation of men. Nothing will be too small from the moment it is useful: we shall have to develop skill at keeping ourselves attentive along with systems of accountability and the play of sanction to maintain perseverance. Briefly, the spiritual doctrine will be a science as complex as human conduct. But it will have to be more complex still. After having given all its rules, it will have to keep repeating that they are all essentially insufficient; because, in the work of salvation, human conduct has the value only of an instrument. Its laws do not bind without appeal, and if we must apply them to the best of our power, we must, nevertheless, and before all else, not use them except in a sentiment of entire dependence upon the principal worker.

But we must use them and this ought to be said very plainly: the ideal thing, in the good instrument of grace, is not a totally inert human nature.

In Christ all the human nature was the instrument of salvation. In order to assume it, the Word did not previously empty it of all initiative; on the contrary: He is life, He made it more intensely living. All its resources of soul and of body, of action and of sentiment, of love and of suffering, have been strained and increased tenfold in order to transmit to our race in all its vigor, the supernatural life. It would be Monothelism to wish to suppress the human energy of the Saviour in order to exalt His divine activity.

The same with us: to cry up pure passivity as a means of union with grace, is to get into Quietism. Human workers, it is true, would be disconcerted if their tool moved of itself in their hands, but that is because man is not master of things and can use them only by some exterior accidents: by their hardness, by their structure, not by their essence. Before God, it is the very being of things that is in dependence. Creator of all, and of liberty as well as of the rest, He can take as an instrument our entire substance, even in what is most personal to it. If He had wished only inert tools, He would have seized hold of stones and of pieces of wood. But in choosing us, it is a living, thinking instrument, all trembling with interior spontaneity, that He wishes.

We would lack docility to His grace if we offered Him only a deboned human nature. It is by acting that one becomes the instrument of the Pure Act; let us be ourselves, and ardently, in order that He may be able to use us in our entirety.

Humanism then, once more; but once more also, supernatural humanism, made up of humility, obedience, abnegation, and charity. The glory of our nature is that it has been inserted into a work which surpasses it.

The Word has assumed a human nature as an instrument of salvation for the entire human race.

This universality of action ought to pass from the Head into the members. It is for the redemption of the entire universe that each one is an instrument. To say that God saves man by man means that God saves all humanity by all humanity.

It is impossible then to regulate the supernatural attitude by considering only isolated individuals: grace, like Christ, is human in a larger fashion. Made to flow into all by the same Man-God, it continues to be, in each one, a thing of the entire Mystical Body. The Catholic spirit, the missionary mentality, the ecumenical pre-occupations, are essential to this life and to the spiritual doctrine which is its science. One narrows souls, if one speaks to them only of themselves, or of their order, or of their country.

As our action is composed of influences coming from the entire Church and destined to have reactions on the entire world, it cannot be understood except in this ensemble. It is then, at base, a thing of universal charity.

Furthermore, the only one who can direct it is He who understands the working of grace throughout the entire universe, that is to say, Christ alone. Whence the necessity of obedience.

Our manner of praying ought also to be Catholic. No one makes a total prayer by himself alone, any more than anyone has total sanctity. Members of an organism, voices which unite with others to form an immense harmony, we are integrating parts of a whole, and our meaning is not in ourselves alone.

It would be possible to develop at length the Catholic aspect of the spiritual doctrine. It would even be very important; for it would show the union of all spirituality with the Church, with the magisterium, and through them, in a new way, with Christ.

But it is time to stop. What precedes suffices to show how Christ, first principle of grace in our humanity, is also first principle in the science which explains how our humanity ought to act in the embrace of grace. He is the transcendent type of the Christian attitude, and we need only make the Christological dogma explicit in order to find in it the rule of our actions.

Besides, the spiritual doctrine is so dependent on the Saviour, that it is not so much an abstract science as a living docility before the unique and ever living Master, who is Christ.

The formula is so true that we can conclude by reversing it: Christ is so perfect a Master that He is, in His own person, the résumé of all the spiritual doctrine. *In ipso erat vita, et vita erat lux. . . .* He Himself has borne witness to Himself: *Ego sum . . . Veritas.*

II—SOTERIOLOGY

Up to the present our exposition has been incomplete: it has not considered sin in us, nor the quality of Redeemer in Christ. We must now fill up this lacuna and see what Christ did in the presence of sin, in order to conclude what we should do.

It is always the chief who should be considered first, if we are to properly assign to the members their formulas of action.

But Christ is the surety for our sins. The Incarnation had, as its reason for being, the original sin and the crimes of men. Perhaps even, without the fall, it would not have taken place. At least God has not revealed to us anything certain on that subject. The surest thing about the Incarnate Word is that He came as a Redeemer, and that Jesus, in fact, is inseparable from our sins.

His Incarnation itself was the first and the principal of the means which He used to purify us. As the Fathers and the Doctors teach, vying with one another, it included such an exaltation of our race in Christ, our Chief, that by its own virtue it was capable of rendering us all immaculate before God.

But to this justice which, in principle, has been acquired for us, an obstacle presented itself in us: original sin and our actual sins, together with their results. What was then sufficient, if we consider only Christ, our Chief, was incomplete if we consider ourselves, the members. A miracle, without doubt, or, more exactly, a direct operation of God, could have arranged everything and grace with a victorious movement would have penetrated every soul.

Only, such was not the divine counsel in the Incarnation. Wishing to sanctify humanity by humanity, God wishes also to destroy the sin of men by the co-operation of men, and, so to speak, in a human fashion.

The humanity of Jesus also, in its human fashion, will have to deal both with sin and with the effects of sin.

Sin has no part in it, nor the effects of sin, which include a moral exhaustion or even an intrinsic imperfection. Its sanctity and its perfection are categorically opposed to it. So does the Head begin to rid us, the members, of it.

Still more: Not only does Christ not admit sin nor evil tendencies in Himself, but He takes exactly the contrary attitudes. He obeys even unto death, because our sin had been a disobedience; He loves God and souls even to the sacrifice of Himself, because sin had been a sensual egoism.

As for the effects of sin which imply no intrinsic imperfection, Christ takes them without stint. They are chastisements, certainly, but, in themselves, they do not constitute any weakness, and He will undergo them for the sins of others. They will come to Him then from the exterior: from His executioners or from His free will, which will give access, in Himself, to sorrow and to torturing foreknowledge.

Nothing will be lacking there. From the crib to Calvary His life will have something opposed to what we would have dreamed for Him. Messiah, but Messiah humble and hidden, He will do the work of God and of men in poverty, in self-effacement and in contradiction. A day will come when He will be tortured in all His body and in every manner, when He will open His soul to impressions even more dolorous for Him, the Holy One: to confusion, to shame, to overwhelming, before the divine Justice, under the sins of humanity.

All will not be consummated until it is all over with Him. It will be required that He disappear from the surface of the earth and, in spite of His Resurrection, it will remain forever true that, from Friday to Sunday, the Incarnate Word was dead.

The proof of it is incontestable; the sepulchre is still there, and on His glorified body, the blows which killed Him are still visible. Only, they are today streaming with splendor.

For Christ underwent these sufferings and death to save the world: they have been the matter of His acts of love and of sacrifice, and they have a glorious and eternal aspect in the effects which they have produced.

It remains to draw the conclusion from what the Saviour has been to what the Christians whom He saves should be.

The Incarnation, we have just finished saying, has a connection with sin: the reason for it is a struggle and an expiation.

The serene perspectives which we have considered up to the present allow then the uncovering of only a part of the truth about our conduct. The supernatural life which the Incarnate Word causes "to inflow" in us, is a life of struggle and of war.

Sin is, in fact, in us, and grace wishes no more of it in us than the Word wished of it in Christ. We must then, quit ourselves.

Abneget semetipsum. And to know how to quit ourselves, it still suffices to look at the Master and to follow Him: *Et sequatur Me.*

To follow Him, yes. All the faults in the world do not prevent us from being His.

On the contrary. Christ, we have seen, is essentially Redeemer; He is, in fact, and as He came, inseparable from sin.

Our very crimes then can attach us to Him. They can furnish the elements for our holiness, magnificent shades of humility and of confidence for our love. Peter would not be Peter, and his physiognomy would not have all its supernatural beauty without the trace of tears on his cheeks. Augustine, without his *Confessions,* would not be Augustine.

In the same way as He uses Satan to form His elect, God makes use even of our past sins to shape our souls. It all consists in taking our sins as He takes them, in order to detest them. "Shall I then," as Paul says, "multiply faults to make grace superabound? God forbid!" The divine plan integrates sins, but in an inverse sense, by making us flee and deplore them. We must consider them as the worst of miseries, and they will become for us stimulants for union with the God of mercies.

God wishes to disengage us from our miseries, but through ourselves.

In Christ, it is the human nature which serves as an instrument for the divinity to work the redemption of men.

In us also. Humanity is the instrument which God deigns to take up in order to purify humanity: He saves man, as He divinises him, by man.

The first condition is to be between His hands.

The first reason why the humanity of Jesus consumed our sins in itself is because it was united to the Word and in virtue of that union.

The same thing is true in our case. The great means of delivering ourselves from our sins is to unite ourselves more to God by the sacraments, by prayer, by love. The disinfection of our interior is not the preliminary condition to all entrance of grace. It is the result of that entrance: it is life which, by the force of its invasion into us, makes death fall back.

It is not for that reason any the less true that, in every spiritual system, the purgative way must come before the unitive way. Not that man can in reality rid himself of his stains otherwise than by union with God. But because, in psychological experience, that which attracts and ought to attract the most attention in the beginning is the fight against faults and especially against self-love. At this time the conscience is greatly encumbered with material preoccupations, impressions, sentiments. Besides, what it perceives best when grace is penetrating it are the complaints of sensibility and of the lower part. Life is being lived at that level, so it is there especially that the conscience ought to act. Later it will become more capable of a more enlightened co-operation, one more suited to it. But from beginning to end the task will remain the same: the conquest by the true life of everything that is mortal in us.

This will then be a struggle. Our nature, which God uses as an instrument, is penetrated with evil of which we must be cured. Our nature, itself, is not evil, certainly; but evil, original, habitual, actual, has placed it in a certain opposition to the very work which it ought to accomplish.

The operation will have then something paradoxical about it, and God, often, will make us do the contrary of what we would have planned.

More still: the Redemption has been an overturn. As Scripture and the first Fathers have already pointed out, Jesus has opposed contraries to contraries: to our rebellion, a total obedience; to our pride, a crushing; to our sensual covetousness, an immolation.

This procedure we must continue.

To be Christian is to turn oneself against oneself; it is to detest, to overturn something in oneself; past sin and its persistent effects.

To weep is not enough. Christ has set Himself against the current; for us too then the Christian tactic must be the offensive: *Agere contra*. We shall not flee then—save for the exception which will occur to every one—we shall react positively. Against egoism, principle of all evil, we shall practice detachment, humility, mortification; or rather, to keep the lead more surely, we shall insist on what is positive in these virtues, on generous, humble, mortified love for God and the neighbor.

In Christ the struggle has been even to the Passion, even to sacrifice, even to death. He has taken on Himself all the effects of sin, to make of them, as we have said, the remedies for sin.

Such should be our attitude also. And we would like to pause here a moment, for we have come to the Christian doctrine of suffering, one of the pearls of Christianity, one of the great chapters of the spiritual doctrine.

Let us go back to the beginning, to the Incarnation. When God decided to become man, humanity was no longer the marvel which had gone forth from His hands. Soiled and wounded it lay, an immense sick body, over all the surface of the earth. It is on it that God took pity. Despising neither His work nor ours, He became man, not only in the philosophical sense of the word, but son of man, heir of the heavy human past, man in the historical and concrete sense of the term. He has then taken our miseries and our sorrows. They occupy too large and too legitimate a place in our life for the Word not to assume them too, in assuming truly the descent from Abraham.

He has taken them then, and He has allowed the wave to inundate His soul even to the depths.

He has not taken refuge, to escape them, in a stoic hardness; He wished to feel all the confusion which overwhelms our flesh and our soul before them: it is as a man that He has endured the sorrow of men.

But human sorrow, in being thus taken up by the Incarnate Word, has been transformed. In being made one with God, it has acquired a divine value and it, the ancient vestige of sin, has become an antidote to sin in becoming the principle of a higher life.

It retains its virtue in us through attachment to Christ.

To suffer then is no longer merely our lot as men and as sinners, it is a supernatural vocation. Man is born for pain, they say, as the bird to fly—and the Christian, like Christ, is born to suffer and to die. The life which he receives in Baptism, is, by essence, a destructive life, destructive of everything sinful in him, and of all the old man in him.

So it nourishes itself on mortification. Its instinct of self-preservation, its will to grow, express themselves, by a sort of reversal, "in a diligent care to seek more and more continual abnegation in all things, as much as shall be possible."

It is not however necessary, in order to fulfil the function of suffering in a Christian way, to tense one's soul to superhuman efforts. On the contrary, patience should be human, as Jesus Christ was. It is useless to pretend that tortures cause no pain. It is useless even to wish to endure them beyond one's strength. Let each man suffer with his own resistance: it is concrete humanity, composed of men of courage and of others, which is united to God in Christ. The lot of many will be "to carry their cross with littleness, joining to the sorrow of carrying it the shame of carrying it badly." The essential thing is that, when each one has carried his part and his own way, the Mystical Body of Christ gives their plenitude, their pleroma, to the redemptive sorrows of the Chief.

We ask ourselves even, if we should not say more, and if the essential thing, when God wishes that we suffer, is not simply to suffer. This, evidently, is only an opinion, which we mention in passing, but it is too much in keeping with the ideas expressed in these pages for us to pass it over in silence.

We wish to say that acts of positive acceptance, of patience, of sorrowful love, are without doubt very salutary and meritorious, when suffering touches us. But these are acts, meritorious as acts, and different in themselves from the suffering endured. Are they necessary in order that our suffering may have some salutary result? Would it not suffice that we should suffer without positive rebellion in order that, truly, if we have grace, *aliquo modo,* if we do not have it, our sufferings may expel sins by union with the sufferings of Christ?

The wording of the Christian dogma about the death and the Passion of Jesus seems to indicate that, in themselves, abstracting even from the intense love and adoration of which they furnished the matter, they have had a considerable efficacy in the work of salvation. Might we not say as much, with due proportion, and in the measure in which they are united to Christ, of the members of the Saviour; especially since, in virtue of the dispositions in which Christ suffered, all our sufferings, in Him, have been offered to God for the salvation of the world? The dignity of Christ is, by participation, ours: when the body of a man suffers, when a human soul is tortured, that is not a trifle in the sight of God. He who sees us, chooses us and loves us in His Incarnate Son, does not divide those whom He has united. The sorrows which our flesh endures are the continuation and the complement of those of the Saviour. In the persecuted Church, according to the testimony of Jesus Himself, it is Christ Who is again tormented.

The vocation and the grace, which attach us to the universal Redeemer, attach our expiations to His sacrifices: so truly is it in virtue of this sacrifice that they have been given to us, in order that, in Christ, humanity may make satisfaction for itself.

That is the explanation of the singular esteem which the Fathers of the Church and spiritual authors have for suffering. They often have the air of considering it useful in itself, and their exhortations to renunciation and to suffering do not seem to indicate that the Cross is worthwhile only because of the virtues of which it is the occasion and the stimulant.

In Purgatory the pains expiate of themselves, *per satispassionem.* Could they not produce something analogous in us during this life, the more so because, it should be noted, for a thing as difficult as suffering, the simple absence of rebellion is already the act of a well-disposed will?

Suffering, in sum, is by essence a passive thing. Since

Christ takes it as it is, in us and in Himself, can we not say that it is received with the indispensable dispositions, from the moment when it is received at least passively and without refusal in the superior part of the soul? We could then say that, just as Christ takes our activity in all its active elements, and that He sanctifies us by our acts, so He unites our passivity to Himself in all its passive components, and that He purifies us by our sorrows, *non ex opere operato, sed quasi ex passione passa.*

Whatever may be the fact about this opinion, and we leave it to the reader to evaluate, it is certain, in any case, that in the conquest of sanctity, sorrow ought to play a considerable rôle. The most frequent image of Himself which God shows us, in the Church, is the crucifix, and the food of our supernatural life is the victim, the host, of a perpetual sacrifice: we live always on death, as on bread.

If such is the worth of suffering, what will the value of death be!

The Man-God died for our sins.

We also then, His members, ought to die.

The Man-God has vivified and resuscitated us by His death.

It is then by our death also that we shall live.

In the Man-God death was not a necessity of nature, but a redemptive act and an instrument of salvation.

In us also. To die, for us, is something other than a physiological phenomenon. It ought to be an act, and a solemn act, of cult and of resurrection. In advance or at the moment itself, we should make of it a sacrifice.

A special grace is ready for the task: the grace of perseverance; a special sacrament is prescribed for it, at least in general: Extreme Unction. For our part, let us try to co-operate in this matter as instruments, by allowing God to come and take us, without rebellion. *Vive moriturus.*

As the scars have remained in the glorified body of Jesus, the sufferings and the death remain in the Mystical Body.

They remain there in their own proper nature: bitter by their banal realism and their imperious brutality.

But their very hardness, which makes them chastisements of sin, makes of them also, in Christ, remedies for sin and sources of beatitude.

They continue then here below after the Incarnation, but under a different banner. They too are glorified.

All that is human has been transfigured at the contact of Jesus without being altered.

Integral realism in an integral optimism, Christianity takes the entire man, and exactly as he is, but for the purpose of rendering him in his entirety, and through the full sum of his resources, like to God in Jesus Christ.

Sin itself does not efface this general note of the divine economy. God overturns sin and turns against it all its effects.

Also, even in this liquidation of human passivity and in what are, at first sight, its negative and pessimist elements, the Christian doctrine remains essentially positive and optimist. Its optimism is even singularly absolute and does not believe it should deny either evil or sorrow, because it feels itself of the stature required to change them into good.

The rôle assigned to penance, to the struggle against self, to sorrow, is immense. It can even appear primordial. But it is transitory and essentially accidental. Evil, all evil, remains always that which should not have been: it is present then only to take its departure, and all that remains of it serves only to expel it.

So suffering can never be total. Since its reason for being is to beget for beatitude, the innermost heart of everything is the eternal life, and it comes to us through everything. One should then fast, but with a joyous face, and the saints in their rudest penances will weep with gladness as they reflect that they are only pardoned sinners.

Even while suffering, even while struggling, all one does is love God and men. Hatred for self, yes; obstinacy in destroying nature in ourselves, yes; all the force of these traditional formulas is required to express the ardent battle which life, in us and with us, wages with death. But these formulas should be rightly understood. One who would see in them the expression of a radical misanthropy or of an absolute antagonism towards our nature which God has created and which Christ has divinised in Himself, would completely misinterpret them. It is through respect for our human nature, through charity towards man, that Christianity sets up such limitless requirements.

To sum up this entire article in a few words, we would say that a spiritual doctrine, like the Christian doctrine in general, is not in the first place a declaration of war, but a formula of union.

The fundamental truth is that God has created everything, that Christ has redeemed all of us, and that, in Him, human nature forms only one person with the divine nature.

Union with God, union with Christ, union with all men in Christ and in God, that is the essential, and in a certain sense, the whole thing.

The first, the unique precept even, is to love God and the neighbor.

And also, since God is not accessible except through the

humanity of Christ, and since the humanity of Christ is no longer visible here below except in men, the centre of all spiritual doctrine and the great means of sanctification is love of the neighbor, zeal for souls.

To contribute, in ourselves and in others, to this mystical prolongation of the Incarnation, which is the divinisation of the human race, is our entire duty, and it should constantly preöccupy us.

For this divinisation, if we except miracles and the efficacy of the sacraments, should be produced by our efforts. Let us act then, let us work with all our human energies and with all our human prudence. And let us suffer also, with all our body and with all our soul.

But in this integral deploying of all our resources for the divine service, let us always remember that we are only instruments. Humility then, obedience, detachment, prayer; but no depression and no mutilation. This integral dependence aims at realising us in our entirety, in the hands of God in union with Christ.

This is the Christian program.

The author of these lines begs leave to add a word. It seems to him that this program corresponds exactly to the one which Saint Ignatius Loyola proposes to his children. So it will not be surprising if, often, it is the ideas and the very formulas of the saint which quite naturally flow from his pen.

Literary dependence, filial rather, which it would have been hard not to declare.

CHAPTER V

Holiness of Christians, Holiness of Members

A CHRISTIAN is a member of Christ: that is the résumé of Christianity.

A Christian should act as a member of Christ: that is the résumé of Christian asceticism and the code of all sanctity.

But, to be a member of Christ implies two aspects, two attachments. In the first place, the attachment to Christ, for the member ought to adhere to the head. Then, the attachment to all Christians, for the member ought to adhere to the entire body. These two attachments, in fact, constitute only one: for a member, adherence to the chief or adherence to the other members is the same attachment, the one which gives life to the member. *Multi unum corpus in Christo, singuli autem alter alterius membra.*[1]

Christian sanctity, in consequence, since it consists in acting as a member of Christ, consists in acting with the same double attachment. Attachment to Christ in the first place: all our virtues can be only a flowing, an influx coming from the Chief. Then attachment to the members: all our virtues can be only an element, a part, a member in some sort in the only sanctity which is total, the sanctity of the entire Mystical Body of Christ.

Since these two attachments constitute only one, as we

[1] Rom. XII, 5; I Cor. XII, 14.

have just been saying, to speak of one is to speak of the other. Each one, however, is a different aspect of the same reality, and in order to know this reality fully, it is helpful to consider them separately. The preceding study has treated of the first; this and the following one speak especially of the second: of the essential necessity which each individual Christian sanctity has of uniting itself to the other sanctities, and of the insufficient, incomplete and partial character of the individual sanctity, when it is considered merely as an isolated entity.

I

Incompletion, we say. Not that Christian sanctity transforms only a part of our being, while leaving the rest pagan. No: the Council of Trent teaches [2]—*in renatis nihil odit Deus:* there is nothing in us which is not divinised at Baptism. Not that our efforts should be confined to certain virtues only and have no interest in the others. In the first place, because, psychologically and logically, the enterprise would be contradictory: we should take away with one hand what we might build up with the other. And also because, from the moral and theological point of view, it is with all our heart that we must love and serve God. Not to make God reign in one part of our wishes, of our preoccupations, of our sentiments, would be the same thing as saying that grace should not take possession of all our being, and to say that, as we have just been recalling after the Council of Trent, is against the doctrine of Justification.

Everything in us ought then to become holy. But, and it is here that the incompletion appears, all ought to become holy, not in the manner of a whole, but in the manner of a part in a whole. Total, when we consider the nature which

[2] Session 5, Canon 5.

it ennobles, Christian sanctity is partial when we consider the glories which it confers and the heights to which it makes us rise, *quoniam sumus invicem membra.*[3]

Incompleteness then, but incompleteness of an order apart.

Incompleteness, in the first place, which is, as we have just been saying, the incompleteness of a totality. Intrinsic incompleteness, in other words. It does not consist in the absence of a complement which should have been added from without; it resides in the most internal substance of our supernatural being.

Incompleteness then, but constituting incompleteness. In the supernatural order it is as necessary to be completed by others as it is to be ourselves. *Credo unam sanctam, catholicam et apostolicam Ecclesiam,* says the Symbol of Nicea-Constantinople. *Unam sanctam,* the two words are not placed together by chance: the Church is holy by that which makes her one, that is to say, by the common attachment of all her members to Christ, and she is one by that which makes her holy, that is to say, by the very justice with which she animates her members and which is, in all, the participation of the same justice of Christ. In the same way, the members of the Church are holy by that which makes them one, and they are one by that which makes them holy, for that which binds them one to another is the incorporation of all in the thrice holy Word which was made flesh. But, precisely, this common incorporation, as it constitutes their totality, makes them parts and members one of another.

Incompletion, besides, which is not merely the incompletion of a totality, but which is intended to confer on this totality a totality more complete: that which makes us need

[3] Eph. IV, 25.

one another ought to make us rich with all the treasures of the divinity, for these treasures, in Christ, are given to the totality of the Mystical Body.

Briefly, incompletion without parallel, supernatural incompletion which ought to confer on Christian sanctity something unique in its kind and altogether special.

And in the first place, we can conclude, there is no separate and individualist holiness. Between each soul and God there is no private and reserved path along which one may journey protected from his neighbor. There is a unique way, which lies open before all souls at once, and this way is Christ. *Ego sum via,* He has said: through Him, and through Him alone, one goes to the Father.

On this unique way there are no isolated bypaths: it is the way itself which moves onward and which advances those who travel along it. *Via viva,* says Saint Paul to the Hebrews, in speaking of Christ. The progress of all is one in its principle; it remains one in its unfolding. The efforts which are made are solidary, and complementary one to another: they enter into one another. As a drop of water in a wave is carried along by the entire mass, each Christian, in his ascent towards God, is lifted up by all the others.

We speak here evidently of the efforts made by those who are already members of Christ. But it would not be difficult to generalize the affirmation, and to extend it to everything of a truly salutary kind accomplished here below. All men, in fact, are by vocation members of Christ; everything that is good for eternal life, in whatever manner, concurs in the incorporation of men in Christ; and everywhere Christ is the Christ of the Church and the Christ of unity. We can say then that everything which is in the line of sanctity, and by everything holy in it, is in the line of unity. But, abandoning this generalisation, which would complicate the exposition and which each one, with the help of a few distinctions, can easily make, we speak here only of men already attached in fact to the Mystical Body.

For them, no separate sanctity; for them, even, no salutary action, no good deed which they can produce alone.

It would be wrong then to demand of them complete good works, works finished in themselves, presentable by their own excellence alone. Why should it be required of a member who, in his being, is not a complete whole that he be complete in his action?

Evidently each one must force himself to have the fewest possible defects in all his works: he will still have quite enough of them. Besides, it is only by putting all his resources into his efforts, that he will make them "partial" in the proper manner, in the manner which corresponds exactly to the manner in which he himself is a part. But to pretend that they are completely finished is an illusion: one would have to be blind not to see the defects which riddle them; one would have to be impious to snatch them from the unique ensemble in which they are realisable.

Every action of a member is taken up again, sustained, implied in the action of the whole. So with the good actions of Christians: they serve only to continue what others have begun; they prepare what others are going to finish; in themselves alone, they have neither their beauty nor their explanation.

One should not despair, for example, if he finds in his acts of virtue, even in the best of them, deficiencies and narrownesses, unawarenesses and failures. One should not be astonished if, often, in spite of all his good will, he does not even think of what he is doing, if he forgets to offer up his action before commencing it, if he loses sight of the very act which he is placing, while he is forcing himself to do his best; if the very attention which the work requires prevents him from performing it with a spirit actually straining towards God. One should not be distressed because sorrow, when it becomes a little strong, consumes the energies which would have served to change it into resignation and into oblation.

All this would be disastrous, if it were necessary that the member should glorify himself in himself. But all this is normal and excellent, if the member should glorify himself only in the Lord and in "the Body" of the Lord.

Our good works are only pieces, by themselves incomplete and unintelligible. But should they be anything else? Each block of stone in an arch is, in itself alone, an odd shape and a defiance of equilibrium. But the very singularity of its structure and the obliquity of its position, which, precisely, render it incapable of standing alone, are they not the very things which will constitute its solidity in the whole, by attaching it to the others?

So with our actions: their insufficiencies and their excesses are like the hollows and the excrescences which articulate the members: they constitute the gears by which they engage one another. What matters it if one become distracted, despite all his good will, in the very midst of the actions which he has just commenced for God—if at that moment another renews his attention, and if he is one with that other? Suppose one does not succeed in offering his sufferings to God when they become intense and overpowering; what matters it still, if another, then, presents to God, in our name, all suffering and all action here below? There is no room certainly for any proud self-sufficiency, ut this is the triumph of unity, it is the communion of aints, it is the solidarity of members: *pro invicem sollicita unt membra.*[4] The essential thing is that each one humbly lo his best, however little it may be; the whole thing is hat each one remain in the unity of Christ. In unity all is ommon and, in it, each one, having done only his own art, has none the less done all.

It is just as impossible to form a judgment of what Chrisian sanctity is outside the whole, as it is to attain it outside he whole. It is then an error and a cause of unjustified everity to consider a Christian or a class of Christians part, and to find then that the work of grace has collapsed n them. One sees, for example, only the working classes nd declares, a little hastily perhaps, that, as a group, there s no longer anything Christian about them. One takes hree-quarters of the persons who have been baptized, and ronounces that their minds are completely taken up with he things of this world, with the bread which perishes, and vith trifles. One sees only too quickly the scandals of every ort which have unsettled them, the lack of instruction and of formation which attenuate their responsibility, and one sks oneself where, in their souls, is the work of the Saviour.

Without doubt, there is still much to be done for the postolate, both among strangers, and in our own regions. But that is not the question. Can we say of these souls, or of these groups of souls in which we see little of Christianty, that they are almost not Christians? In our opinion his would be an error in point of view: it would be to judge hem apart, as if they were isolated, when the Christian ife is an attachment. The sanctity of each member of the Church is constituted in different manners, *in mensuram*

[4] I Cor. XII, 25.

cujusque membri,[5] by the sanctity of the entire Church. The sanctity of the crowds—and who knows if he is not of the crowd—is, in a certain measure, in the measure in which the body of Christ is one, the sanctity also of the best and of the most humble—and who would dare to say that he is one of them? To evaluate a part of the body, the entire body must be seen. But, God alone can have a view so vast and so penetrating.

We do not have to judge. If we seek out these deficiencies to apply a remedy to them, that is excellent; but if our purpose is to despise our brothers, though it be a little only, let us not search them out. When we ascertain them—to the extent to which they can be ascertained—let us strike our own breasts, let us increase our sanctity, let us press more closely up against the others, in unity.

In unity (this is another consequence) in unity alone can sanctity be understood. To divide it, even if it were the better to examine the pieces, would be to destroy what we wished to study.

To make this clear, the best thing is to consider sanctity in its stage of full development, that is to say, in heaven.

In heaven, assuredly, there are different degrees of glory: some see God more perfectly than others, according to the greatness of their merits, the Council of Florence affirms.[6]

But these degrees do not indicate separations; on the contrary, they only serve to show the different manners in which each one is united to the others in being united to Christ.

[5] Eph. IV, 16.
[6] Decretum pro Graecis, Denz. 693.

The saints are not like stars, which shine each one with ts own brilliance, removed from the others by abysses of lacial space. They are one. When their radiant holiness s revealed, their incorporation with all in the same body s revealed at the same time, and it is just as radiant. On arth we could not see how perfectly they held together in Christ. But when Christ shall appear, then also will appear vhat unity there was in all the members of His Mystical Body.

The temptation would then be entirely absurd—it is rue that they are all absurd—to consider holiness as a way vithout promise. The most beautiful places are taken, we night say: no one will ever again be Mother of God, nor oster-father of Jesus, nor apostle. The extraordinary vocaions, which suppose exceptional graces and which lead to nusual sanctity, are very rare and the ordinary person cannot pretend to them. Before the mass of human beings, efore us, the perspectives which open up are banal: a anctity of the millionth or the billionth degree, magnificent n itself, assuredly, but very mortifying for self-love. At est, we shall be lost, drowned, indiscernible, in the immense troop which no one can count. "No one can count t," [7] that is very true; we shall not even be a number.

We shall not be a number. We shall, all of us, be the whole.

The view which we have been studying, according to which individualism breaks up the gladness of unity into separate sanctities, is as false as the individualism is narrow. When the life is one, when the splendor is one, each one possesses all of it. So in Christ: each one, when he is definitively united to the members of the Saviour, enjoys

[7] Apoc. VII, 9.

the happiness of all; each one in his own manner certainly for each member has his place; but each one in truth, for the body is one.

Congaudent omnia membra.[8] The members have their own way of rejoicing: it is "to rejoice with," to rejoice all together. The saints have their own manner of exulting in the gladness and the glory, it is to exult in unity. The joy of the greatest constitutes in part the happiness of the smallest, and the most resplendent, far from eclipsing the others, share their radiance with all.

But the unity of the Church militant is the same as that of the Church triumphant. It is in a preparatory stage, it is as yet imperceptible to our eyes of flesh, but it is not less real.

We must then conclude that the life of grace, while it has certainly, its degrees, has also its unity: we live only by unity: the unity of Christ.

In consequence, if it is true that each one receives as his own the grace which sanctifies him personally, it is not true that he receives it in separation from the others; for it is by incorporation in Christ that he receives all the grace that is given to him, and incorporation in Christ is, identically, incorporation in all the members of Christ. There is a distinction, yes; that is of faith. But there is no isolation. The members, in the body, are distinct, and even different, only that they may be the better united.

Grace then is not a matter for dispute or for jealousy. He who has received less—and besides how can he tell how much he has received?—cannot feel distressed because others have received more. Even for him, it is good that others should be more favored than he, because what is given them as their own is also given to him as his own.

[8] I Cor. XII. 26.

In the unity of the body, in the indivision of love, even those who receive the least have received the whole.

Mystery of grace, mystery of difference and of inequality, and mystery too of equality and of unity, it is the mystery of the Christian life.

Those who have abandoned the Christian life and the unity of Christ can no longer comprehend this mystery. The Protestants, for example, speak of a unique sanctity, of an equal sanctity in all the members of Christ. It is the very sanctity of the Saviour, they explain, which is imputed to all the faithful and which, in all, covers with His personal innocence, always the same, their personal misery, always lamentable. They say this. But let us look carefully: this sanctity which superimposes itself on our malice does not make us holy ourselves, and it cannot be said that the sanctities of the members are truly all equal, because it cannot be said that the members are truly holy in themselves at all.

The Catholic doctrine is altogether different. There is no question here of a sanctity equally exterior to all. All, the Church teaches, are sanctified in themselves; all are sanctified in their own degree and in their own manner: each member is placed in the body as God has wished [9] but all are placed so by a sanctity which remains one in its source and which constitutes the unity of all in its unfolding, for the members of the body, however numerous they are, are only one body.[10]

This synthesis of equality and of difference, Saint John Chrysostom explained to his faithful.[11]

[9] I Cor. XII, 18.
[10] Ibid. 12.
[11] In I Cor. hom. XXX P.G., LXI, 251-252.

The members, he said, do not differ from one another by nature, nor by their life, but by the arrangement of their positions. "Now," says Paul, "God hath set the members, every one of them in the body as it hath pleased Him." (I Cor., XII, 18.) He says very well "Every one of the members" to show that all have their function. It cannot be said, in fact, that God has placed one and not another: on the contrary, each one finds itself situated as He has wished. In this way, it is good for the foot to be placed as it is, and not only for the head: if it changed its position, if it abandoned its place to take another, even if it seemed to have profited by the change, it would have lost all and behold it would decompose; it would no longer have its proper position and it would not reach another.

"If they all were one member, where would be the body? But now there are many members indeed, yet one body." (Ibid., 19, 20.) See then how Paul argues and how he carries it off. That which made them believe that they were not all of equal dignity, that is to say, the great differences which they remarked between them, this very thing serves him to show that they are, and in this very thing, of an equal dignity. How? I am going to tell you. "If they all," he explains, "were one member, where would be the body?" This is what he means to say. If there were not among you great differences, you would not be one body; and if you were not one body, you would not be one only and unique thing among you; if you were not one only and unique thing you would not all have the same dignity. If, then, all of you had the *same* dignity you would not be a body; if you were not a body, you would not be one; if you were not one, how could you be of equal dignity? But now, because you have not all the same gifts, you are a body; being a body, you are one only and the same thing, and you differ in nothing one from another inasmuch as you are of the body. It is then the great difference which is among you, which engenders equality. So the Apostle is able to continue: "Now, there are many members indeed, yet one body." Thinking of these things, let us reject all jealousy, let us not envy those who have graces greater than ours, let us not despise those who have received the smallest. So had God disposed things.

This divine disposition is a lesson for us.

II

Each Christian sanctity is the sanctity of a part. So Christian asceticism is the asceticism of a part.

Not, of course, that it neglects the individual, for then what would it be interested in? There is nothing else in humanity or in the Mystical Body of Christ. It contains then, and almost exclusively even, rules for the particular examen, tactics against faults, etc. But it gives these rules in a Catholic spirit; because the purpose which it assigns to them is to form, not merely a perfect, honest man, but a Christian united to the other Christians in the one body of Christ.

In a purely individualist asceticism the fundamental disposition would be the aspiration towards personal moral excellence, the desire of perfecting oneself. This desire is very praiseworthy, incontestably; in fact, if it is properly understood, it is the necessary stimulant of all progress; but, unhappily, it is too easily misinterpreted. In our minds, which tend towards self-sufficiency, it becomes quickly and without our perceiving it, a call to I know not what spiritual ambition, a mask which covers, under devout appearances, reserves of vanity, of egoism, of dryness of soul, of obstinacy. Then, and this is the principal objection, to Christians whom God wishes to sanctify in union with the entire human race, it does not state the essential truth.

The essential thing for members is that they be united with all the other members; the essential Christian virtue is then the virtue which unifies all the members of Christ, that is to say, charity.

Charity is in the supernatural life what the instinct of self-preservation is for life in general. In every living thing, the primordial function is the dull tendency which unites it to itself, the cohesion, if we may so put it, the solidity with which it clings to its own existence. But, in the supernatural order, our own proper being, our only total and complete being, is the entire body of Christ. Our first duty, the first condition of our life, is then to adhere, and with all our strength, to this entire body, that is to say, to have charity.

The only life which we may live is the universal life of this entire organism; we must then succeed in feeling, in desiring, in willing, as parts and as members, in the immensity of the entire organism. But it is charity which works this happy transposition. It is then charity which adapts us to the real, to the splendid real, which is ours. Far from leading us astray in a land of mirage, far from absorbing us in vain tendernesses, she, and she alone, renders us solicitous about the only task which must be accomplished, the salvation of the human race.

However astonishing it may appear, the formula is rigorously true. If we are to make progress in virtue, we cannot do without the knowledge of our dominant fault, and no more can we do without certain notions on the missionary apostolate. The one as well as the other determines the dispositions required for self-study.

Does this mean that a person must at the outset throw himself headlong into works and be free to neglect his own sanctification? By no means; the whole does not grow greater, unless the parts develop; in order that the entire Church may gain in sanctity, each Christian must force himself to sanctify himself.

It is not then the heresy of works which is here proposed. In fact, there is not even any question of works. We speak of the motive which leads Christians to undertake all their works, of that interior and invisible thing which is the source of all Christian action, and we say, or rather the entire Church, after Jesus Christ, declares, that this thing should be love, love of God and of the neighbor, love of God in the neighbor.

Works—in the sense in which we here understand the word, for we are not Protestants—works are not always necessary. Often, in fact, Providence undertakes to show that it can get along without them, by effecting or by permitting mishaps which render them impossible. But what is indispensable is the charity which urges men to them. If this should be diminished, the salt would have lost its savor, and what would maintain in the Church the ardor for apostolic labor?

Evidently, if charity is sincere, it will show itself in works: love which does not act, when it could act, is a lie. But this exterior action, if it gives an exterior expression and, as it were, a body and a new fervor to charity, borrows all its force from charity. Definitely, charity is all; it is she who converts, who dedicates herself, who sanctifies, and, if the rest is useful, it is because the rest must come from her.

After charity, and right alongside her, we must mention another virtue which is also necessary to those who are members: we mean obedience.

Charity makes us love in the manner of a member; obedience makes us will in the manner of a member. Both, consequently, from different but very neighborly points of view, give us the attitude of parts attached to their whole: the one by co-ordinating us with the other parts, and this is charity, the other by subordinating us to the ensemble of the other parts, and that is obedience.

We shall speak of obedience at length in another place, to show how it unites men to God and permits them to effect divine results. Here we wish to say that it unites men to the entire work of God, that it teaches them to will in the manner which is suitable to a member united to all the other members, to "will with," with all the body, with all the regenerated human race, and that thusly it permits them to perform fully human works, Catholic works.

Or rather, since obedience constitutes precisely the unity in charity, what it permits men to perform is not so much a multitude of works, as one only—an immense work, the Catholic work, the salvation of the entire human race in Christ.

The fact is, that the sanctification of a Christian is not a purely individual thing. To speak truly, there is nothing purely individual in the Church: in a living organism, between what concerns the part and what concerns the whole, there cannot be an adequate distinction.

As we have explained, the most personal good works of a Christian should find their completion in the works of others; it is the needs and the forces of the whole which determine for each member his physiognomy, his work, his resources. Some ought to pray for all, others should be charitable for all, still others must teach, or evangelise, or care for the sick, or chant the divine office, and always for all and in the name of all. How can we know, from our point of view alone, that which cannot be decided except from the point of view of the ensemble?

Ah! if a man's only duty were to scour his own virtues, strictly speaking he might believe himself competent. Of course, he would not be competent; for who knows both the supernatural perfection which God wishes to place in his soul and the depths of his soul where God wishes to place it? But, at least, his illusion could be understood.

But now, in the presence of the immense work by which God wishes to sanctify all men, and all of them together, and all of them by one another, and all of them, even, by all the procedures of all the others, who can believe himself qualified: who can deny that, if he is not to grope his way along like a blind man, he must allow himself to be guided, he must obey?

Obedience, as is clear, appears here as the dependence of the members on the ensemble. That is a secondary aspect of it, certainly; it is, in the first place, submission to the authority which holds the place of God. But this aspect, secondary though it is, is interesting: it shows the universal and catholic element in it.

It shows also in the superiors whom one obeys a function which is important, though it is, to be sure, secondary also. It makes them appear, not formally as vicars of God and of His Christ (that is what they are in the principal order and we shall say it in another place) but as representatives of the supernatural organism which is the Church; or, if you wish, as representatives of Christ, not formally inasmuch as He is God, but inasmuch as He is the unity of His Church and the source of life for all Christianity. To obey them is not then merely to obey God, it is also to obey the work of God, to obey the grace which works upon humanity, which is, after all, the same thing.

It shows also that obedience is indispensable (and by a special claim) to the active and to the enterprising. It is the most active parts of a machine which must be most accurately adjusted to the others; it is the priests, the missionaries, the apostles, who must be the most closely attached, the most exactly subjected to the work to which they wish to consecrate themselves more entirely.

It shows finally, as we shall see again in another place, but from another angle, what a splendid thing obedience is. It consists, not in wishing little or in wishing less, but in "wishing with", in wishing with all regenerated humanity, in wishing, consequently, in a manner desperately and supernaturally human.

Obedience is then altogether like to charity, and it is not well practiced except in the spirit of charity. Like charity it is an "ecstatic" virtue, a virtue which makes us go outside ourselves and which permits us escape from our limitations and from our impotencies. Like charity, it is a "unitive" virtue, a virtue which attaches us to God and to humanity, a virtue which makes of our will and of all human wills, one only will, in the unity of the Mystical Christ.

CHAPTER VI

Prayers of Christians Prayers of Members

CHRISTIAN prayer is like Christian action. Martha and Mary are sisters and should resemble each other. The same quality of parts, the same *partialitas,* which demands of every Christian that he attach his efforts to those of all the others, demands of him also that he attach his prayers to all their prayers.

The manner of being of a Christian is to "be with," to be with Christ, as a member with the Head, to be with the other Christians as a member with the other members. The manner of willing which is suited to him is to "will with"; the manner of praying which is required of him is to "pray with."

So, to know how one of the faithful ought to pray, it is not the individual who should be first considered. It is the prayer of all Christianity. For it is the prayer of the group which shows what is and what should be the prayer of each member.

But, to know what the prayer of Christianity is, it is not Christianity which must be considered first, but He from whom Christianity comes in its entirety, that is to say, Christ. It is in Christ that we see what the Church, His Body, is; and it is in the Church, the Body of Christ, that we see what the faithful are. So it is in the prayer of Christ that we see what the prayer of the Church is, and in the prayer of the Church what the prayer of the Christian is.

Certainly the prayer of a Christian, since it is the prayer of an individual, ought to have an individual character, something spontaneous, interior, invisible from without. But this personal aspect, in our view, is not different from his very personal attachment to the group. So it cannot be considered outside of that attachment: that is evident. We shall establish it again, merely by speaking of the prayer which we ought to make in the Church and in Christ.

Let us see then Christ and His prayer, and, in Him, may we see ourselves and our prayers.

I

Prayer occupied the life of Christ here below; it even composed, in a certain sense, all His substance; since He was in Himself the Man-God and since, therefore, He realised in His single person the perpetual oblation of humanity to the divinity. This prayer of all His instants, that of His days of toil and that of the long nights which He passed in prayer on the mountains, He united and brought to the maximum of intensity in a supreme oblation, when He offered Himself up entirely. All His acts of love and of cult, all the piety and all the religion which He brought into the world in Himself, converge towards Calvary and towards the Sacrifice of the Cross.

This was a unique sacrifice, one of transcendent perfection, the most perfect ever offered by this Pontiff who infinitely surpasses all the pontiffs. It is a sacrifice, consequently, which is not a prayer alongside other prayers and comparable to them; which is not among prayers the most august and the most powerful; but which is, in truth, the prayer, the prayer unique and total, the one which takes up in itself all the prayers which have ever been offered here below, to render them acceptable.

And this, not merely because He who prays is God; not merely because amongst men He is the purest and the most holy; but especially because in His unity of Man-God, He is the mediator between our race and the Father; because in His humanity, which subsists in the Word, He is the Head of a Mystical Body, and no man lives before God, no one loves, no one prays, except by living and praying in Him.

Also, His prayer subsists perpetually, precisely because of its unique perfection and because of the perpetual rôle which it must fill. Jesus left it to His own in memory of Him, and without ceasing to be His holocaust, or rather, because it is continually His holocaust, it is, across the ages, the holocaust of Christianity and the everflowing source of the piety of Christians.

It is the Sacrifice of the Mass. The Mass is the Sacrifice of Jesus Christ inasmuch as this Sacrifice is continued and renewed in the Church; it is this Sacrifice considered in the act of its efficacy, in the communication of its virtue which it makes to us.

The Mass is also, like the Sacrifice of the Cross and by the same title, the prayer without defect and without equal, the perfect prayer and the absolute prayer, the prayer so total and so sufficient that no supplication need be added to it, that all prayers derive from it, that all prayers find in it their spirit and their strength, that it gives to all worship, which is practiced here below, its centre, its meaning and even its possibility.

Also, as it is always indispensable, it is always renewed. From the east to the west, over all the surface of the earth, at all the hours of the day, the most august act that men can place ceases not to be accomplished.

More still: from one oblation to the other, it gives itself a sort of prolongation. And it is of this prolongation that we must speak especially, for it is in it that we are going to find the prayer of Christians.

But this prolongation is double, for the Church in which it is produced, has a double aspect. It has a body and a soul, a public life and an interior life. In the two, this Sacrifice from which all Christian life derives, finds a sort of perpetuity.

II

In the body of the Church, in the public and exterior life of the Church, the prolongation consists in the liturgy. What continues there is the exterior and visible aspect, the "body" of the Mass, if we may so express it. The Mass is essentially constituted by the words of consecration, pronounced by an ordained minister, over the bread and wine. To this sacred action, the Church, as a public and visible society, has given a sort of context which is also visible. This is, in the first place, the ceremonies, the supplications, the lessons, of which the ensemble of the Sacrifice is constituted. There are then the psalms, the hymns, the lessons of the breviary. These surround and prolong the liturgy of the Mass, as this liturgy itself is the accompaniment and the frame of the Sacrifice properly so called. Thanks to it, the Sacrifice is never completely finished. From one oblation to the other, and while this same oblation goes on propagating itself over all the earth, each local Church remains grouped about its altar and the prayer of Jesus is continued in the prayer of the Church, without a break and without cessation.

No more than one can divide the body of the Chief or the Church of Christ, can one separate this solemn supplication from the act in which Christ, in the Church and by the Church, offers Himself to God with the Church: it is a part of it, or rather, it is its soul.

Such is the liturgy in its magnificent totality. But it is not this totality which, for the moment, we wish to consider; it is only a part of it, only the exterior element, the words, the rites and the ceremonies which serve as a frame for what is essential in the holy Sacrifice and in the confection of the sacraments. It is in connection with this part and with it alone, in fact, that the question of the relation between the liturgy and private devotions, which occupies us for the moment, can be proposed; so it is this part which the term liturgy will designate.

This liturgy is a magnificent prayer, not merely because of the inspired character of almost all its formulas, not merely because of its plenitude of meaning, of its adaptation to our nature, of its discretion, of its antiquity (all this, in fact, is only accidental to it) but especially because of its very essence and of its reason for being. It is the holy context given to the Sacrifice of the Saviour by those who are the authentic representatives of the Saviour; it is the official prayer of Catholicity; it is the voice of the Church, inasmuch as she is, at the same time, a visible society and a society of religion and of worship.

Since it serves as a context and a prolongation to the holy mysteries, something of the grandeur of these mysteries is prolonged in it. Because of this, it is, like them, the prayer, the prayer unique and absolute, the Catholic and total prayer. This it is, in its own special manner, by title of authentic and official expression. Any prayer not attached to it in any manner, neither immediately nor mediately, any prayer which does not have in it, by any title, its formula and its exterior expression, is not truly a prayer of Christ and cannot then be truly a Christian prayer. Outside the Church there is no salvation, we must assert; in the same way, we may continue, in the sense just explained, outside the prayer of the Church there is no prayer.

But this ought to be stated precisely. The liturgy is, essentially, a vocal prayer. The very thing which constitutes its grandeur determines its nature. As it is an exterior and visible prolongation given by the Church inasmuch as she is a visible society, to the Mass inasmuch as the Mass is an exterior and visible rite, it is and can be only an ensemble of words, of chants, of actions, of exterior and visible ceremonies. Everything about it is regulated, even to the least details. While he is performing it, the celebrant ought to disappear as a private person and no longer be anything but the agent who lends his lips and his arms to full Catholicity. Even if he says Mass in an isolated chapel, even if he is alone when he recites the canonical hours, he still speaks in the plural, because he speaks in the name of the entire Church; even if he says his breviary in a very low tone, he should still move his lips and form, as Moral Theology says, *aliqua vox tenuis,* some shadow of perceptible pronunciation, however slight it may be; because it is of the essence of this prayer to be an exterior prayer, a prayer of the Church, inasmuch as the Church is a visible society. Meditations, fervent reflections or even attention to the sense of the words which he pronounces, are not strictly necessary. The essential thing is that the minister, in the name of the Church, should say properly and should wish to say properly, the words which the Church dictates to him.

Evidently, he can add to this recitation pious reflections, movements of devotion; he can even arrange to follow the recitation which is of rule by a second recitation. But this is no longer an official prayer. And even if he should of his own movement insert into the imposed formulas meditations according to his taste, or any words, however devout they might be, he would to that extent corrupt, in an unhappy or even culpable manner, the prayer which he ought to say in the name of all.

These other prayers, these acts of personal devotion, the liturgy often suggests. We see it expressing, to God and to the Christians who hear it, the movements which arise in the secret of souls, movements of repentance, of joy, of praise and of oblation; movements of which it is the expression, as the cry on the lips is the exterior formula of the joy in the heart, but movements which are not itself, and from which it ought to remain, not separated certainly, but distinct.

The time has now come to speak of this personal devotion.

III

It also is attached to the Mass. The Mass, in fact, as it is an exterior rite, is a hidden reality. The words of the minister over the bread and over the wine are only the sign and the cause to which God has joined a prodigy, or rather a series of prodigies invisible to our eyes. In the depths to which faith alone attains, Christ is present, and He is present as an oblation, and He offers Himself to God as a host and to men as food, and in Himself He offers all men to God.

Just as the Mass has a prolongation in its exterior aspect, it has one in its interior aspect also. The first prolongation was the liturgy, inasmuch as the liturgy is the exterior prayer which is made in the Church considered as an exterior and visible society. The other is interior; it is realised in the interior of souls, and it is the individual prayer, Christian devotion.

Like the liturgy, personal piety can be understood in two ways. In the first place in its full totality, inasmuch as it comprehends in itself, as its soul and its all, the prayer and the Sacrifice of Christ Himself. Then, in a more restricted manner, inasmuch as it is only the piety of Christians. For the same reason as in the case of the liturgy, it is in this second sense that we shall take it for some pages, as the context will sufficiently indicate.

It is then the prolongation, the true prolongation of the prayer of Christ. For, the act of worship of Christ Himself, His Sacrifice and His Mass, is accomplished only by rendering the victim present under the form of food. It must also be eaten. Communion, as Christian doctrine teaches, is an integrating and necessary part of the holy Sacrifice. The minister at least must receive Communion as minister, that is to say in the name of all the Church; Christians also must receive Communion, and it is greatly to be desired that they do so often and even every day.

But every Communion, even if for good reasons it does not take place at the liturgical moment, is Communion with the Christ of the Mass; there are no other hosts to receive than those which remain over from a Sacrifice. The host, always and everywhere, is the victim of an immolation, and, when it enters into one of the faithful, it is the Sacrifice itself which, in some sort, passes into those who are present to it and it implants itself in them.

For the future their existence should be a prolongation of what He is, and their prayer a continuation of His.

So the prayer of the Chief takes up in itself the prayer of each member, by the very act by which the Chief takes His member up into Himself and makes him live in Him. The prayer of a communicant is the prayer of Christ and his very own at the same time, and much more Christ's than his own.

It is also the prayer of all the faithful. For what Christ does in one, He does in all. In making them all one in Him, He makes all their prayers one in His prayer. The one who prays in me is absolutely the same one who prays in all the others who have received Him. There are no longer separate Christians, there are no longer separate prayers. There is now only one man, the Man-God, the Man-God with His own; there is now only one voice which rises from the surface of the earth. It is His, but it is His, grouping and uniting in itself all the voices. And, *qui vos audit, me audit;* God himself, in listening to men, hears the voice of His Well-Beloved Son, of His Son who came to dwell among them.

Nothing shows as well as meditation on the Eucharistic mystery what the members are, precisely inasmuch as they are members, and what the prayers of the members are, precisely inasmuch as they are the prayers of members: prayers which are all united together by the very thing which is their origin.

So we can never sufficiently emphasize what a lesson in prayer the Thanksgiving after Holy Communion is. Not merely because it presents a soul better disposed for the sacramental action, and because this sacramental action is union with the very Sacrifice of Christ, but also because it teaches what it is to pray with Christ. He was there on the altar in the exercise of His prayer, and behold He inserts this prayer into souls with Himself. *Semper vivens ad interpellandum pro nobis,* in us, as in heaven, He intercedes. And the soul knows well enough what this prayer is: the Our Father, the Gospel, the Church, the Liturgy tell it to her. Let the soul then unite herself with it, let her too make this prayer, let her cause to arise voluntarily in herself the aspirations which are Christ's and which at this moment spring from what is most profound in her: her implantation in Him. Let her make this prayer, wishing everything that He wishes, desiring what He desires, begging for what He has at heart, for all His human race which He came to save, for all His Church and all His saints, those here below, those of heaven and of purgatory. Let her make this prayer, and let her also keep silence, accepting it, ratifying it, assimilating it in the silence of conformity.

Sacred moments, precious moments, of which she should not, through her own fault, lose any particle. Instants of grace, whose marvel she should at leisure meditate, and meditate profoundly, especially at the moment when it is accomplished, in order that she may fully understand its lesson. Better than anything else, they can teach the members what it is to pray as a member, in the prayer, absolute and catholic, which is theirs, because Christ is theirs.

But, we must not think that this unity is ended when the sacramental presence of Jesus Christ ceases. The effect of the Sacrament is a permanent union. Christ, through the virtue of the heavenly bread, wishes to remain in us and us to remain in Him, and to become one with us for time and for eternity.

The same thing is true of our prayer. It is not only at the moment of Communion that it lives by the prayer of Christ. It is always. It is always that all should pray with Him, in Him and by Him, if they wish their prayers to be salutary. It is also always that they should pray together, since in Him they are always together.

So, and the principle should be emphasized, there are no isolated Christian prayers: they would cease to be the prayers of Christians; a Christian is a Christian and acts as a Christian only through the bond which unites him to all his brothers in attaching him to Christ. That which gives him his interior life makes that life universal and catholic. That which gives rise to this prayer and makes it a Christian prayer is the same thing that makes it universal, catholic, public and united to all Christian prayers.

Not, certainly, that private piety is public in the same manner as the official prayer; it is public, but differently; it is public in its own proper manner, corresponding to the characteristics of its nature. The official prayer is the prayer of the group considered as a group: it is determined by the authority which rules the operation of the group and it is said in the name of the group. Private prayer is the prayer of a part of the group, and it is said in the name of this part, and by this part. The official prayer is the voice of the entire Body of Christ; private prayer is the voice of the members of this Body, the voice of members praying as members, not inasmuch as they are a body: they are not the Body; but as united with the Body: they are not what they are save by union with the body.

But, official or private, all Christian prayer is essentially catholic. Whether it be the whole which speaks, or a part of the whole, it is always the entire organism which lives and which tends towards God.

It is important to tell and to retell this to the faithful; for this principle is capital in the spiritual doctrine. By very constitution their private piety is the piety of a part; it is "partial"; it demands, in order to be fully what it is, that it be united to a whole. No Protestant individualism, then, no ignorant and narrow presumption, no effort to make for oneself a little devotion apart. *Ut non sit schisma in corpore*. By tearing itself away from the prayer of all, the individual piety would break with life.

IV

So, and this is the first consequence, between private prayer and the official prayer, there is no opposition, nor even any separation. Both are the prolongation of the same reality, both are the prayer of the Christ of the Mass, which continues in the Church; both are the prayer of the Chief, and of the Chief as Chief, and even of the Chief in the act in which He has been and in which He is always constituted fully Chief, that is to say, of the Chief in the act by which He united Himself to his Body in uniting it to God.

The liturgical prayer is this prayer as it is prolonged in the supplication of the Body, inasmuch as the Body is a visible organization; private prayer is this same prayer as it is prolonged in the prayers of the members inasmuch as they live their personal lives. But both, taken in their totality, their totality so essential that outside of it they are nothing, coincide and are identified in that which is their principle and their all. It is for this reason, let it be said in passing, that it was necessary, in order to compare them and to see clearly their relation to one another, to make an abstraction in each of them from what it has in common with the other, and to consider them, as we have done, only in what is peculiar to each of them. Without this, from the point of view taken in these pages, we would have ended by confounding them. But it is for this reason also that both, even in what differentiates them, remain profoundly united to each other, remain even, radically one only and the same thing. They are like the two aspects, the one social and official, the other interior and personal, of only one mysterious reality, which is at the same time social and interior: social even to unity and to immanent and interior unity; interior even to those last depths of the soul where the life of each member is rooted in Him Who constitutes the social unity of all.

Besides, accord between the two does not have to be obtained by violent efforts; it results from the very nature of things. Let Christian piety only know what it is, what bonds attach it to Christ and to the faithful, and, at once, it will be practised in the same public spirit, with the same solicitude for all souls, as the official piety. Let it understand the life which animates it, the aspirations which Christ wishes to arouse in it, and it will find them formulated in the liturgy. The liturgy, being the authentic expression of the prayer of the entire body, is also the authentic expression of the prayer of the members. Nowhere could the members find subjects for reflection which suit them so much, cycles of meditations so adapted to them, formulas so sure and so eloquent, such finished models of the attitude which they should take before God.

That is not the same thing, evidently, as saying that private piety ought to be a precise copy of the official piety, and that it is enough, in order to have the liturgical spirit, to recite exactly as priests do the orations of the Mass and the psalms of the breviary. The simple faithful do not have, as a rule, either the duty, or the mission, or even the power to make an official prayer: delegation is lacking to them. Neither the formulas of the Mass, nor those of the breviary have been composed to be precisely an individual prayer, a prayer of a member. It even happens often that a too literal fidelity to the liturgy as, for example, the effort on the part of one of the faithful to read as quickly as the celebrant all the prayers of the Holy Sacrifice, interferes with piety. Too much preoccupation with the letter stifles the spirit: in his endeavor to keep the markers of his missal moving, the individual forgets what is going on, and he no longer thinks of uniting himself with all his heart and with all his soul to God and to all his brothers in Christ, who is giving Himself.

Please understand us correctly; we do not say that they should not use the missal, far from it: where else would they learn what the Mass is, and what the prayer of the Church is, and what the prayers of the members of the Church should be? But we say that the faithful should make use of it, not in the manner of the priest who says the prayer of the group, but in the manner of the faithful, who are parts of this group. They can make use of it with a liberty which the official minister does not have; they ought to make use of it, when they are not taking part in the sacred functions in an active and exterior manner, as a theme of Catholic interior life, they should meditate upon its prayers, they should dwell upon them at need, they should repeat them, but they should not strain after a literal fidelity, which, in their case, would have no meaning.

Private piety ought to unite itself to the liturgy, not by taking itself for a liturgy, which it is not, but by being itself. It ought to enter into this union in its own proper manner, for, if it ceased to be itself, what would be left to it to unite to the liturgy?

Let it be itself, and it will be the piety of members, and it will have its place in the whole, and it will be united to the piety of the whole. To be liturgical is not a duty added to its other duties; to be liturgical demands neither suppression, nor modification, nor new constraints. It is, before everything else, the obligation to conduct oneself in a catholic spirit, in communion with the human race.

Such is the spirit: the letter will follow. By absorbing it the faithful will desire to pray with the rest of the faithful, to pray with their priests and in the prayer of the Church, to assist at the offices of their parish and to participate actively in them.

Allow us to insist: there is here an important point of contact between private piety and official piety. The official prayer arranges within itself the place where the prayer of the faithful can be inserted; we speak of the responses of the Mass, of the chants of the multitude at the singing of the Divine Office, and also, in a special but very elevated sense, of the sacramental and spiritual communion. Nothing permits the simple faithful to make the liturgical prayer as this active intervention does.

But, it must be added at once, this intervention is still insufficient to give the liturgical spirit.

In the first place, because, in fact, it can only be rather rare. And also because, at the most august moments of the liturgy, it is reduced to almost nothing: at these moments, what is officially demanded of the faithful is rather their private prayer than responses or chants. The canon is said in a low voice. Apart from certain chants, the faithful, at the Consecration, have only to adore in silence, to lift up their hearts, as the Preface has commanded them. At the Communion also: the liturgy makes provision for only a little in the way of responses and of chants for this moment. The Church places the principal Priest and unique Victim of the Christian sacrifice in the hearts of her children: then, almost at once, she is silent. What does this mean, if not that the holy action transfers itself to where the Pontiff has just gone, and that the liturgy has only to continue in the secret of the soul in private prayers?

Finally, and this is the last reason, intervention, even active intervention, in the Divine Office cannot suffice to render our piety liturgical, because it constitutes of itself alone only a union in externals. It consists only of words, of gestures, of actions. That is very good certainly. But it is still only an act of the body.

But, in private piety, the exterior act, though it may be necessary, and perhaps often more important than we think, is secondary. The essential thing is the interior; the essential thing is adoration in spirit and in truth; the essential things are mental prayers, prayers which we make while trying to forget both ourselves and everything else, prayers which we offer, as Jesus Christ has counseled us to do, in the secret of our souls, where only the eye of the Father, who sees in secret, can reach.

We must not believe that these things, because they are interior, cannot or ought not to have any public element. This would be a refined individualism. We must not believe that they cannot be public except through some superadded intention or through the choice of a subject of meditation or because of the place in which we pray. Our Catholicism is not of the surface merely; neither is the Catholicism of our prayer. It touches its remotest inwardness and even what is more interior to it than itself is, that is to say, the source from which it comes: we have to act and to pray as Catholics only because, primarily, by our substance, in Christ, we are Catholic. Our prayer comes from Christ, it goes to Christ, it seeks union with Christ, or it is not Christian. But Christ is everywhere the Christ of the Church and of unity. So, while it buries us in recollection, it can, by the same operation, enlarge us in catholicity. Our prayer can be public and universal through the very thing which renders it interior and personal; for its source is at the same time both more interior to us than we are to ourselves, and more catholic, more world-embracing than existing humanity is.

V

This must be said and repeated, lest exhortations—and very necessary they are—to the liturgical spirit end by throwing discredit on private devotion. The liturgical spirit ought to be, before everything else, a spirit. It ought also to manifest itself in acts, that is incontestably true. But if it goes no further forward, it no longer exists.

The liturgical spirit is, before everything else, where the faithful are concerned, of course, a thing of the soul and of individual conviction. It dwells in the will, the will to live and to pray in Christ and in the Church. The more profound, the more interior, the more private this will is, the more real and efficacious it will be. And it will not cease, for that reason, to be a Catholic reality; for it is within especially, in the very substance of the soul where the grace of Christ transfigures us, that we are Catholics.

For private piety then the exhortation to the liturgical spirit is, in part, a call to the interior life, a counsel to go so deeply into ourselves that we shall reach even to Christ, even to the Christ of unity.

It is the splendor of the Christian life thus to unite attitudes which seem opposed, in Him who is at once the explanation of what is most universal in the Church and of what is most interior in our souls.

The Lord's Prayer has an important lesson in this matter. The Saviour, as He wished that we should pray, wished that we should pray in the plural. The Pater is said, according to Saint Thomas,[1] "in the name of the entire Church, *in persona totius Ecclesiae.*" When we say it, we say it with the crowd, not a crowd with which we might mingle outside ourselves in noisy gatherings, but the crowd of the Christian people, with which we live within ourselves in the silence of solitude.

The Pater, also, is said for all. This résumé of the Gospel, as Tertullian remarked,[2] represents the form which our every desire should take:[3] it makes us ask "in the plural" with all the human race and for all the human race.

The Pater, also, teaches us to pray, not as individuals but as members. We say it, not because we have made it up, but because we have been instructed to do so by Divine teaching, and because Christ has commanded us to do so in virtue of His authentic mission.

Priests have the breviary; the faithful, and the priests also, have the Pater. All have a mission to say it. Certainly the delegations differ. The priest is consecrated, he has a special and official mandate, he has more developed formulas. The ordinary faithful do not have these, but they are not left without a vocation. An authentic order of the Saviour, which the Church recalls to them, tells them to pray and tells them how they should pray. They pray God, in the name of Christ, with the Church.

After the Pater we might mention, in the same order of ideas, not a prayer, but an association of prayers, the Apostleship of Prayer.

[1] S.T., IIª IIªᵉ, Qu. LXXXIII, art. 16 ad. 3.
[2] De Oratione I, P.L. I, 1153.
[3] St. Augustine, Sermon LV. P.L. XXXVIII, 379.

This work also has an important theological bearing. We should not consider it a little devotional affair. It is the Catholic organization of prayer. It consists in making all the faithful pray, all together, in union with the prayer of Jesus, for an intention designated by the Sovereign Pontiff. So their prayers will go to God, sent up to Him from all the Christian people, united to Christ, in the name of the Pope.

This is so thoroughly Catholic a type of prayer, that this association seems to us to correspond exactly, in the domain of prayer, to what the great work of Catholic Action is in the domain of works. Catholic Action makes the laity participate in the work of the hierarchy; the Apostleship of Prayer makes them participate in the prayer of the hierarchy, in this sense, that it gives them, even in their interior life, cares and preoccupations which are authentically universal and ecclesiastical, and it mobilises in some sort all their desires and supplications, all the impetratory and adorational value in all their activities, to the profit of the great Catholic interests. Exactly in the same manner, Catholic Action mobilises all their activities to the profit of the great Catholic crusade.

This shows clearly enough the importance of the Apostleship of Prayer, and the necessity of fully understanding its inner meaning and its ecclesiastical and Catholic character. It will teach the faithful what their true interests as Christians are: the interests of Christianity; it will accustom them to desire and to ask as members of the great Catholic family; it will make them see, in the hierarchy and in the Pope, the leaders of prayer; it will teach them that, in the work of the supernatural apostolate, the principal energy is the hidden energy of prayer, of charity and of interior desire; it will show what a formidable thing it is to be Catholic and to set in motion, when one prays to God, the energies of all regenerated humanity.

So, little by little, we have arrived at the place for treating no longer merely of union with the prayer of the whole, but of union with the prayer of the other parts. We must now consider this second union more at length.

Recalling the principle, we know that the prayer of each Christian is the prayer of a part, and hence a partial prayer; a prayer, consequently, which has its full explanation and its true physiognomy only when attached to the other prayers.

Is it not a fact that this truth is very often forgotten and that this forgetfulness is a fruitful source of discouragement and disgust? We wish to pray as we should, we wish very much to pray in such a manner that our prayers may dare to present themselves before God. And all we succeed in making is distracted and drowsy prayers, meditations composed of momentary fervors and ridiculous or humiliating distractions. The constant reckoning up of so lamentable a result ends by changing presumption into disgust; we come to detest these prayers which no longer arouse in us any uplift of spirit, and we pray no more except as we have to under pain of sin.

As if God demanded anything more of us than our hearts, our hearts made of mud, as He well knows; as if these deficiencies could not have the result of rendering us more humble and more suppliant, more prayerful, in other words; as if, especially, the insufficiency of our isolated prayers should not teach us not to pray alone.

An isolated prayer is no more presentable than a member torn from the organism. Our prayers considered in themselves alone are partial, incomplete as prayers, lacking in fervor, attention, in everything that is most essential. But we must not be surprised that the prayer of a part is a partial prayer, nor that what is most necessary in it, its ardor and its recollection, should come to it only by its attachment to the other parts.

Instead of being discontented about these deficiencies, we can and we should receive them with a joyous heart. Some of them because we can by our own efforts lessen and suppress them, and because this struggle will be the homage which God expects of us. The others, those which spring from our personal mentality, from our special and very imperfect manner of thinking and of willing, because they have for their author the God who made our temperament and our soul, and because they indicate our place and our rôle in the ensemble of men and in the prayer which all together make before God.

They are not obstacles and lacunae with nothing to compensate for them except in the individualist hypothesis. In the Catholic system, they are exigencies and means of attaining union.

Christian prayer is an immense total prayer; it is like a symphony.

In a symphony no instrument plays the whole piece. Each one has its score. Some scarcely do more than repeat certain heavy notes, always the same; others specialize on long silences with, from time to time, a brusque explosion, or a few lonely arpeggios; others outline at intervals, but in veiled sonorities, the general theme; others finally sing what the rest are suggesting: certain limpid notes whose sinuous curve dominates the rest. They sing and repeat the theme, then their voices, having blended for a moment, are silent, and others lift themselves up in their place. The melody passes from one to another, repeated and repeated again without ceasing, developing and asserting itself, and, within itself, sweeping the whole along. In it everything is balanced, everything is complete, all is perfect harmony, and all the notes of all the instruments blend in one unique song. And this song no one renders by himself alone, so rich is it; but all, attached to the others, express the whole of it, it is so one.

So with Christian prayer. Each member has his part to play; it is indicated to him by his temperament, his kind of mind, his capacity for attention and for fervor. These particularities make his prayer a personal and unique prayer, for there are no two individuals the same. Because of them there is a manner of loving God which he alone can realise, a note of a special quality which he is alone in being able to give. And so, these particularities, while they make his prayer personal, mark for him the place which he ought to fill and which no other can fill for him in the prayer of the group.

Let him pray then in his own way, doing his best against his wanderings and his torpors, but without being astonished or despairing if in his supplications there are many lacunae. In an orchestra, must all the instruments be trumpets, and must they blare away without cessation all at the same time? Must each individual make a complete prayer and one which is adequate in itself alone, although each one is a member and cannot pray except with the whole?

Prayer is community singing. Some will produce only heavy and dull prayers; others, only efforts against drowsiness; others, even in spite of all their good intentions, will often have only sleepy half-dreams on a religious theme. Others will do a little better; others better still; certain ones, at times, will make a prayer that is almost complete, almost presentable. These last are probably souls unknown to others and to themselves; but they too, as far as we know, lose themselves in the ensemble; they pray, then distractions come, or the cares of life take hold of them and others continue their prayer, and then others again. The prayer goes on developing without ceasing, passing from one to the other, but always, what each one says has for its accompaniment, its meaning, its very physiognomy, all that the others say. And this meaning is that of the whole; no one has said his prayer by himself alone; but each one, united to the others, has said all, with the others.

This prayer is not merely the prayer of men: alone, men are powerless. It is above all the prayer of Christ. Also, always, the prayer of Christ dwells here below for the purpose of arousing it. This prayer of Christ is the Mass, which continues the Cross. And the Mass is prolonged in the liturgy and in Christian piety. Both liturgy and Christian piety are two aspects of one sole reality; the one is the public expression, the other is the continuation in the interior life of souls of the same religion of the Saviour, which He communicated to His Mystical Body in the unity of His Church.

CHAPTER VII

All Priests in the Unique Priest

IN order to see in what sense it can be true to say that all the faithful are priests, although ordained ministers alone are priests; in order to see how this "priesthood," which is common to all, squares with the exclusive priesthood of certain ones, what we must look at in the first place is neither the faithful nor the ordained ministers, but Jesus Christ.

Jesus Christ in Christianity, as He is the unique source of life, of strength and of hope, is also the unique source of light and of unity. In Him all the truths which come from Him, like all the grandeurs and all the graces which come from Him, are united and, hence, He is the explanation, the synthesis, the unity, both of all His work and of all His doctrine.

That will be our point of view in this treatise. It is, certainly, a partial and particular point of view. But the manner in which we shall consider it, within the limits of this study, will have to be still more partial. For this inevitable incompletion, we now beg your indulgence.

We offer an apology also for using a word in a sense which is not its ordinary sense: the word priesthood, priest, to designate the eminent religious dignity of Christians. But, alas, there is no other, and the sum of our considerations, while giving a brief explanation of the meaning assigned to it, will guard, we hope, against wrong ways of understanding it. There is always danger of such misinterpretation.

Let us consider then the priesthood of Jesus Christ and with the purpose of seeing, in Him, the entire Christian priesthood. Is it not in Jesus Christ that God Himself sees the entire world and that He accepts our worship?

How is Jesus Christ priest?

Priests, in general, are intermediaries between God and men; they present to God the prayers of the crowd, they call down on the crowd the blessings of God.[1]

Their role is to express outwardly a religious process which should take place in souls. For, we are anxious to have you note from this moment something which we shall have to consider often and which, besides, is evident,—the exterior priesthood cannot exist alone. Alongside it, altogether like to it, what we may call an interior priesthood, an invisible priesthood, should be found. Every man should interiorly rise above himself, should strain to open himself to God in appeal and in hope, and this interior action corresponds exactly, in the depths of the conscience, to what the sacerdotal function is, on the external scene.

In the purely natural state, this interior "priesthood," this personal and invisible "priesthood" would even have been the principal thing. It alone would have given a religious meaning to all the hecatombs and to all the solemnities, and the rest, without it, would have been only theatrical pomp and a soulless body of religion, a corpse of religion.

In the supernatural state the facts are very different. There, it is no longer men who establish a priesthood

[1] Heb. V. I.—St. Thomas, S.T. III^a^, QU. XXII, Art. I,c.

according to their own views, it is God Himself who gives them a priesthood according to His personal designs.

And it is in Jesus Christ that He gives this Priesthood, just as it is in Him that He gives the entire supernatural order.

At once the priesthood of Christ appears in its grandeur.

In relation to what we have called the interior priesthood, it is not a result, but a principle. It does not come from a centre self-designated by our cult, but everything central, everything real in the worship of regenerate men, comes from it. *A Domino factum est istud.* "Behold the days come," saith the Lord, "and I will send forth a famine into the land . . . of hearing the word of the Lord."[2]

We must not then picture this priest as a chargé d'affaires deputised by the crowd: it is of himself that He is priest. We must not imagine that He is, like the pontiffs of the ancient law, an elect person whom God has deigned to choose and to consecrate: He is priest independently of all ulterior designation, in virtue of His very composition, if we may dare so to put it, and of His structure. His consecration is nothing other than His personality, and His anointing, it is He: He is the anointed, He is the Christ of the Lord, because He is the Man-God.

The Man-God, that is the whole thing: what He is, is the résumé of all He does. What else is He but the assumption of a human nature in a divine person, the unheard of condescension of a God who has wished to be only one with man, the most total of flights towards God in the most complete of descents of God toward men, that is to say, what else is he but the priesthood itself, the priesthood perfectly and divinely realized?

Without doubt, it is in His human nature that He is

[2] Amos. VIII, 2.

priest: in this nature alone, He has that inferiority with relation to God and that union with men which the priesthood implies. So also is He Prophet and King, Mediator and Redeemer, Source of grace and Head of a Mystical Body: He is all this as man; but also, He is not all this in plenitude except because He is God. The same is true of His sacerdotal rôle: He has it as man; but He has it in perfection, because He is God.

But, for Him, to be God is an infinitely simple and easy thing, since it is, identically, to be what He is. Also the absolute perfection which His divinity gives to His sacerdotal character, He has without straining upwards, without rending Himself—it was no fault of ours—He has it merely by being Himself.

Others have had some participation of the priesthood: He has it in its entirety, or rather, He does not so much have it as be it. He is all the priesthood, the priesthood supereminent and personified, because He is the double oblation both of man to God and of God to man, and He is these two oblations so totally that they meet in His unity.

Besides, He is not a priest among priests, greater than the others or holier. He is the unique Priest. Just as the angels, because they are pure forms, contain in themselves their entire species, He, too, because He is the pure priesthood, exhausts in Himself, if we may use the expression, all priesthood.

Nevertheless, there are other priests than He.

It must be so: He has been seen so little and in so few places. And it is everywhere and always that men have need of a visible priesthood. They have need of it because of their nature, which requires empirical ceremonies of worship, which insists also on public acts of religion; and how would these be possible without a priest? They have need of it also because of the economy of the supernatural, which everywhere makes use of visible and human means to communicate invisible grace.

But these other priests, as is plain, are necessary, not because of any imperfection in Him, but because of our indigence.

And it is His superabundance which renders them possible. Precisely because He is priest in a unique manner, without parallel, transcendent; He is priest in a universal, mystic, overflowing manner: *fons totius sacerdotii,* as Saint Thomas says; [3] *catholicus sacerdos,* as Tertullian expressed it.[4] His priesthood, from this point of view, is like His grace: catholic.

Here, we must stress the point, we are at the place where the divine springs forth in humanity: in the Heart of Christ.

It seems, in fact, that to apply to the priesthood of Christ the ordinary doctrine on the subject of the grace which is in Him, is enough to give us a theory of His universal priesthood.

The grace of Christ, which sanctifies His individual humanity, at the same time that it is individual and private grace, is also grace of "Chief," of mystical "Head"—universal grace. It is destined to act on all men, to diffuse itself, to "inflow" into them through the very thing which renders it strictly personal, that is to say, through the hypostatic union. As the Greek Fathers say, it results from a unity of hypostasis with Him who is life itself, and thence, it is altogether necessary that it be rendered vivifying for all men, that is to say that it be the source of supernatural

[3] S.T. III^a, QU. XXII, Art. 4,c.
[4] Adversus Marcionem IV, 9.

life, the source of grace. As the Scholastics say, it results from the closest possible proximity with God, and it is necessary, in consequence, that it be, in all mankind, the principle of union with God, that is to say, once again, the principle of grace.

In these two explanations, it is scarcely necessary to underline certain words to have them speak, no longer merely of the grace of Christ in general, but of that particular grace which constitutes Him priest.

He is supernatural life for all men, say the Greek Fathers. That is exactly true: it is, then, all men who in Him are lifted up to God to be animated with a new life, and it is to all men that God descends. Is that not the priesthood and the universal and mystical priesthood: the offering of all to God and the descent of God to all in one alone?

He is, for all humanity, the principle of union with God, say the Schoolmen. Again, that is very true: in Him, it is all humanity which is lifted up to God, and it is into all humanity that God enters. In other words, in Him, it is a universal consecration which is brought about and a universal priesthood which begins.

And this priesthood, exactly like the grace of the Chief, is universal and destined to flow into all through the very thing which makes it unique and absolutely superior to all. The hypostatic union with the Word, which renders this priest transcendent in relation to all humanity, is precisely what enables him to sanctify in Himself all humanity.

So it is in all humanity that we must seek for the breadth and the length, the height and the depth of such a priesthood. Not that in humanity it should receive the addition of some new extension, but because it is only in humanity that it can express the plenitude which is in it.

Here we should consider all the religion of men in order

to show how it is the religion of Christ. But, to abridge the matter, without, however, distorting it, we can take man's entire religion in the act which is its most elevated and most complete expression—sacrifice. Besides, it is on this point, as we shall see, this point at which worship appears at its maximum of intensity, that the accord between the priesthood of Christ and the priesthood of men manifests itself most clearly.

Sacrifice. But what is sacrifice?

Formidable question, complex question, question to which happily we shall be called upon to reply here only in part.

Let us leave to one side all that relates to those states which, in fact, have never existed; let us consider only the order of Providence which has ruled the human race since the promise made after the fall. It is exclusively a supernatural order, the order of a redemption first prepared, then effected, then continued, in Jesus Christ. Wherever grace works on men (and has there ever been one of them, however degraded, on whom it has not worked?) it is towards the God who has been rendered accessible in Christ that it directs them.

But, in the supernatural state, what man has to do, all that he has to do, is to cease being only himself in order to be in God with Christ. Already in the natural state, something of this kind, but on a lower level, would have constituted his religious attitude: to surpass himself in order to go to God. In the supernatural state, the same double process is required, but in a manner differently total: it is the Infinite Himself who comes to lay hold on man and to effectuate the union.

In the supernatural state moreover (but this time no longer because of God but because of man) a complication arises: sin. Man is a sinner. This means that, in the measure in which he is a sinner (and all of him is sinful although not totally sinful) he is opposed to union with God, and that he ought to be suppressed, that he ought to die to the extent to which he is a sinner in order to go to the most Holy.

This is an outline of the complete attitude which is prescribed, in the presence of the Infinite, for the men we are: to die in order to pass within the Most-High, to pass away.

To express himself to himself, to profess publicly this attitude, man—aided, of course, by grace—can invent signs, ceremonies, rites: these will be sacrifices. All of them, we believe, will have in a more or less marked way the same double aspect: a negative aspect, a gesture of quitting, of renouncing, of dying, immolation, abandonment of the profane, mortification; and a positive aspect, a gesture of offering and of ascent, consecration, feasts indicating union, affirmation that God, in a certain manner, has come closer.

Is this what those of the ancient sacrifices which were celebrated in good faith wished to signify, confusedly and gropingly? Perhaps, for even then, the Psalms tell us, *misericordia Domini plena est terra.*[5] In any case, this is what the levitical sacrifices typified, as a thing to come and as a thing already begun.

But this was accomplished only once. One only God, one only Christ, one only altar, one only faith; the plenary Sacrifice is unique, as the supernatural order is unique, in Jesus Christ, our Lord.

This was the Sacrifice of the Cross.

This was then the supreme act, in which the supreme Pontiff was Priest to the supreme degree; it was also—but

[5] Ps. XXXII, 5; CXVIII, 64.

it comes to the same thing—the act in which the Man-God acted as Man-God to the supreme degree. Then, in fact, the Man entered into men, by becoming for them and in them Justice, Peace and Holiness, and Food; then also, God entered into God by returning to the Father. Then and forever He became the perfect Sacrifice: the Host which will be forever elevated from the earth towards heaven, nourishment and the total gift which will descend without ceasing from heaven to the earth.

From the point of view of the senses, *oculis insipientium,* His death seemed to be a disaster, the collapse of His work and of His life. In reality, it is a sovereign realisation: never has He been so much Himself and so living.

All the events of His life, also, converge towards it as towards a climax. From without, it seemed the effect of intrigues and of jealousies; within, it is the expression of a very different logic from that of destruction and of hate: the logic of love and of its restorations. The wheat-seed bursts in the earth, not because moisture disintegrates it, but because its fecundity distends it. It is too laden within itself, bearer that it is of thirty and sixty and a hundred for one, bearer of harvests and of fields beyond the range of vision, and it is beneath the pressure of what it is that it is broken: the seed is not itself, it is not seed, except in causing itself to spring forth. *Nisi granum frumenti . . .* So with Jesus, the seed of divine wheat: He has never been so magnificently Himself, so fully Man-God, *in actu ultimo et perfecto,* as in bursting forth to attain His fulness, as in opening Himself out through obedience and love in order to go to the Father and to go to men. *Quomodo coarctor!* What tension, what anguish, to have in Himself the life of the world, and what an explosion!

How clear it is now that the entire development of this

life, all the procedures of this existence, advanced towards this sovereign expansion, so truly that all their import is summed up in it alone, and that consequently they have their redemptive virtue only when considered in it!

But, as this act takes up in itself the whole Christ, Christ takes up in Himself all men, and the Cross of Calvary, consequently, dominates not merely all His life, but all the earth also.

In virtue of His mystical union with all men, it is all men who in Him are dead to sin;[6] in Him, it is all humanity which has entered into God; as it is into all humanity that, through Him, God has descended.

So when this act is terminated, everything is accomplished. All that the holocausts and the ceremonies of other ages had attempted and sketched out, everything good and supernatural which may have been in the ancient hecatombs, all that men had ever attempted in their veritable religious acts, every most tragic and most essential element which was ever in religion before that time and then and always, all this, finally, is achieved. *Consummatum est*. Now the worship of men is plenary; the work of the Supreme Pontiff is done. *Et inclinato capite tradidit spiritum.*

What the Incarnation does in the order of finite natures, this oblation does in the order of finite activities: the centre, the summit, the whole; it is the full expression of the Incarnation, the perfect and actual entering into possession of all humanity by the God who became man.

As all creation is summed up in the Man-God, so all created action is summed up in the Act, the absolute and pre-eminent act, the act in which the Man-God acts to the maximum as Man-God. For all human acts have their last and necessary expression in the religious act, and the

[6] Rom. VI, 10, VI 2-11.

religious act has its plenitude in sacrifice, and sacrifice has its plenitude in the Sacrifice of Calvary. So the Sacrifice of Calvary is the last seal and the complete recapitulation of human action in general.

That this total immolation of Him who is all in all is a sacrifice, that it is even the greatest of all sacrifices, need not be stressed; it is too evident. But what should be noted is that it is The Sacrifice, the absolute Sacrifice, the total Sacrifice. Outside it, in the supernatural order, no sacrifice is possible. What could one present to God which has not already been offered up in this Lamb, immolated since the beginning of the world? *Toti non fit additio.*

Also, one who sees in this Sacrifice only the exterior, sees nothing; it has another immensity besides that of the scene on Golgotha. Just as the Priest and the Victim who is there on the altar dwells in all men, and all men in Him, and as He makes them all live, so this sacrifice dwells in all true sacrifices and all true sacrifices in it, and it renders them real and efficacious. In it, in it alone, we must see all of them. It is one, they are multiple, but in it, which is one, they, though multiple, are one. There is no imagination here nor any figure of speech, but ultra-realism, so to speak: they are in it much more truly than they are in themselves; for, in themselves alone, as supernatural sacrifices, they would be nothing; and, in it, they are in their source, in their centre, in their zenith.

Let us then see them in it, in order to see them as they are in themselves. At once we shall discover how everything is harmonised, how—it was the original question—the sacrifice which the Christian life is goes along with the Eucharistic Sacrifice, and how the priesthood of all the faithful squares with the priesthood of the ordained ministers.

First the Christian life. As the life of Christ was one long sacrifice, and as it was such only by consummating itself in the oblation on Calvary, the Christian life is one long sacrifice and it is such by consummating itself in death.

What is it, in fact, if not a perpetual exigency for renunciation and for death, for perfection and for life; if not a call to quit the world of sense and of sin in order to mount towards God? And this escape in this ascent, this breaking with self in this flight towards God, what else is it but a sacrifice?

This sacrifice certainly is not ritual, but real; not figured, but effected; not represented externally, but implanted within; but it is a sacrifice which kills none the less; and it is none the less a passage towards God. *Sacrificium Deo spiritus contribulatus;*[7] *devotionis nostrae tibi, quaesumus, Domine, hostia jugiter immoletur.*[8]

Some day even, this sacrifice will go even to immolation: the day when it will be necessary for us either to revolt or to be obedient even unto death. It will be necessary then to allow the will of God to be accomplished in us and ourselves to be suppressed, and, in a realism which would be brutal if it were not splendid, to love God more than ourselves, in order to find ourselves again in Him. Then, in us also all will be consummated, but this consummation will be nothing other than the full realisation of what should have been done in miniature every day: the offering of ourselves.

We could stress this point and show that dying should

[7] Ps. L., 19.
[8] Secr. Dom. III Adv.

be an act, not an act in the series of our acts, but an act which closes and fixes this series. Only, we should have to introduce some metaphysical considerations—and also make an effort to free ourselves from physiological considerations—which have no object when there is question of the cessation of all physiology—and this would be too heavy a burden for an exposition already overladen.

Whatever may be the fact about this matter, Jesus Christ, in dying, offered and consecrated our death, and this enables it to assume in our human action a moral and religious value. Our entire life ends in sacrifice and this last moment shows the meaning of all that has preceded. To live, is to offer a sacrifice, a sacrifice which is prolonged, while waiting for death—which is the paroxysm of life—to consummate it; to live, is to pass from vanity to truth, from death to life.

And this passage is Jesus Christ; and more precisely still, the passage, the sacrament of passage, *Pascha, id est transitus,* is Jesus Christ in His death and in His Eucharist. It is by dying that He snatched us from our past and that He gave us access to the Father, a Host holy and pure,[9] eternal redemption.[10] His death is then all; and our death is all also, and these are not two sufficiencies, but one only. It is necessary that we suffer, and nothing else is required; it is sufficient, absolutely sufficient, as God Himself is sufficient, *Deus meus et omnia.*

Nothing else is required . . . But then, you will say, what about the Mass and the priesthood of the priests? Are these useless things?

[9] Ord. Missae.
[10] Postc. Dom. XIII, Pent. et fer. III, post. Dom. III Quadr.

Ah! the Mass and the ecclesiastical priesthood are not something else; they are the union of the two, the union of the priesthood of Christ with what we may call the priesthood of the faithful, and the very flowing of the one into the other.

The "priesthood" of the faithful, the long sacrifice which is the Christian life, are not efficacious, are not even possible, unless they are the Priesthood and the Sacrifice of Christ continued. It is required then that, as long as they must endure, that is to say, through all the ages, they be placed in contact, in immediate contact, with the Priesthood and the Sacrifice of Christ, with the Cross, *in mysterii salutaris transeat consortium;*[11] it is required then that, in a certain and a real and a very real fashion, the immolation of Jesus remain present, present to all the Christian life. It is in the Mass that this presence occurs and it is the ecclesiastical priesthood which effects it.

The sacrifice of Christ, on its side, is not merely, as we have seen, the empirical fact of Calvary; it is the total, absolute, universal sacrifice, the sacrifice of all humanity in its Mystical Chief. It ought then to extend, in all truth and reality over all the Christian life, and that is what it does, inasmuch as it is rendered present in the Mass by the ecclesiastical priesthood.

Of course, strictly speaking, this presence, this extension, this contact could have been purely spiritual. But the plan of God, in the order of the Incarnation, for our so material race, is not to follow invisible ways. Everywhere, in Christ, then in the Church which continues Christ, it is by visible means that invisible grace reaches men. So (we should expect it) the priesthood of Jesus Christ applies itself to

[11] Postc. Dom. I. Quadr.

the Christian life: by an exterior ministry, by a sacramental economy, by a "terrestrial substance which confers what is divine." [12]

Assuredly, the Eucharist as a Sacrifice is not formally the Eucharist as a Sacrament: the Eucharist as a Sacrifice is the means by which the Eucharist as a Sacrament exists, and the Eucharist as a Sacrament is the means by which the Eucharist as a Sacrifice penetrates into the Christian life. But there is only one Eucharist: the Sacrifice is not effected except by preparing a food and the Sacrament is not given without establishing communion with an immolation.

So the Sacramental Sacrifice places itself between the historic Sacrifice of another time and the Mystical Sacrifice of all time. "Between," we say; it is for want of a better word: but we must not think of any intermediary uniting separate things. There is question only of union, there is question only of the prodigy by which Christ, through the act by which He passes to the Father, passes also into men.

The Mass is that by which the Cross becomes the Christian life, and it is essential to the Cross to produce the Christian life and to the Christian life to be produced by the Cross. The Mass is the Cross, but the Cross inasmuch as it is the cause always present and always actual—let us repeat it: always present and always actual—of the Christian life. The Mass is the Christian life considered, not in itself, but in that which is more itself than itself, in its gushing forth always real, always contemporaneous, always immediate—yes, let us repeat it, real, contemporaneous, immediate—from the pierced side of Jesus Christ.

The Mass exterior to the Christian life and to Calvary! But it is Calvary itself considered in its expansion, *quoties hujus hostiae commemoratio celebratur, opus nostrae re-*

[12] Secr. 2ae Missae Nativ.

demptionis exercetur;[13] it is the Christian life considered in its source: *sacrosancta mysteria in quibus omnis sanctitatis fontem constituisti;*[14] it is that which, interiorly, essentially, unites the two in the unique Christ.

I have the conviction, but I do not insist, because this is not the place for it and it would require a number of distinctions, I have the conviction that, when one sees the place which the Mass occupies in the organism of the Mystical Body, the question no longer presents itself of knowing in what it is essentially a sacrifice, and a sacrifice which is intrinsically sacrifice, and a sacrifice so relative to that of the Cross, that it adds nothing to it and borrows all from it. But for this it is necessary to take the doctrine of the Mystical Body very seriously and in a very realistic sense. As truly as Christ remains with us all days, so truly is the act in which He expresses Himself to the maximum an act which remains with us all days. It remains, not bloody, not visible, but sacramental; not new and apparent to the senses, but real, as real as in another time, *sola offerendi ratione diversa.* It remains, one because of Him, multiple because of us, plenary because of our incorporation in Him, so "intrinsically sacrifice" that it contains Christ Himself intrinsically, and even as "intrinsically sacrifice" as possible, for it contains Christ precisely inasmuch as He makes His sacrifice itself pass within all His own, through all the ages. It remains always identical with itself, and the cross which dominates the altar is not a simple memorial, but the sign of an indefectible persistence: it is always the absolute sacrifice, the one outside of which no true sacrifice is any longer possible, but it is this sacrifice taken at the place where, descending among men, it makes

[13] Secr. Dom. IX post Pent.
[14] Secr. St. Ignatii.

itself multiple like them to take up all their multiplicity in the unity of Christ: *ut et ipsi in nobis unum sint,*[15] asked Jesus on the evening of the first Mass.

Descendat nunc de cruce, ut videamus et credamus,[16] they cried to Him on Calvary. He has never come down. The altar, always, is the Cross standing erect, and the priest, the principal priest, the unique priest, is always He.

The other priests, the ordained priests, have not, in reality, a priesthood which originates in their own persons. They only lend their hands and their lips and however unworthy, however sinful, alas! they may be, the grace which comes through them is neither less immaculate nor less august. Another, The Priest, acts through them; their power, in the acts which they perform in His name, is equal to His, and their baptisms, their absolutions, their consecrations have the same worth as His, because in reality they are His.

Fremens et tremens dico: there is not less in our hands, in our poor sinful hands, when the words have been said over the bread and over the wine, than there was in His own hands, in His holy and venerable hands, on the evening when he instituted the Eucharist. Unheard of dignity of the Christian priesthood: it has Jesus Christ and it gives Him—*quod habeo, hoc tibi do—;* more still: it is Jesus Christ who gives Himself, and who gives Himself as Christ alone knows how to give Himself, with a donation which never ceases.

I am anxious to say this, to say it very loud, for fear that, from what has been said about the grandeur of the faithful, some may arrive at a lesser esteem for the ordained priest-

[15] Jn., XVII, 21.
[16] Mk., XV, 32.

hood: the priesthood is Jesus Christ always leaning over the world and always contriving that we shall live by Him.

But this dignity of the priesthood is essentially a dignity which comes from another, from Christ, and which consists in sanctifying others in Christ: no priest, not even the Sovereign Pontiff, can absolve himself.

Without doubt, the Sacrament of Orders which priests have received and the ministry which they exercise, places in their lives graces, helps, stimulants to sanctity. But all this does not sanctify them in order that they may be priests in a greater degree, but in order that they may be Christians in a more perfect way. The fact is that all the sanctity which Jesus Christ has brought into the world, all the sanctity which the ecclesiastical priesthood communicates, is Christian sanctity, and there is no other, and he who would not be holy through it, would not be holy at all. Christian sanctity has its degrees, its progress, its history, *donec formetur Christus in nobis;* the priesthood and the episcopate do not have them.

But, this Christian sanctity consists in what we called, a few moments ago, the spiritual priesthood; it consists in dying to self and to one's own pretended sufficiency in order to live in God, in Christ with all men.

Once this fact is understood, the relations between the ecclesiastical priesthood and the spiritual priesthood appear clearly.

The ordained priests have, in their ministerial priesthood, a transitive priesthood, a priesthood destined for the sanctification of others; it does not sanctify them themselves except by leading them to quit themselves in order to pass to God, that is to say, by intensifying the spiritual life which they have by the same title as other Christians.

The faithful, on their side, in the presence of the official priesthood, are receptive: they do not give, they receive; they do not consecrate, they are consecrated.

But they are truly consecrated. Baptism has made them intrinsically holy and intrinsically marked for such a reception. The Church which offers it to them is the Church to which they belong, the Church which, in their unity, they are, and the consecrated ministry has no title to its office except inasmuch as it represents this Church.

They are consecrated, not in the manner of completely passive terms which receive action and do not react. We must not imagine division of that kind in the mystery of reconciliation. They are consecrated in the manner of members who form only one, mystically, with Him who consecrates.

The consecrating action, far from slackening and dying within them, should prolong itself and, as it were, rebound. The Sacrifice of the Mass ought to be continued in their own sacrifice: it is, precisely, the Sacrifice of the Cross, inasmuch as this Sacrifice, through the ages, seeks and gives rise to a mysterious increase.

It is for this reason that their rôle in the sacerdotal functions, while it is a passive part, does not permit them to be inert. It is of them, in Christ, that there is question at the altar; it is their own sacrifice which is offered and which begins there, the sacrifice of which their life also will be the subject; it begins, and the reason it begins is so that it may come and lay hold on them. At the very least they should have their word to say in it and their actions to perform.

Ah! yes, let them have an active participation, let them understand, let them see, let them respond and let them chant: their devotion could not be at a better school, nor closer to the source: source and school of sacrifice, of humility, of union, of the ecclesiastical spirit.

But let this participation be, above all else, interior.

According to Dom Capelle, the liturgy and public worship on the one hand, and the interior life and private piety on the other, are not mutually exclusive. Quite the contrary: they live the one on the other, the one with the other. What then is the soul of the liturgy, if not Christ, the Christ of the Mass and of Communion, and what is the soul of the interior life, if not Christ again, the Christ of Communion and of the Mass?

If the Mass is an exterior and visible function which claims, for that reason, an assistance of an exterior and visible order, it is also a mystery of interior life—and what an interior life: that of Christ making all His own live within Him and within themselves!—and it demands, therefore, an interior assistance, an assistance which takes us to the profoundest depths of our interior life, of our own interior life and of the interior life of all Catholicity.

Besides, the closer the decisive moment comes in the great action, the smaller the external rôle of the faithful becomes. At the Consecration they have nothing more to do than be silent and believe. The visible priest, for that matter, has scarcely more to do: his person should disappear in order that Christ may be all. *Ut sit Christus omnia in omnibus.*

There is no longer any question of speaking, then: all is act, all is terribly serious. There is question, if one wishes to be entirely united to the Sacrifice, of becoming oneself a sacrifice. Not an isolated oblation, not a schismatic immolation, but a member-sacrifice, a sacrifice derived from the Mass and nourished by it.

Ah! do not say that I am mixing everything up; that we are concerned with a matter of public worship and of ministerial priesthood, not with one of asceticism and of spirituality! Certainly distinctions must be made, and I believe that I have noted them, and they are obvious enough. But we are in the place, in Him rather, whence everything comes, and where all, consequently, should meet again. All Christian life, all renunciation of oneself to give oneself to God and to souls, all sacrifice and all interior "priesthood," come from Him and from Him alone, and He is there on the altar, precisely inasmuch as He gives them.

When then one of the faithful who is reading the Mass in his prayer-book feels the great breath of charity and the spirit of sacrifice passing into him, let him not put them aside to return to the text of the Mass: he has just touched, in his own interior, the interior of the Mass, has just coincided, by his right as a member, in his own interior sacrifice, with the sacrifice of Christ authentically continued!

No separate prayers certainly, no devotions in isolation! But, in Him who is the universal priest, through this Catholic Sacrifice, a Catholic and universal devotion! It will be only the more interior for that reason, because it is our interior itself which is Catholic and universal. And it will be only the more interior to us, for it will come, in us, from Him who is more interior to us than we are to ourselves, from Christ who dwells in us and we in Him.

Interior life, spirit of devotion, of sacrifice, of "priesthood," it is to this that the Church Herself, through the liturgy, invites us. "By the frequentation of this mystery, teach us, Lord, to despise what is earthly and to love what is heavenly."[17] "Grant, we pray Thee, O Almighty God, that we may become members of Him whose flesh and blood we receive."[18]

It is not only the Missal which so speaks; Christ does also, and He does not merely speak: He acts. For Christ does not wait until, by their spirit of devotion and of sacrifice, the faithful come to meet the priesthood; it is He who first comes; it is His Sacrifice which comes, and the Mass is precisely the Sacrifice of the Cross, inasmuch as it comes.

You know this perfectly, but it is so magnificent to consider! The Eucharistic Sacrifice exists only under the form of food; it is ended when the priest, when the faithful, take this food, when the Church communicates through her official representative and through her members.

Behold the sacred banquet has taken place; there are still some prayers, but very short ones, one final word and only one: "Go; the Mass is over. . . ." It is finished!

It is finished? No. Not more than Christ was finished when He died. When He died, He commenced His great terrestrial life, His mystical life. So too the Mass. Finished? No. It commences, it recommences always its work of limitless invasion. We see nothing more at the altar; it is because all has passed within souls. With the Victim, with Christ, it is the Sacrifice which has entered into Christianity, to lift up there an immense sacrifice, the sacrifice of Christianity. *Sacrificia quae sumpsimus,*[19] nourished by the Sacrifice which was the principle of all the martyrs,[20] we too become sacrifices: *nosmetipsos, Domine, tibi perfice*

[17] Postc. Dom. II Adv. et passim.
[18] Postc. Sabb. post Dom. III Quadr.
[19] Postc. S. Nicolai; cfr. Postc. fer VI post Dom. Pass.
[20] Secr. fer. V. post Dom. III Quadr.

munus aeternum.[21] That which should form our thoughts in us, and more than we ourselves form them, is the heavenly gift,[22] and in return for what generosity!

So, through the Mass, the Cross becomes the Christian life, that is to say, the passage of all Christians into life. And from the rising to the setting of the sun, through all the nations, there is offered to God a sacrifice which is one, one pure oblation.

And a living oblation, living with a living unity. The Mass is a prayer which lives in itself, because it lives of Christ; personal piety is a prayer which lives in itself, because it lives of Christ. In Christ, each of them while living in itself, lives in the other. The unity of the two does not have to be effected by simple human efforts; it exists and it is operative because it is living, in Christ. Let men yield themselves to it, let them cooperate with it, and all Christian devotion will appear one, because, in Christ, it is one.

In Him all is reconciled! His historical Sacrifice and His historical Priesthood, through His sacramental Sacrifice and His sacramental Priesthood, are prolonged and receive their pleroma in a mystical Sacrifice and a mystical Priesthood. And all this does not go forth from Him: everywhere He is Himself, but everywhere differently; here inasmuch as He is Chief, there in an efficacious sign, there again in His members, but nowhere is He divided.

"Glory to Thee, Lord, for Thou hast purchased us in Thy blood . . . and Thou hast made us priests before God!" [23]

[21] Secr. fer. III Pent.
[22] Postc. Dom. XV Pent.
[23] Apoc. V., 10.

CHAPTER VIII

The Mystical Body and Contemporary Humanity

Deus qui solus novit congruentem suis temporibus generi humano exhibere medicinam.
S. Augustine, *De Sermone Domini in Monte,* I, I, P.L., XXXIV, 1231

IN our days two tendencies assert themselves more and more in humanity.

On one hand, the individualist tendency, the desire for an autonomous life.

On the other, the tendency which we shall call "collectivist": preoccupation with a life solidly framed in the collective life of humanity.

I

First individualism.

In a certain sense it is essential to man: in this sense, that man, being a person and an end in himself, demands the right to direct himself and to act only for reasons which he has understood and which he has, in this way, given to himself.

But in our epoch, individualism has become acute. It could not be otherwise. Every day the press brings to each individual most of the data—at least we readily believe it does—on the most diverse problems; it discusses them before the general public, and, as a matter of course, considers each reader a judge. A strong head is needed to resist this daily intoxication of being set up as an arbiter of the nations.

Besides, each one knows that governments fear opinion, and that opinion is himself—at least, that is what he has been led to believe, and there is some truth in it—each one also is an elector; he knows that the masters of the hour have canvassed for his votes and will canvass for them again: they have pleaded with him and will do so again; so he accustoms himself to considering them as at all times amenable to him. In a number of countries besides, public order is based on the play of parties, that is to say, on the recognized right of each one to constitute himself judge of the leaders.

To this must be added the critical spirit which the positive sciences and the historical sciences have developed, the conclusion which each one has reached, that it is in the crowd, among the "each ones" that the great leaders of men have formed and asserted themselves.

So the thought takes root more and more firmly in the minds of men that, in humanity, the individual is everything.

On the other hand meanwhile, more and more clearly also, the individual realizes that in humanity and even for the best interests of the human individual, it is the group, it is humanity which is everything.

Assuredly, this dependence of the individual in relation to the totality has existed at all times. Always the human individual has been the termination of an entire genealogy: he has always been made by his two ascendants, and each of these by two others, and so on: the root from which he draws all his sap buries itself through ramifications which redouble without ceasing into an immense throng, the same approximately for all, into innumerable humanity. Always the maintenance of his life has been made possible by exchanges; always the formation of his mentality and of his character has been, in large part, the work of his environment. Always, finally, he has been a man only by being a man among other men, that is to say, he has been what he is, in what is most essential to him, only by being the very same which the others are.

Only, today, this dependence of each man on all men has become closer and more visible. It appears even in the details of life: everyone knows, without being astonished at it any more, that he eats the fish of Newfoundland, the apples of Canada, the bananas of the Antilles, the macaroni of Italy, and the dried raisins of California; that he drinks Brazilian coffee, that he smokes American tobacco, that he has a Swiss watch, and that his brief-case contains Congolian, Chinese or Egyptian securities. For his nourishment, for his heating, for all the economic order by which he lives, it is the entire universe which has co-operated by a medley of exchanges, of co-operations, of relations. Let the crop be bad in Canada, and the baker, faced with that fact, will raise the price of his bread; let Australia, to favor its own glass-works, close its ports to foreign products, and he will be out of work; let a panic occur on the New York Exchange, and the franc which he has in his pocket will find its value questioned; let Japan enter into a struggle with Russia, and his children will be called to arms.

More and more also, it seems, even in the midst of inevitable rivalries, the different classes of society are aware of their solidarity, or at least everything is calculated to make them aware of it. More and more the nations recognize, without daring to act accordingly, that what causes depression in one causes it in all.

More and more, too, intellectual labor is becoming collective: one no longer attempts anything serious without consulting the literature of the world, and researches begun in Tokio are continued in Austria and in Germany.

So, everywhere, every day, man realizes that he is caught in a net whose controlling strands are spread over all the universe, and these strands are of steel and stretched to the breaking point.

They encompass even his interior, even his manner of thinking. His thoughts, often without his suspecting it, are shaped in function of the entire universe and by the entire universe.

In the first place there are the daily papers. They are a true school, a school for children and for adults, a day and an evening school. There is no escape in reading almost nothing except the sport pages and the local news. You will constantly encounter dispatches from the entire universe; the matches themselves, and the races, and the Olympic games, and the records, are they not international? So, little by little, men live in communication with the entire human race; so, little by little, the soul becomes fully human.

Evidently we are not much stirred by the recital of distant events: we are almost cold to the story of a lynching in the United States, or of executions in Moscow or in Mexico. But that is because we are not yet formed: the press has not given the details; especially, we have not yet, by radio, by television, heard and seen the victims. But so, one day, we may arrive at seeing and at hearing. . . .

But, we are making a beginning, and the radio, in this matter, is from now on an unprecedented lesson. It is not a toy, that little set of waxed walnut, so simple that a child can start it going; it is a revelation! A nothing, a contact, the turn of a screw, and behold, we hear Berlin, and then

Madrid, and then London, and then Moscow, and then Vienna, and then the signals which ships are exchanging on the sea. We might say that the nations, questioned in turn, and by the first comer, reply; we might say that we are everywhere, that we implant ourselves, through some long root, among all peoples; or rather that "everyplace" is here, in the very place where we are listening, and that all the peoples are there, in the little clear-toned box. And, even when we cease to lend an ear, the great silent voices continue to re-echo about the globe; through the night they cross and reply to one another, they mingle and multiply; it is the entire earth which awakens and converses with itself, and all men, when they wish, can hear it. And these voices are human; in them each man can find himself and, at these distant songs, at these fanfares, at these melodies, can feel his soul tremble, for everywhere it is the same human soul which is revealed.

Truly, no man is alone. And what will happen on the day when some universal language will be spread abroad and when, from one end to the other of the world, we shall hear ourselves appealed to, when some distant orator will make his reflections, his enthusiasms, his indignations enter into us, when we shall feel ourselves, throughout all the earth, thinking together and willing together?

At certain moments each individual has been able to have some experience of it. All Catholics remember, for example, the days of last October, when they heard, with the entire universe, the ceremonies at Buenos Ayres and the voice of the Pope speaking to all the earth.

At these moments the radio broadcast makes every man experience the collective soul, it forms the sentiment of belonging to the group, of attachment to humanity. What will happen when the experience becomes more universal and more common, and when, besides, the transmission of images will permit us to see what we are still limited to hearing?

In the meantime, the simple radio is diffused more and more widely, and the children themselves pay no more attention to it. Little by little it shapes souls, it teaches every man that he has everywhere other selves, who think and desire as he does, and that, greater than he, overflowing him and penetrating him, humanity exists and even that it is humanity which exists the most here below.

This collectivism—the preceding pages define the term sufficiently—and the individualism which we discussed earlier, are two leavens, and terribly powerful leavens, which ferment in the breast of humanity. Their action in the secret places of men's minds must be intense. So, in our day, within itself, in its concept of man and of the union between men, humanity must change, and change vastly, and change quickly.

But this mentality is what is expressed in society, in the State. Society is indeed imposed on man by God Himself, but it is imposed on him through the medium of his nature, and hence in dependence on the accidental modifications and on the general development which necessarily occur in it.

It is therefore incontestable that at the present hour some accidental, but profound, changes are imminent in the institutions and in the structure of the State. They are imminent because they are already realised and in process of being more fully realised in what the form of the State can only express and make incarnate, that is to say, in the mentality of men.

That is not a prophecy; it is an estimate. Besides, is not

the unrest visible enough; are not changes, radical changes at times, occurring frequently, almost everywhere; is there not more talk than ever before of reforming the régime?

All these signs are not necessarily precursors of cataclysm: they are certainly messengers of modification.

To say that the unrest comes only from the fact that we have broken the ancient frames of life, and that the flood will end of itself when the torrent re-enters its bed, is a pleasantry. What has occurred and what must occur, is profound in a different way: humanity has lived, humanity has grown, humanity has become more strongly humanity, both in the individual and in the group of men. Hence, as it has changed in itself, it must necessarily effect a similar change in externals, in its methods of organization and of public presentation.

What can this change be? That is for humanity to make clear; because it is humanity which is worked upon by the forces which are going to produce it. Isolated reflection can scarcely guess at some of its outlines; it cannot see details or definite features.

Will it be an increase of regionalism and of particularism, giving to each part of the country the exact physiognomy which belongs to it, and this with an increase of the central powers and of the amplitude of the groupings; will it be an ensemble of international organizations, professional as well as cultural, and strongly constituted, paralleled by a loosening of the internal bonds of each State; will it be, in States more solidly constructed, relations, even close relations, of certain provinces with provinces of other States, economic, intellectual, and even political relations; will it be all this at once, or will it be something altogether different? No one knows.

But if the immanent halting-places are not yet clearly in

sight, what is sure is that we are at a curve in the road and it is a sharp curve.

And the question arises, not from the point of view of the facts, but from that of principles: how shall we make the turn?

II

The question is a hard one.

If what is working on humanity is two opposed forces, what can lie ahead except a catastrophe? What is needed is not reflection but flight. But where can we be safe?

No, some will perhaps say, and it is the first answer—the question is not hard: there is not even a question. These very forces, because they are opposed, neutralise each other. So with two locomotives which are placed in contact head to head: it would be useless for them to get up full steam; they would succeed only in holding each other reciprocally immobile.

Yes, certainly, if they don't both blow up. If poor humanity, so in struggle with itself, is not shattered to pieces, at best it will, and by dolorous efforts, reduce itself to impotence.

A second reply would consist in saying that one of the tendencies must win over the other; let it be, for example, the "collectivist" tendency.

Such is, with differing modalities, the doctrine of the totalitarian State, of the State which rules everything and directs everything, which pretends, alone, to form youth to its image and to its use, which pretends to be the norm of all rights and the last end of all efforts.

Certainly, the ancient social frames are no longer rigorously adapted to actual humanity, and we have said above that, among men, the concept of collective unity has asserted itself more vigorously, and that consequently, this same concept should express itself more definitely in institutions also.

But, precisely, the question is to know how. If we must, for this purpose, absolutely subordinate the human individual to the ensemble of men, we involve ourselves in a contradiction. For Society holds all its reality and all its value from the men who compose it: when we dispute the sacred character of men, we deny that there is anything sacred in Society either. So certain diseases destroy themselves by destroying the patient. Menaced in his most inalienable rights, annihilated as father of a family, as a free economic and social force, the citizen ends by being suffocated, and the city is no longer anything but a cemetery.

Of the narrowness of the political concepts which reduce everything to terms of the State and which, as a result, lose sight of humanity and then of the true dignity of men (understanding here the man who is the citizen of such a State) we shall say nothing at this time. It is not essential to the "collectivist" idea.

A third response would be the one which, in an absolute manner, would lift up individualism above collectivism.

It is as unacceptable as the preceding.

For each man every other man is as respectable as himself. For him to call in question their unrivalled worth, is, by the same act, to make his very own uncertain: he has no human ego except through being what they are. It is from them that he receives what is best in himself; in placing them purely and simply below him, it is himself whom, in his own interior, he turns upside down.

What is to be done then? What indeed, if to unite the two opposed tendencies is to invite catastrophe, and if to choose only one of them is to offer ourselves to the blows, and the mortal blows, of the other? What is to be done? Introduce here the classical distinction between individual and person? Yes, without doubt that would be good. But another solution, or rather, the same one appears, but under another form and with wider applications.

The difficulty comes from the antagonism between these two tendencies. To make it disappear, it suffices to show that this antagonism does not exist. And that is the fact. These two tendencies of opposite direction are the expression of one only and the same internal principle, as, in a tree, the force which sinks the roots in the earth and the force which lifts the crest to the skies, are two manifestations of the same vital force.

This unique principle is the very nature of man. Man, by nature, is social at the same time that he is individual; he is then directed, from the very interior of himself, towards the exterior.

Hence, to develop himself, he must at the same time increase in interiority with relation to himself and in interiority with relation to others. To be entirely master of himself, since he is man, it is imperative that humanity be master of itself, and hence that the union between men be close. On the other hand, in order that this humanity may be master of itself, each man must be, as totally as possible, his own master, and hence his personality, his liberty, must be as complete as possible.

All this is based on the very nature of man, on some truths which the Scholastics express marvelously, but which could be meditated upon at length, for they have wider applications than at first appears, and they shatter some narrow frames. The form, they say, is, of itself, the same for all men. This form, in its concrete realisation, is proper to each one, but at the same time, as form, it has, though imperfectly, its own act and its own existence in each man. *Actus, in quo genere est irreceptus, in eo est illimitatus.*

But this concordance, which exists in the nature of man, has been rendered more complete still by the supernatural.

That is what these pages wish to show especially.

The supernatural has rendered it more complete, through what is most essential in it, through the union which it gives to each man with all the others in Christ.

This doctrine of the whole Christ, we have said in another place,[1] sums up all Theology, as Christ recapitulates in Himself all the human race. The present pages would like to show how it also says the last word in the matter of the evolution which is evident in humanity. But this word is much more magnificent than any which man would have been able to find: it is a word which comes from heaven; it is the Word of God.

Individual life first.

In Christ, it acquires a supernatural depth, a depth so great that, for us, it remains a strict mystery; for, in Christ, it penetrates infinitely deeper than all our natural being.

Ego dixi, dii estis et filii excelsi omnes. In Christ, Who is God and the Son of God, men are divinised and constituted sons of adoption. Between them and the secret of the divine life, there is no longer any separation, and the life

[1] Nouvelle Revue Théologique t, LXVI, 1934, p. 449.

which springs from the depths of themselves is one and immanent with a unity which has its principle and its model in the unity of the Trinity itself.

This, evidently, is the absolute interiority. It is this which offers itself to and imposes itself on Christians.

So with the collective life also.

By being one with Christ, all men become one with all the others.

Christ, in consequence, as He is the last seal of God on the reality of humanity, is also the last seal of God on the unity of this humanity. This group unity He seals at the same time in the most august depths of God and in the most interior depths of man, because He seals it in Himself, Who is at once the Word of God and the source of life in the interior of each man.

So humanity which, in the natural order, seeks itself, finds itself in Christ. It finds itself there with the unity which it has in God *eminenter,* but realised in man. Each man remains distinct certainly: one is not man otherwise; but no one is any longer separate: one is not in Christ otherwise.

Before such unity as this, the wildest proclamations of solidarity are dull. One does not say to men: "You are alike, you are near to one another"; one says to them, or rather God says to them: "You are one only, one only with a divine unity": *Omnes vos unus estis in Christo Jesu;* [2] *unum sicut et nos unum sumus.* [3]

Contemporary experience can give to each man the thrill of feeling that humanity seems to exist and that it throbs near him. Christianity gives to every Christian the certitude

[2] Gal. III, 28.
[3] Jn. XVII.

of faith that humanity truly exists, and that it exists within him; because Christ, who is all in each one, is all in all.

Collective life, however, forming only one with the individual life.

As these two lives, in Christ, attain their paroxysm, their union also attains its maximum. Both, in fact, taken in their principle, are exactly the same thing, and the same thing totally one, for this thing is Christ, and Christ is one, exclusively, because He is the Person of the Word.

It is from being a member of Christ that the Christian is divinely deepened in his interior life; it is also from being a member of this same Christ that he is, and to the same extent, divinely rooted in the interior life of all the others. The union with all is then an interior thing, like Christ; and the interiority with oneself, like this same Christ, is Catholic.

Does a man wish to find the entire humanity? Let him enter into himself; within himself it is in His presence that he will find himself, and, in Him, he will find himself—within himself—in the presence of the immense throng which cannot be counted, and which is one in Him.

Does a man wish to find himself? Let him forget himself, let him throw himself entirely into the service of others, and behold! the one who in these others will have received him and who will have received all, will be Christ, and this Christ is the mysterious guest of the most profound places of the soul: in losing himself in Him, he will have found himself.

The doctrine of the Mystical Body is then a doctrine eminently actual.

More and more it impresses itself on the attention, on

the study, on the meditation of Christians, but especially noteworthy is the fact that the profane movement of the world, supposing that it is profane, is approaching it.

This observation should be made: the tumults of our epoch, Bolshevism, Nazism, Nationalisms of every sort, are signs of the times: they reveal the forces which are working on humanity, even when they are deviations from these forces. But what they make plain—and with what force!—is that, in our day, more than ever before perhaps, humanity wishes to unite with itself.

And behold, in our day precisely, Christian teaching places in the forefront the doctrine of this union of humanity with itself.

The doctrine is ancient certainly; but the divine truth is full of ever new aspects. "Every scribe instructed in the kingdom of heaven, is like to a man that is a householder, who bringeth forth out of his treasure new things and old." (Matt. XIII. 52.) It happens that the ancient preaching of the Kingdom, the teaching of Jesus, of Paul and of John, is the revelation, not merely of what God makes known, but also of what the man of the XXth century is seeking within himself without knowing it.

The meeting is not fortuitous. He who made the revelation is the one who made the heart of man, and He made them for each other. The whole Christ, Who is the résumé of this revelation, is also the centre in which God wishes to recapitulate all things. Is it astonishing then, if all this joins up, and if the unfolding of the centuries adapts itself to the history of the Word of life?

The meeting is a lesson. It shows that the teaching of the Church, and, in their way, theological studies, are not responsible merely for religious thought; they have charge also of the destinies of humanity. It shows also that in studying the truth about the Mystical Body, in preaching it, in meditating on it, we follow the directions of the Spirit, we obey the truth, and we serve humanity.

But it shows especially that this doctrine must be lived. The world has need of finding it, not in books, but in souls. The witness which it must have today, the witness which Christ arouses and awaits, the one which will be efficacious, is that of the member of Christ acting as a member of Christ, of the member who wishes to labor and to suffer, with Christ and in Christ, for all the immensity of the Body. To forget oneself, to renounce oneself, in order to belong in Christ, to God and to every man, that is the spectacle which will make manifest to all, in the manner which will strike them, that Christ still lives in His own. Abnegation then, but abnegation which shows itself especially in love and respect for all, in the will to efface oneself in the service of the Church and of humanity, in the giving of oneself to God by the consecration of oneself to all the children of God: it is of seeing this that the world has need.

This need is a petition which God Himself addresses to us: "I was hungry and you gave Me to eat." We can be sure that He answers it by giving generously in our epoch the grace of living as a member of Christ, of living not for oneself, it cannot be repeated often enough, but for Christ, and for the whole Christ. This grace we must receive jealously and correspond with attentively: by allowing it to be lost, we would betray the human race, and Him Who has so loved it.

It has often been said that the Church is the school of respect. It is very true, and the lesson, assuredly, is very necessary for our epoch. But it must be universal respect, a respect which includes all men, and which is thus one of the forms of love.

For it is love which is the authentic mark of Christ, and which ought to be, in the Church, the converting sign. She is, it is her primordial mission, the school of charity. And this lesson for our epoch, is the most necessary of all.

Making plain to men, and that in acts, in devotion, in self-sacrifice, in the giving of self to all, how, in fact, they are all one in Christ, and one with a unity at once divine and human, marvellously human and veritably divine, one with a unity far superior to the unities which they seek by their revolutions, alas, and by their murders—it is this which will convert the world.

Only let the salt not lose its savor! Let Christians who live by this unity, who ought to make it shine before the eyes of men, not hide it under their egoisms of class, of race or of persons, under theories of massacre and of hostilities, of reprisals and of parties. They would be responsible before Him Who died that we might be one, for the loss of their brothers and for the exhaustion of humanity in death.

SOME APPLICATIONS

CHAPTER IX

Christian Poverty

THERE is a Christian poverty; Jesus gave it its letters of nobility in the manger and on the Cross.

There is likewise a Christian virtue of poverty, and Jesus proclaims it indispensable:[1] whoever does not renounce, at least in his heart, all that he possesses cannot be His disciple; to follow Him it is necessary to leave all,[2] and he who wishes to hold to his riches might enter more hardly into heaven than a camel passes through the eye of a needle.[3]

In these pages we intend to make an inquiry into the exact nature of this virtue and to do so by taking the doctrine of the Mystical Body as our particular point of view. In this way we shall not, of course, get a complete picture; but at least we can expect to see its essential points.

Our point of view is, in fact, the centre of Christianity, since it is incorporation in Christ which makes us Christians and gives us all our supernatural life. On the other hand, poverty, which was the object of the first and of the last predilections of the Saviour, which forms the object of the first of the beatitudes and of the first of the vows of

[1] Lk. XIV, 33.
[2] Mk. X, 21.
[3] Ibid. 24, 25.

religion, must touch the centre of Christianity with the utmost closeness. If we are to see clearly what poverty is, that is where we must stand.

It is enough to say that the last word on this subject will not be found in the profane sayings of popular good sense. They have spoken of it however, and, long before le Savetier and the Financier of La Fontaine, they pointed out the great deception of riches. Riches, they tell us, make a man believe that he has great possessions, when, in fact, he has only great cares;—that he has made provision for his future, when he has embarked on a leaky vessel;—that he has all the means for finding contentment, when all he has done is multiply his needs and cloy his satisfactions;—that he is an owner, when he is himself possessed. He must manage his goods, conserve them, augment them, and, from evening to morning, his mind is full of calculation, his heart is hard, and his soul is empty. Insatiate, worried, encumbered, a rich man is indigent, but indigent by his own fault.

These reflections are just enough up to a certain point, and wise with a limited wisdom. We shall abandon them to the Stoics and the Epicureans. They could, it is true, by means of commentaries and retouchings, become an echo of the evangelical warnings about the *sollicitudo saeculi istius* and the *fallacia divitiarum*. But developments would be required, which, for the sake of brevity, we prefer to omit here. Their defect is in considering riches and poverty in their results much more than in their essence; in their outside much more than in their inwardness. And what appears on the outside if not the place where things cease to be themselves? It would be as much worth while to study liberty by looking only at its external manifestations.

Let us then leave the superficial and go to the essence. The question is that of material goods and of the proper attitude to have towards them. So let us see what these goods are and what they ought to be for us; we shall consider the matter first in the light of Philosophy, then in the light of faith.

I

Philosophy tells us that material things have of themselves no absolute value. So an act which would do no more than take possession of them or give them up, would not be either good or bad.

God alone, the infinite Good, the supreme Good, is absolutely good. Outside Him, among finite things, nothing is good in every respect, except the act which tends towards Him, the moral act, and the being which places such an act, the moral subject, man. Such a being alone puts on a dignity which participates in that of the infinite, because he expresses intelligibly in himself, though only in an analogical manner, the good to which he aspires and in which his movement terminates. Man alone, consequently, in the midst of our universe, possesses an absolute value.

But he does not have this value for himself alone. For he does not exist for himself alone. During this life the soul does not exist separate from its body, nor does the body live outside the universe. So, during this life, the whole soul is the soul with the body, and the whole body is the body with the world. The human being, in consequence, so long as we do not make arbitrary divisions, is man in the centre of the universe; it is the universe summed up in humanity.

The body of man, in fact, is built of substances borrowed from all nature; human action is composed of forces levied on all the cosmic energies. Before being in us, they were dispersed to the four winds of heaven and, after the some years or the some hours of their stay in us, they will be sent back again into general circulation. We live of the world, as we live in the world, and if it is true that it is neither the body nor the soul which thinks and acts, but man by his soul and also by his body, if it is true, besides, that the operation of the body is, in part and in large part, the operation of the entire universe, we must conclude, that it is not man isolated from the world who thinks and acts, but man united to things and taking up in his action and even in his moral action, the material things themselves.

As material things are a prolongation of our being, they can receive in themselves a prolongation of our dignity and they will receive it in the precise measure of their attachment to us, and of their union with the action of absolute range which is ours.

To the extent to which man makes them his—and this has a social aspect and ought to be estimated according to the general order which rules in the community—they share in his inviolability. Whence the sacred aspect of private property.

We must then say that the value of material things is real; but it is our very own. Not because they are worth something to us; but because they constitute us. Is it permissible to desire them? Evidently, yes: what attracts us in them is ourselves, but ourselves completed, sustained and aided by what they are. To despise them would be not merely an insult to the God of whom they are images and towards whom they open the way, but it would be an act of contempt towards ourselves, and, by consequence, an act against nature. Is it right to seek their possession? Yes again, evidently, and as much as possible, because this possession makes us be more entirely and because God has created us to be. To put it more precisely, it is right to seek their possession in all the measure in which this possession realises us more completely, that is to say, in the measure in which it renders us more truly, more largely, more nobly human.

Here, as you are aware, the facts compel us to make a reservation and a reservation which can have far-reaching effects. If the possession of material things, because of our bad manner of conceiving it, or for any other reason, should diminish us, if it should hinder the development of virtue, of courage, of disinterestedness, it would become necessary, on the instant, to renounce it. First, the higher goods; then, the others: as much as possible of both the first and the second; but with due proportion. It is a question of dosage and of balance.

In fact, the hypothesis is realised only too often. In general, we may say, the things of this world are so tempting and the covetousness which they awaken is at once so insinuating and so ardent, that prudence and wisdom counsel holding oneself on the defensive before them. As a general rule, the most favorable state for the development of what is best in man will be poverty, a poverty not too complete however; or better, a certain indifference of soul in a kind of *aurea mediocritas*. It is this aspect of things which popular wisdom expresses in the sayings which we recalled at the beginning of these pages.

The renunciation of which there is question is far from being total. It is even the contrary of renunciation; it is an appetite, an appetite for possession, but for calm possession. It is not Christian poverty; far from it; but it is the philosophical attitude which Christian poverty perfects and finishes.

II

Christian poverty is Christian essentially, not merely because it is Christians who practise it, but also because, in itself, in the attitude of soul which it constitutes, it is an entity which is explained only by Christ. Those who have best known Him and most loved Him, have looked upon the Crucified, and have had no need of seeing anything else. He wished to be poor, and they have wished it too. Or rather, since they are His members and since He lives in them, their manner of judging has been much more His than their own. The choice which He made of being needy on His entrance into the world, He has continued in them, and they have continued it in Him and through Him.

From the point of view of practice, there is no more to say: the Word, the Eternal Light, is the superabundant justification of all His acts: to be attached to Him is to be in brightness. One no longer needs to reason, but to do; the more one unites himself to Him by loving Him and by imitating Him, the more, in Him, one will see how good and just it is to live like him.

But, from the speculative point of view, some questions can still present themselves, which we must try to settle as far as is possible here below, if we wish to make a science of Christian action. Even for practice, the little which we shall be able to say will have its value: the "children of the light and children of the day" [4] cannot neglect the least light.

What is then, exactly, this Christian poverty and how is it Christian? How does it correspond with what Christ is and with what we are, we and the material universe, in Christ? Even in the supernatural order, and there more

[4] I Thess. V, 5.

than any place else, virtue consists in a voluntary adaptation of the soul and of the heart to the realities which God has made.

The reply has already been prepared. What we have seen about the supernatural order has set us on the way; we shall only have to take up again, in a larger and more beautiful synthesis, the philosophical considerations we have just outlined.

And this synthesis is a unit: souls are united to bodies; bodies are attached to material things; the only being which would not be a mutilation is man with the universe, it is the human universe, if we may so put it. So was it once; now there is a further unity. To this ensemble the Man-God has joined Himself. He forms one body with the humanity of which He is a member, as humanity forms one body with matter. More still: the plenitude of grace which He possesses, the superabundance of divine life which springs up in Him, makes Him contain in Himself, as in a source, all the supernatural life of our race. So He constitutes in Himself the unity of humanity much more perfectly than humanity constitutes the unity of the world. So also, because of Him, humanity, unified supernaturally in Him, constitutes the unity of the world more perfectly than before. *Ens et unum convertuntur*. All our universe, lifted up in its being to a transcendent dignity, is lifted up in the cohesion of its being to a supernatural unity. From Christ to men, from men to things, the bonds are close, through God and in God, strong with a superhuman energy. And the effect of the Incarnation, because there is no break in continuity, extends, step by step, even to the stars, to plants and to pebbles.

The Fathers used to say that the world is like a harp: merely by touching one string, the divine goodness makes it vibrate throughout. In the last strings the sound is attenuated in prolonging itself, but it is not extinguished. The effect of the Incarnation, in the same manner, goes even to the end of the world. Only, in material things, it is not, in any manner, the infusion of grace. It is merely the conferring of a new dignity: the dignity of being the setting in which the Mystical Body of Christ lives, the setting in which it is eternally true that Christ Himself has lived.

So, what is by itself only the human universe, becomes through Him the Christian universe. In the natural order, it is by the universe, with the universe, of the universe, that man forms his body and his actions, even including his acts of thinking and willing, at least in part. In the supernatural order all this continues, but on a higher plane. The universe, in giving to man his flesh and his blood, furnishes the matter of which the Mystical Body is made, the matter of which the physical body of the Saviour was made. It serves, in the Sacraments and even in all the events which occur in it and which Providence directs, for the growth of the Mystical Body. Besides, as Saint Paul teaches us, it has, through man, some relation to the order of grace. "Because the creature also itself," says the Apostle, "shall be delivered from the servitude of corruption into the liberty of the glory of the children of God. For we know that every creature groaneth and travaileth in pain, even till now." [5] And, in fact, when at last we shall be given our definitive exaltation, material things will receive some prolongation of it, because they themselves are our prolongation. The newness of life which will unfold itself in us will shine in them; there will be a new heaven and a new earth,[6] and they will reveal themselves through eternity before the eyes

[5] Rom. VIII 21, 22.
[6] Apoc. XXI, 1.

of flesh of the elect, like a splendid mirror of the divine goodness.[7]

While waiting, "all nature groans in the sorrows of childbirth." The rocks were broken at the death of Christ; the rending continues, we might say as long as the Mystical Body of Christ endures on the earth. The universe, however beautiful it may be, is a universe of suffering and of blood, of destruction and of death. The struggle is going on everywhere: the streams flow while wearing away the mountains, the mosses grow by nibbling at the rocks, and the animals live by the mutual slaughter which their meals necessitate. It is as if the universe adapts itself as much as it can to the actual stage of men, to a humanity which goes towards life only in mortification and death.

We shall not develop this point further.[8] What we must do now is make some applications with regard to the possession of material things in relation to poverty.

III

Henceforth, then, all things belong to Christ, and they belong to Him, it must be said, as being something of Him, mystically.

Formerly, man was the last of the ends included in the universe, God being the last end of man and of the universe. Now, it is Christ who is the last end of the universe, and man is no longer that last end except in Christ. Man is no longer even fully himself except in Christ.

So the things which, formerly, should have been ordered to man without the need for further considerations, should now be ordered to Christ. It is all over then, in the case of individuals, with the right of possessing totally, absolutely,

[7] St. Thomas, S.T. Suppl., Qu. XCI, Art. I, c.
[8] *The Whole Christ,* Mersch.

without being deterred by anything on earth over and above their titles by a sort of *dominium altum*. Private property, in the sense of possessing for oneself alone, without explanations or relation to a higher order of things, is no longer the last word. Men, themselves, exist not except through Christ; let them not possess then except through Christ! Through those who are His members, it is He who is the Master and the Lord, and, if one dares to say it, the last proprietor.

Proprietor: the word is almost ridiculous when applied to Him and, in using it, we must at once cut out every selfish connotation which it evokes. There is no question of property in the sense ordinarily intended by earthly property-holders. He who did not wish to have a stone on which to rest His head has not come to confiscate everything for His own profit. He, the priest of the total sacrifice, who wishes to keep nothing for Himself alone, not even His Body and His Blood, does not dream of laying up treasures. He came only for others; if then He ought to enter into possession of everything, it is not by taking away anything, it is in giving everything, that is to say, in giving to possess all, through Him and in Him, but much more perfectly than before, one hundred fold and for life eternal.

His Kingdom will have no end. So with the possession which, through Him, one obtains over things. God will conserve these things through all the ages, for Christ and His elect, while supplying by His virtue what is lacking to their feebleness.[9] And humanity, in Him, as it has entered into a new and eternal manner of possessing itself, will possess His universe in a manner new and eternal.

It remains to be seen what this new manner is.

It is, before all else, a change of spirit, not a social over-

[9] St. Thomas, *Summa Contra Gentes* IV, 97.

turn; and it is possible whatever may be the economic régime.

The principle of private property is not questioned: it is of natural right; it simply ought to enter as a component part into an order which will overflow it on all sides.

That ought to be said, and plainly. But we must add at once that it is only of natural right. The fences of artificial brambles which it demands are not the purest expression which the Christian ideal could find, and the most fraternal greeting which one could address to his brother is not to warn him that the foot-paths of a grove have been sown with wolf-traps with him in mind.

Once more, please do not misunderstand us, for the subject is a delicate one. We in no wise pretend that private property is an evil or an inevitable makeshift. We affirm, on the contrary, since it is certain, that it is a good, and a good necessary to men. But we add that men have been elevated by grace to a greater dignity, and so private property too should be lifted up to a like altitude in order to remain always the régime which is suited to men.

Men have received the gift of existing in Christ: let their possession then be possession in Christ. We mean to say: let it find its rules in His precepts, not in the simple ideas and whims of men, and let Him who is truly the Lord of all things, direct all through them: *tu solus Dominus*. Let a man make use of his goods to be charitable and to be religious, for the good of those whom God commands him to love, for the good of bodies and especially of souls, for the good of the family to which he belongs, for the good of all Christianity.

This manner of possessing is possible in every state and many Christians practice it in the world.

But, we must add, it is only in the religious life that it is fully realised.

There, in fact, and there only, all is so arranged that Christ directs, even in details, the use of the least things and even to the smallest semblance of a proprietary act. There the domain of Christ is recognized by an irrevocable act, by a vow which places between His hands the disposition of all things. There an organism, visible and perceptible, Superiors, the Chapter, the Council, speaks in His name and expresses clearly His will, and, as this organism is approved by the Church, and as the Church is Jesus Christ continued, we can be certain that, in hearing it, we are hearing only His voice.

Such a state implies a certain degree of indigence: the members ought to follow the paths which the Chief has followed, and the Chief wishes to continue in His members His struggles and His expiations.

This must be set forth at length. The entire supernatural life is, in fact, an immense expiation. Sin is here. It must be suppressed. It has consisted, very often, in an irregulated attachment to material goods. So its purification must consist in an immense detachment. Christ has begun this detachment in Himself, or rather, He has realised it in Himself with such plenitude that it ought to prolong itself in all the Mystical Body to express there its totality. Man ought to be mortified, inasmuch also as he is the centre and the reason for being of material things: this centre, henceforth, is Christ, and, in Christ, it is God. We must disappear, that He may be all.

Christian poverty is then a struggle and a self-effacement: it includes sufferings and renunciations.

Christian poverty is, also, a dependence. This dependence is a clearer expression of the reason why Christian poverty exists, and it is more characteristic of it than all the privations. Or, if you prefer, it constitutes the first of the privations; for it is the privation of unconditional domain, and this privation mortifies the pride of the spirit, while the other privations are only privations of use, which affect only the sensibility, and for a short time.

However, neither of these privations, in our opinion, is essential. The essential thing in a member is adherence to the chief; the essential thing in the manner of possessing proper to members is union with Christ. The dependence and the conformity of attitude come after, and they are the negative or secondary aspects of this union which is primordial.

Poverty is, in the first place, a union, a union with Him who is the Master of heaven and earth, and in Whom, alone, one wishes to possess all.

Poverty is love, a love which, in giving itself, gives all the rest and which no longer wishes to see anything or to put a value on anything except through the eyes of Jesus Christ.

Poverty is a consecration, a transfer to Christ, an elevation to the divine level, of what would, without it, be only the conduct of a rational animal among the things of which he has need.

It is also an act of worship and of religion. It is such, not merely in virtue of the vow which seals it, but by its very substance. It is in itself an oblation and a sacrifice, because it is the total offering made to Christ of all that one is as the centre of the universe, and of all that the universe is inasmuch as it has its centre in man; or rather, because it is the sacrifice of Christ, of Christ despoiled of everything on Calvary, continuing itself in the Mystical Body.

It is a sacrifice, yes, but in the Sacrifice of Christ, and the sacrifice is a passage, the passage from death to life; it is also the entrance into life eternal.

Man effaces himself inasmuch as he is the centre of the material universe in order that Christ alone may be in all the first, yes. But he possesses Christ in himself; so, in giving Him the first place, he gives it in some sort to himself. As member of Him to whom the nations have been given as a heritage, as child of God, he becomes the centre of the universe, in the Lord, in a more sacred manner, in a manner which participates in the primacy of God.

IV

Poverty is not merely an attitude which one takes before Christ; it is also an attitude which one takes before men.

As we have just been seeing, in fact, poverty is the mode of possessing which is suited to Christians inasmuch as they are members of Christ. But, as members of Christ, they are members of one another. To possess in Christ, is then to possess in union with others. But, at least by vocation of God and by the tendency of grace which works on all souls, all men are members of Christ. To possess in Christ, is then to possess in union with them all.

Besides, Christ, inasmuch as He is the centre of the universe, to Whom all things and all ownership should be brought back, is not so much Christ inasmuch as He has quitted this universe, as He is Christ inasmuch as He has remained here. Inasmuch as He has departed, what need has He any more of our miseries and what meaning would there be in a use of things which should be to His profit? While, inasmuch as he dwells among us, inasmuch as He has a Mystical Body, He remains in connection with His creatures, and He even has need of them. "I was hungry," He says, "And you gave Me to eat; I was thirsty and you gave Me to drink; I was naked and you clothed me." [10] Very certainly, there is only one Christ. But this unique Christ can be considered in different ways, and we mean to say that, when we point Him out as the term to which all possession and material things should tend, we speak of Him inasmuch as He is the Head of a Mystical Body.

But the head and the body form only one organism; *caput et corpus unus est Christus,* as Saint Augustine so often says. To say that the head is the supreme proprietor of all things, is to say that the body is also, through it. To say that all possession ought to order all use of goods towards the last master, is to say that it ought to order it towards the entire body. Since God has given all to Christ, and since Christ has given all to men, who are His members, it is to men that, in the last analysis, all belongs. What each one has as his own, he has, not in the manner of an individual separated from the others nor of an absolute despot, but in the manner of a part existing for an ensemble. He has it, in some sort, by title of representative of this ensemble, by title of manager, if we may so express it, he has it in order to procure the good of all.

These formulas, as we are well aware, have something disquieting about them: they seem to cry up the most complete collectivism. They do nothing of the kind, however, and we shall explain ourselves soon on this subject. All that need be noted for the moment is the peremptory manner in which they set aside egoism. The supernatural manner of possessing, which has been showing itself thus far as essentially Christian, appears now as essentially "Catholic": to such a degree should it bring back all to Christ

[10] Matt. XXV 35, 36.

and be in Christ, to such a degree should it bring back all to men and be in communion preoccupations, of desires, of intentions with all men.

But in what should this Catholicism consist?

Catholicism dwells, in the first place, within; it consists in the unity of life which joins through the centre each soul to all the souls which live by the same Christ. From this depth it ought to spread abroad in acts.

So with the Catholicism of the manner of possessing: in the very first place it ought to reside in the soul. It ought to consist in the certitude and the will of not being alone and of not having alone; in the preoccupation, the habit, the tendency of relating everything, through oneself, to the happiness and to the salvation of all regenerated humanity. The result will be as if there were for all goods only one possessor: this organism of grace in which all men, according to the plan of God, are vivified in Christ. All is for Him. Everything belongs to Him, and the individual act of possessing is not a small detached whole which wishes to retain something for itself alone, but rather a sort of element which is organized into this great ensemble and which, not seeking its own good except in the good of the ensemble, wishes in the first place the good of the ensemble.

Once the soul is disposed in this manner, action will follow. One will give alms, one will aid good works, one will support the missions, and one will be happy to so act. One will consider generosity, not as an astonishing and admirable attitude, but as the only manner of acting which is suited to the grace which one has received. By structure, by essence, a member insists on living for the others; when he communicates what he has, he does no more than act in the only manner which is connatural to him and he is only a useless servant.

Not, certainly, that this liberality is an obligation in strict justice. We are not concerned with justice here. Justice supposes essentially the otherness of the contracting parties, their opposition, and almost their possible hostility. Here these subdivisions have been overpassed and one is in unity.

Words become too poor when there is so much richness to express. Justice and liberality, charity and respect, possession and detachment, are all here together, and it is not exactly any one of them.

It is an attitude which is complex and one; an attitude which consists in the will to live of Christ and in Christ, and which possesses as many different aspects as this life itself does.

If followed to the end, the Christian virtues lead back to this centre, in which dwells all plenitude.[11] At their extremities, since they terminate in Him, while retaining their own modalities, they are continued in one another.

If a name must be given to it, and it seems altogether necessary that it should have a name, if we are to talk about it, let us call it Catholic poverty. But we must not forget that, in Him who has renewed all things,[12] words themselves assume a new meaning.

In the natural order, property has a social function. It justifies itself, in part, because it is the indispensable stimulant to stubborn labor, to economy, to the development of the universe, all of which are indispensable to the common good as they are to the good of each individual.

[11] Col. I, 18.
[12] Apoc., XXI, 5; II Cor. V, 17.

In the supernatural order, the same thing is true, but in a much larger sense: the social aspect of property, like the social aspect of our being itself, receives supernatural completions. Not, of course, that a wave of Communism should pass over the world, carrying away hedges and fences; but an immense love ought to invade our souls, sweeping out narrownesses and hardnesses. Grace does not suppress the distinctions between the different associations which it unites; families, groupings, fatherlands remain; but it breaks down the walls of separation.[13] In the same way, it does not suppress either the distinction between properties, or boundaries, or public registers; but by effacing in souls jealousies, egoisms, incomprehensions, it takes away from these necessary determinations, what would otherwise be division or antagonism. Above the subdivisions and the allotments, whose only contacts with one another are closed and rigid walls, it devotes all its energies to spreading abroad an immense love which should, in some sort, drown all these hardnesses in the consciousness of a universal solidarity and of a Catholic unity. So, in an organism, at the joints where the bones touch one another, Providence has inserted delicate tissues and anointing secretions, to change into smooth action what would have been rigidity, and into an easy adaptation what would have been a smashing blow.

Even in the natural order, the first proprietor is, in a certain sense, the collectivity: in this sense, that material goods are ordered in general for human nature, which is spiritual, before being ordered for such or such a man in particular. If, after all, they are ordered for such or such a man, it is because human nature does not exist in itself, but merely in particular individuals. It is also because this

[13] Eph. II, 14.

ordination (given what are in fact the propensities of men) is the only means of making sure that these goods will be conserved, kept up, developed, and thus of obtaining mediately that they will be truly useful to the collectivity. Private property thus vindicates itself in two ways; but, in the two ways, it presents itself as a social function, relative to the ensemble of men.

In the supernatural order also, it is true that nature in general does not exist formally, in the manner of a universal subsistant. But it exists eminently, since all men can and ought to be summed up in Christ. This recapitulation is, certainly, still in process of being effected; it is realised only in germ and on the supernatural level. So it has not yet succeeded in revolutionizing the natural economic order. But it is not nothing however, and, for those who have the grace and the will to live truly the new life, it gives a new concept of humanity and, by way of consequence, a new concept of the relations between humanity and the human universe. In the measure in which all humanity is realised by summing-up in Christ, it becomes the centre to which, by their very nature, material things should be brought back; it becomes, by right, the great proprietor, if we may dare to use the word, to which all belongs and in function of which use should be made of things. Besides, this new humanity is endowed with new leanings, among others charity, and this, in the measure in which it enters into human hearts, renders them capable of not damaging and destroying what is intended for the good of all.

Evidently, it consists in a change of principle more than in a change effectuated in the concrete: it demands a new soul, a new attitude of will, and not a new distribution of material goods. As such, it is possible everywhere: it is only a change of direction, and a progressive change. Let a man possess, not as an egoist, but more and more as a brother who, in Christ, forms only one with his brothers: *et pro invicem sollicita sunt membra.*[14] But is not the direction the all-important thing?

In the meantime, we repeat, it does not exist except inchoatively. And there will always be Christians who will desire, were it by casting themselves into the sea, to rejoin Christ more quickly.

"Mine" and "Thine" separate ever, and it is good for members to live together. When one forms only one body, why should one have many goods?

So the vow of poverty of the religious orders has arisen in the Church. It comes not merely from the fact that, on the one hand, community life is useful in many respects, and from the fact that, on the other hand, it cannot be stable except by a certain renunciation, on the part of all, of their individual properties. It comes also from the fact that this renunciation itself and this poverty are an attitude which the members of Christ take inasmuch as they are members, and from the fact that the members were created to live and hence to possess in common. Everything holds together in the unity of the Christian life; each aspect gives the explanation of the others, as, in the unity of an organism, each part glows with the life which animates the whole.

Comments have been made about the Communism of the religious orders, and also about the Communism of the early Christianity of Jerusalem. In the actual signification of the word, it is nonsense. Communism is an economic régime, and a materialist economic régime, which intends the enslavement of the individual to the collectivity. The manner of considering material goods in the religious life is

[14] I Cor. XII, 25.

an act of faith in a spiritual and supernatural union, and it is an exaltation of the individual, who is animated henceforth by a life larger than his very own. It is true that a man no longer possesses anything for himself alone. But it is just as true that he forms only one with the entire organism, which possesses all.

The vow of poverty, we have seen, is a holocaust offered to God; we see now that it is an oblation made to all the human race, an oath of comradeship, so to speak, which attaches each man of us to all the others.

From both points of view it is a sacrifice and an act of worship. But is it not God whom we love in the neighbor? And does a man love without sacrificing himself? And does a man sacrifice himself without depriving himself of anything?

To repeat once more, how truly is it the essential weapon for combatting egoism!

The individual will no longer be the one to decide about the use of goods; it will be a public person, the superior. And this public person will have to take into consideration not merely a number of religious and a monastery, but also the whole Catholic Church. So is avoided, as much as it can be, for it is very subtle, a certain form of egoism, collective egoism.

The superior ought to represent the entire Catholicity. He does not hold his power from the members of his convent, but from the entire Church. It is She, the Catholic, who gives him his authority, and who points out to him how he has to make use of it; it is then She, She who speaks in the name of all the Mystical Body, who will rule through him the use of all things; the Mystical Body, so, will be the veritable proprietor.

Without doubt, each superior ought to watch with special

care over the community which is entrusted to him and over the works which are assigned to it. But he will exercise this supervision as over a part which does not exist except in a whole, by a solicitude which, while busied with the part, never forgets the whole. And religious houses, even the poorest, will know how not to forget the Catholic interests.

V

Before the neighbor, poverty is then charity; before Christ, it is worship and religion. And before things, before the universe, what is it?

It is a kind of worship and a kind of charity. Something, in fact, of the attitude which it takes before the Saviour and before the neighbor extends even to this material world, which is a prolongation of man and in which the Saviour has willed to live.

In material creatures, poverty no longer sees the simple display of a splendid variety. She sees a belonging to Christ. Christ has breathed our air, admired our flowers, and sprinkled our soil with His blood; all this, henceforth, is consecrated and, in all this, the most real thing is what He has left of Himself. Just as the goodness of God shone in His human face, just as His charity expresses itself in the generous actions of those who are His members, something of His sweetness, of His beauty, and of His grandeur, shines through all His universe. *Tui sunt coeli et tua est terra.*[15] In its entirety, this universe is too august to serve only individual needs. In its entirety, it has become sufficiently holy, sufficiently consecrated, to be ordered only to the service of Christ, of Christ and of His Mystical Body.

No use is forbidden, since all can be related to the Lord.

[15] Ps. LXXVIII, 12.

But a state of soul is rejected: a certain pride, a certain self-sufficient arrogance, a certain pretence at elevating oneself into the last end of things. This hollow vanity is often inspired by wealth: it does not square with the grandeur of the universe or with the true dignity of the members of Christ.

A certain humility is now required, together with a certain charity. The world . . . , but it is of our family: by nature we form a part of it; by grace we are more united to it still. In Christ, the unity of creation has received a divine completion; matter has become susceptible of salvation,[16] it will revive for the life eternal, our souls will be reunited to it forever and it itself will be spiritualised and glorified in an ineffable manner.

Henceforth, a little of the love which we owe to ourselves, a little of the love which we owe to humanity, ought to descend even to it. It is the flesh of our flesh, the bone of our bone; we must then cherish it; we must even, in a certain sense, cherish it with charity, since it is attached to Christ and to His Mystical Body.

This sympathy for all that is, is not a little tenderness that we refuse to men in order to give it to things. That would be bad. It is love for men, so vast that it embraces all that touches them. Love, like the good, is diffusive of itself; the more ardent it is, the greater the flames it throws out; when it burns with a divine ardor, it is all the earth which it wishes to set on fire. We shall then, in Christ, love men with theological charity, as far as they go, even to the end of the universe, even to the grains of which our bread is made, even to the great trees of which the Cross was formed.

This love, magnanimous and generous, has nothing in

[16] St. Ireneus, Adv. Haer., V, 6, I; etc.

common with the parsimonious idolatry of the miser. If, in things, we love men and Christ, we shall not hesitate to use them, and as largely as possible, whenever there is question of aiding the neighbor or of honoring the Saviour.

This love is disinterested also. Poverty is not economy, still less prodigality or negligence. It is not a financial institution, a sort of co-operative of production and of purchase permitting easy gains. Does one make a vow of poverty, of detachment, to rid oneself of the perpetual necessity of saving? We shall respect goods by not squandering them; but we shall respect our souls by not crushing them under the fear of expenses.

This love is luminous too, and it makes us understand. Egoism is opaque. It allows men to see in things only their use value, and their relation to self, that is to say, the thin superficial layer by which they touch the rest, and not their inwardness. Poverty, poverty respectful and loving, in disencumbering us of ourselves, gives us leisure and room to admire and to possess within our souls the true majesty of the real.

Poverty gives us the awareness, everywhere, of a belonging to Christ and of a mystery of grandeur. We can open our eyes; they are ready to discern, at the least indications, accumulated magnificences in all which is. It is not by chance that the Poverello of Assisi was one of those who have best understood nature. Poverty, in releasing his soul, has made it quick to vibrate.

Finally, it is human love. If sympathy for things is one of the most delicate marks of the love for men, Poverty, by facilitating this sympathy, shows how well it is calculated to develop in us whatever is most profoundly human. We must not let it be said or believed that we are indifferent or blind before the universe, as if the brightness of the beyond hid from us the real world where the Father has placed us, or as if pre-occupation with begging veiled the splendor of the world to our parasitic eyes. Would it be because we are the children of the Creator of all, and members of Him who has restored all in Himself, that we would be incapable of seeing the world as it is; or would it be because everything is an image of God and a vestige of Christ, that it would be less august?

VI

Poverty, we cannot say it often enough, is exactly the contrary of contempt. Contempt is not Christian, and besides, it is usually stupid. Poverty does not say that things are nothing. That would be false, since they are. It does not say that they are evil, which would be more false still, since they are the work of God. It says that we, we are covetous, and that we must not enslave or imprison ourselves. It says that things are beautiful and grand, too beautiful and too grand for us to seek, in them, ourselves alone.

It is true that it includes a negative aspect, and this aspect is important. It supposes mortifications, sacrifices, privations. But these renunciations are negative only in part, and that the least part. Before all else, they are a deliverance, the deliverance from our narrownesses; and they are love, the love of Christ and of the universe in Christ.

Do not all the virtues demand certain suppressions, the suppressions of their contraries? Chastity and Obedience, to speak more especially of virtues which the vows of religion range alongside poverty, do they not imply, the one, abstention from conjugal love, the other, the sacrifice of one's own will?

But, in them, these abdications are only the reverse side of a conquest. Obedience renounces willing with an individualistic will: but it is to arrive by that means at willing in Christ and with Christ, in the Mystical Body of Christ, and with this Mystical Body. Chastity forsakes conjugal love, but by so doing it makes men love more strongly and more largely, it makes them love Christ in all the extension of His Mystical Body. We suppress, at bottom, only restrictions; we do not mortify the man except to divinise him: behold how one penetrates into the divine and into the Catholic; one wishes, with God, divine things; one produces, with all Christians, the birth of all humanity in Christ.

In the same way Poverty. It leaves only to find, in a more perfect form, what it has abandoned. It breaks with everything exclusive, restricting, limited, in individual ownership; and it acquires under a better and more developed form the element of true possession which was contained in this ownership.

It can keep things in all their being, in their use as in their substantial inwardness, and even in the increase of dignity which the Incarnation adds to them.

It holds them with the force of all the human race, for it holds them in the unity of the Mystical Body and by all the Mystical Body.

The act of possessing, itself, otherwise so earthly and so narrow, becomes marvelously total. It is no longer merely annexing; it is worship, universalism, admiration for the universe; it is charity especially, charity for Christ, charity for all men, charity, in an analogical sense, for things, charity blending with the use of material goods.

Plenitudo legis est dilectio. So Poverty shows itself as a total thing, including in itself (from a particular point of view, it is true) all perfection, as each of the angles of a triangle, even the smallest, comprehends all the triangle.

As it is perfection, so is it beatitude. *Beati pauperes,* blessed the poor, they are kings, the Kingdom of God is theirs. They are the truly rich, not because they have renounced all, but because, in renouncing, they have acquired all. He who leaves his goods, or his fields, or his house, for the sake of Christ[17] will receive them again a hundredfold, and life eternal. Even here below he will possess all these, but in a manner so perfect that it makes him dream of the plenitude of eternity.

Christ, in Himself, has made beatitudes of what seemed a curse. Of poverty, which seemed pitiable and threadbare, He has made something royal and opulent, a magnificent adaptation to the splendor of the human universe, a mysterious union with God who has made all things, in a sacrifice which unites to itself His sacrifice, which is entrance into God and penetration into all humanity.

But this Poverty is not any poverty at all: it is the Poverty which is His, as this sacrifice is His, Christian Poverty.

[17] Matt. XIX, 29.

CHAPTER X

Love, Marriage, Chastity

THE Word became flesh and dwelt among us.

Henceforth, human nature is no longer simply human nature. Men are brothers of the Word, members of Christ, children of God, temples of the Holy Spirit; they are a holy race, a divinised race.

In consequence, a thing as totally and essentially human as conjugal love is changed too. It is no longer simply human love; it is a thing of grace, an act of divine life, an exercise of charity; and the fire which burns in it is the fire which Christ brought here below, the celestial fire which the Spirit lights.

When we speak then of conjugal love, we must be mindful of this marvellous ennobling.

That is what we wish to do in these pages. We wish to speak of it as of a thing which finds its last and eternal gladness in the happiness (totally limpid, but vibrant like the splendor of the sun) of what is called the Nuptials of the Lamb. We wish to speak of it by showing how, even here below, it tends, of its own movement, to prolong itself, to lose itself, or rather, to transfigure itself in a human love more totally human than itself, and divine also, in pure and generous Christian charity.

The duty is urgent in our age more than in others, of making those who have received the Sacrament of Matrimony see all the splendor, the immaterial splendor even, of their state. They must be shown how their state has its place, its very own place, in the Church of God, among the martyrs and the confessors, the virgins and the pontiffs. They must know of what spirit they are and what it is to transmit life in the generation of children of God, in order that they may see how their state itself sanctifies them, how it allies them with the saints, how it lives with a superior love, which is capable of sustaining their souls in the days when constraints or privations impose themselves on their bodies.

The duty is urgent also of intensifying among the educators whom God charges with forming the future heads of families, a respect for marriage alive enough to be communicated to others. We are aware that the subject is a delicate one. Most Christian educators are vowed to perfect chastity, and they can never have too jealous a devotion to the angelic virtue. But they must endeavor to conceive of perfect chastity in such a way that they will be able, in loving it, in preferring it immensely to marriage, to love marriage also; and to love marriage not merely as another state of life, but, if possible, simultaneously and with the same love, though in an inferior degree.

For this, in our opinion, we must bring back religious chastity, marriage, and also (for there is a close connection between all of these) the rigorous precepts of purity, to their first principle, which is love, human love, or rather, as we shall see more and more plainly, which is charity.

Such is our plan in these pages. It is very clear. It consists in sketching out, in broad outline, a treatise on Chastity, an essentially positive statement of the Moral Theology on the Sixth Commandment, a statement which may be summed up in the requirement of respect for a profoundly venerable good.

In broad outline, we say. There can be no question of a complete treatise intended to provide a solution for every case which might be presented. Complete and accurate treatises may be found in any of the great works devoted to this subject. All we plan is a study of the principles, concrete enough to make plain the attitude of soul which they require, and to direct and explain their application. But our study is restricted to the general rules, to those which, precisely, express the spirit of the precept.

Too often, perhaps, preaching and teaching appear to limit themselves in these matters to cries of alarm. We speak of dangers, of enemies, of easy illusions, of abysses concealed under flowers, of death-dealing pleasures. As if nothing were required except an immense prudence before multiple perils.

Perils there are—yes! We can never repeat often enough that the only security, in this matter, is a perpetual vigilance—and confident vigilance too, of course.

But is not the whole world one in proclaiming that the source of prudence is ardent love of the good menaced? Is not the entire Christian tradition unanimous in pointing out the good in chastity, a good intimately united to charity?

I

Let us dare then to begin with a eulogy of love. It is a duty. The priests of God are anointed to claim what belongs to the Lord. But love is His; it comes from Him. *Amor ex Deo natus est.* We would be guilty of a betrayal of trust if we allowed the halo to be snatched from this divine thing.

The infamies of men, the degradations to which they have been led by the impure spirit, concupiscence itself, change nothing of the essences of things. Love comes from God.

God, in His love for men, had so much confidence in them and so much respect for them that He entrusted to them the conservation of their species. He has then, in creating them, implanted deep in their being, along with the instinct of self-preservation, another tendency almost equally energetic, and almost as completely identified with them. We mean conjugal love, the instinct of conservation of the species.

The rôle of this love is an august one. While other natural activities produce only things, this one produces a man, and it is from this love that God awaits those who will be His children of adoption.

In no other activity—of the natural order, of course—is the divine co-operation engaged to the same extent. The procreative action implies, so to speak, a creative concurrence, since the child, its term, cannot exist without a soul and because God alone can create souls.

What we are going to say will at first appear shocking. But it is only a particular manner of presenting a truth which is altogether traditional, and this truth, seen from this angle, is too important not to be stressed. In no other place—still, of course, in the natural order—is God present as He is there. For in no other place is His activity so immediate.

Then too, of its very nature, love is a sacred thing and an element of religion. So we now begin to perceive how fitting it was that, in revealed religion, marriage should be a sacrament.

Amor ex Deo natus est. Love is then a thing of God.

To sin against it, is to sin against God where He is most present in the natural order.

To sin against love is also to sin against the race, against this humanity which God has made to His own likeness and which He has loved to the point of giving to it His only Son.

Love, in fact, has its reason for being, its energies, and thence its requirements, not from the individual, but from the species. The individual is the carrier and the agent of it, not the master.

Love is an act of the species, in this sense, that it is destined to perpetuate the species, and that, in it, the species realises itself and acts in the measure in which it can be realised and can act.

It will be necessary to develop this idea at some length, as we shall have to make use of it in what follows.

The species of which we speak, humanity in general, cannot exist in itself. Only individuals, only men, exist. It is by the multiplication of these that the species seeks to realise all the richness of the human type which it contains and to find itself quite entirely expressed.

The ideal term of this movement, as also of every social element in our nature and of all the efforts which men make to come closer together, is the unity of humanity, that is to say, the realisation, in an existence unique and complete, of all that humanity implies of energy and of inherent capacity. But forces are by so much the more powerful as they are more unified and more compact, and unity is the principle of multiplicity. So the unity of humanity of which we are speaking is fecund, and the origin of the multiplication of men.

But, in the natural order, it is impossible and contradictory that this unity should be adequately realised: to repeat, there exist only multiple individuals. It is not nothing, however. It is the cement and the *raison d'être* of all society. And, besides, it finds a sort of outline of existence and a beginning of actuation in conjugal society. We mean to say that, in marriage, the individuals are the instruments, almost the passive instruments, of a force which overpasses them, which is in them, but not for them, and which, in making use of them, does more than they do, themselves. In marriage, it is humanity which, as far as is possible to it, asserts itself, takes a definite position, completes itself, and finds its unity and its fulness, in individuals and not in itself, for in itself it cannot exist.

Incarnating the unity of humanity, love is august and venerable with all the nobility of our race. God, who has so admirably established, and, more magnificently still, restored the dignity of our substance, places on us a strict obligation to respect it with all the respect which He requires of us for ourselves.

We are at the corner-stone of social morality. To disturb the position of this stone, is to imperil the whole structure. Respect for the lives of our fellow-men, for their reputations, for their goods, is only the consequence of a more fundamental obligation: "Remember thou to respect humanity." To insult it at its source and in the very centre of its unity, and to take as a toy the august function which alone assures its existence, is to sin grievously against the first principle of all society and against the essential subordination of the individual to the species.

So the conscience and the psychology of the individual who sins against this love is bruised and wounded unto death.

Precisely because it is an act of the species, this love profoundly affects the individual. It perfects him and exalts him to the point of making him coincide, in some way, with humanity itself, and of constituting him principle of man.

That is why it plays a formidable rôle in human psychology. It is one of the most perpetual stimulants of action, one of the most incessant solicitudes, and one of the most important factors of human morality. It completes and forms the mentality of each sex through their mutual influence and through the education of the children. It leads the man and the woman, by a movement insensible and exacting, from preoccupations egoistic enough in the beginning, to a splendid life of devotion and of forgetfulness of self.

It is plain what respectful attention is required by this so central, so essential—and so delicate—point of human psychology and of human morality. At this first beginning of human conduct the least irregularity provokes catastrophies. Hence, to turn this piece on itself and to change into a sensualist egoism the movement of the giving of self, is, in perverting one of the principal incentives of its attitude, to make an attempt on oneself and to pillage one's soul.

Nothing debases like this disorder. When it is established in the heart, respect for oneself and for humanity is banished, and one sacrifices, without embarrassment and without emotion, the dignity of the human person and the lives of his fellows—the small and the great.

So the worst chastisement of the peoples who pervert love—after the eternal sanctions, of course—is not in the rarity of births and the ruin of health. It is in the debasing of characters. Their souls have no longer the courage to live, and their wills are sick, stricken by a wound more hideous than all the pus that flows from it.

One point remains to be explained before establishing the principles of the natural law on the subject of love.

Love, like man in whom it is found, has, like the humanity which it is designed to perpetuate, two aspects: a corporal aspect and a spiritual aspect. The one is common to it with the lower living beings, the other is proper to it. The corporal aspect of which we speak is the organic activity of generating, in which human love is embodied, and through which alone it is efficacious.

Given the unity of the human composite and the close connection between our souls and our bodies, to arouse this activity is to make love itself pass into act. Superficial intentions change nothing in these primordial functions. Whether one wishes it or not, the emotion which accompanies the activity of which we are speaking is the psychological bond through which our will is engaged in our organism and is held there. The very thing that renders it appetible is that it is the sensible and corporal aspect of love and that it completes a man in that way; it would not exalt him, it would not attract him to this extent, if it were not, in some sort, the paroxysm of his humanity, the summit upon which, by becoming principle of man, he becomes man to the maximum. This activity is then intrinsically bound to love, and one cannot arouse it voluntarily except in conformity with the natural law, which is the law of love, and of which we shall treat in the course of this study.

As is plain, the extent of the activity aroused is not the point at issue; the malice consists here, not in the effects produced, but in the abuse itself of a function, and of a function which is of itself generative of man. Of itself then, the matter is grave; its gravity can, assuredly, have degrees; but it remains essential.

In other matters, in the case of charity or justice, for example, the external action of the body and the voluntary decision are not so closely united, with the result that it is possible for the external action in itself to interest in only a relatively mild way the will to be good or to be just. In consequence, in these matters, one can have acts which, although intrinsically evil, will be so only venially.

But such is not the case here. The will acts precisely inasmuch as it forms a unit with a well-determined organic function and can do nothing except with it.

Nowhere then is morality so bound up with corporal activity; nowhere is the activity of the body so intrinsically of the moral order; nowhere does the absolute value which our soul gives to our flesh appear more clearly or in such rigorous requirements.

Nowhere, either, from another point of view and for the same reason, can good faith, or demi-good faith at least, endure longer, in spite of shortcomings numerous and grave.

It is the counterpart of the preceding remark. It too should be clearly formulated.

The conditions are not the same here as in the case of the other precepts of which we have just been speaking. They concern the will inasmuch as it rules, by title of spiritual power, our corporal acts. In this superior zone it is limpid and it can see its act to its uttermost depth and can judge it.

In what concerns purity, on the contrary, the will interposes inasmuch as it incarnates itself in an organic activity. As such, it is not luminous, and only a will energetically determined upon right action can, with a great struggle, make brightness penetrate into these depths. But too often, in softer souls, a demi-obscurity endures, favorable to illusions. Rarely, we think, for after all it is a question of the natural law, rarely is the lack of light sufficiently total to completely excuse faults. But, more often perhaps than we may believe, the apparently grave faults of others are lessened by a certain unawareness.

On this point besides, more than on others, moral teaching has been formulated in humanity only by successive approximations. Revelation itself did not tell everything in the beginning. We are aware of the fact that, in the Old Testament, God did not speak, even to the holiest of the Patriarchs, of the precept of monogamy, for example. Yet it belongs to the natural law, at least among its secondary requirements, as the Moralists say.

This progress, however, is no indication that Moral Science is, because of its development, artificial. On the contrary, it proves that it is natural. Our sensitivo-rational nature is, through the body, subject to time and to the law of growth. The natural law and the requirements of Moral Science, especially in what concerns the will inasmuch as it does not act except in and by a material function, cannot but follow the history of the development of our race. In themselves, of course, their prescriptions exist once man exists. But, for man, they become conscious, known, and hence obligatory, only in the measure that man knows himself better, and in the measure that he acquires a more complete awareness of the most profound requirements of his being—those requirements in which, to sum up, morality is the most corporal and where the body most affirms its moral value.

It remains to settle what these requirements are.

The Sixth Commandment consists entirely—it is our thesis—in a demand for respect: "Respect love, in the name of God."

Let us examine the requirements implied in this formula. For love has, through the gift of God, its nature, and we are going to see how, whatever we may feel and whatever we may say, its nature enjoins upon it, by order of God again, its natural law.

Love is a union. Conjugal love is the union of the man and the woman. The act of love then should be an act of union. One who wished to place it without loving anyone, for his isolated individual enjoyment, would direct towards emptiness the impulse of his being; he would by effecting the act, contradict human love essentially.

The act of love is the union of the man and the woman. And this states clearly enough what being alone is worthy of it and what union alone it admits.

What we have just been saying has in view also the sanctity of the matrimonial union. It would be enough, we believe, to prohibit abortion, even if this were not homicide. One sins against the unity which one has willed by destroying it in its natural term. Especially, it must be added, as the unity of which there is question is ordered to the good of the species and as it is not then to the individual that it belongs to make or to unmake it. In placing the action, in fact, he has set in motion forces which overpass him: humanity which perpetuates itself, God, if we dare to say it, Who creates souls, the child who is a human being. Willingly or unwillingly, such an act possesses a range and a unity which do not depend on him, and which even, coming from an authority higher than himself, force themselves upon him.

What has just been said about the immortal being in whom the union of the man and the woman terminates of its own proper movement, through the divine concursus, suggests that this union cannot be a transitory event, but that it demands indissolubility. That is what we must now consider more closely.

Love, we repeat, is a union. It is impossible without a reciprocal donation of self, by which each partner renounces his life as an isolated individual, in order to become one with the other.

But, for a man to give "himself" is not a momentary thing. He is not, in fact, restricted, as animals are, to having only a vague and fugitive sensation of himself, only an obscure apprehension which is effaced with the present perception. He thinks and judges in function of the past and of the future and, when he reflects on himself, it is of all his life that there is question. This manner of knowing himself, of "possessing himself," indicates the manner in which he ought to give himself, under pain of self-contradiction: he ought to give himself for his entire life. If he wished the conjugal union, but pretended not to renounce by the same act the right of taking himself back, he would give himself while refusing himself, and would therefore go contrary to the essential requirement of love. Marriage is then a contract which the natural law wills to be indissoluble.

Death alone can break it. Then, in fact, the object of the contract is suppressed, for there is then no longer a possibility of a reciprocal giving between souls united to bodies and inasmuch as they are united to bodies. Once the body is separated from the soul, love and the conjugal contract are without object and exist no longer, at least in the same way. It is certain, in fact, that after death, and especially after the resurrection of the body and its glorification in a spiritual state, a special love, a particular charity can prolong between the spouses what was, during the terrestrial life, conjugal love. But of that, we have not to speak here.

There has been talk about the death of love: once sensible love has disappeared, they tell us, the married persons have lost the bond which united their souls, so now they have only to separate their bodies. Error evidently. This could be true if man were not rational as well as "sensible." But human love is something other than a sentiment; it is essentially—though not exclusively—a procedure of the soul and a willed giving of oneself. For that reason, because of that in which the grandeur of our race consists, it must be more solid than the affections of the heart and it must lift itself above what passes with time. When tender feelings grow cold, they must be made to glow again; that is all. To submit human love to the instability of sensible and animal psychology, is to trample on the grandeur of humanity in its primary origin, and that is a more serious thing than to trample on it in one of its individuals.

The indissolubility of marriage ought to go along with its unity. The fact is that the love of which we are speaking cannot, like charity, multiply its objects without dividing and lacerating itself. Because it is material, it must be limited, under pain of mutilation. One who wished to love, but without relinquishing by the same act the right of giving himself to another, would make of his donation a refusal to give himself, and so would sin against the natural law.

Finally, the last requirement where Christians are concerned, the union of the man and the woman ought to be a Sacrament. It is the will of God that His children should be united by grace. We can discern reasons of fitness in the reality of things. Love, we can say, plays in human life—and hence also in Christian life—too grand a rôle, it is too fecund, both in good works and in dangers, not to have need of a consecration. It is also too necessary to the Church, to which it furnishes her future children, not to be a thing of the Church. Finally, and this "mystical" consideration appears to us the most decisive, marriage, we have already seen, realises, to the extent to which it can be realised, the natural unity of humanity. But, as we must now note, as we shall explain more at length in the course of this study, this unity of humanity is realised, but supernaturally and with a higher kind of perfection, in Jesus Christ.

It is the great truth of Christ living in the Church, of the Mystical Body of Christ. In Christ, through grace, in a mysterious and real manner, regenerate humanity is a unit.

Hence, in Christianity, marriage, by its essence, that is to say, by the union in which it consists, has relation to Christ and it includes an activity of the Saviour inasmuch as he unites humanity in Himself, that is to say, inasmuch as He is still acting in the Church. There is then an action of the Church which is an action of the Saviour Himself, who, as such, is the principle of supernatural life, and who sanctifies and "supernaturalises," in marriage, the fruitful union of humanity. In other words, marriage is a Sacrament.

And, as is evident, the Sacrament in marriage is not a benediction superadded to it; it is the very essence of marriage, of the contract of union and of love. It is this which participates in the union between Christ and the Church, between the Word and humanity.

And it is this, it is the essence of the contract, which, elevated by grace to a higher dignity, receives new perfections.

Marriage is one and indissoluble of itself and as a contract. As a Sacrament, it receives a divine unity, and it is sealed with the seal of the Trinity in a divine indivisibility. The love of which it is constituted ceases to be purely human and becomes an aspect of theological charity.

The Council of Trent puts it magnificently: "The sacramental grace of marriage leads conjugal love to its perfection. It confirms its indissoluble unity, and it sanctifies the partners. It is Christ who has merited this grace by His passion." [1] "It is Christ our Lord," as Leo XIII says, "who has united more closely, by the bond of divine charity, the society of the man and the woman, already indivisible by its nature." [2]

Over the love of the man and the woman hovers the image of the crucifix. It is a symbol and a consecration. Marriage is a thing of Christ and of the Church; it is a state of charity, of devotion and of redeeming sorrows, and its rôle is to bring up young Christians in the love of the Saviour.

By essence, in the natural order, marriage is what furnishes educators to children; for what is education, if not the long extension of birth; and who is adapted, prepared, willed by nature itself for the formation of mentalities and characters, if not those who, through heredity, have furnished the soil to be cultivated? In the supernatural order there is something similar: the Sacrament of Marriage prepares for the young Christians the educators whom they will need for their lives as children of God, and it prepares

[1] Denz. 969.
[2] Litt. encyl. Arcanum illud.

for them the environment in which their regenerate souls will be able to grow. Not that marriage sanctifies directly the children who are born of it; it is Baptism alone which gives entrance into the sanctity of Christ. But it sanctifies the partners as partners; it divinises their union; it merits for them the graces which their state requires; and what is this conjunction, this union, this state, if not that which, by nature and by grace, is destined to furnish men to humanity and children to the Church, *ut populus Dei et Salvatoris cultui addictus in dies augeatur?* [3] That is its principal end, its *primum bonum.* Also, in the forefront of the graces which it brings to the parents, is the grace of bringing up their children in the fear of God. The Christian education of children, assuredly, is a thing of the Church, and the rôle of parents, in this matter, cannot be conceived except in union with and in dependence on the magisterium of the Church. But the union and the dependence has not had to be set up by an arbitrary and adventitious delegation, it belongs to the nature of things and to the Sacrament of marriage which has been conferred. In virtue of the natural law and of the sacramental grace, the parents have the mission and the authority to form their children to the image of what they themselves are and ought to be, to form little Christians and obedient sons of the Church. And it is a constant source of wonder to see what marvelous skill Christian piety, joined to the maternal or paternal instinct, gives them in this direction. The Church will never dream, save in case of unworthiness, of replacing them; she cannot dream of it: their mandate is a derivative of her own; only a derivative, but a true derivative: in contesting it, she would bring her own rights in question. But, also, because it is a derivative, she watches over this teaching and she

[3] Pius XI Litt. encyl. casti connubii.

repeats without ceasing its importance: even when given by the parents, and as given by the parents, it remains hers. It is only later on, when the child is born to the personal life and when it requires a more complete instruction, that, without setting aside the parents, far from it, she who teaches the parents will also teach the children directly.

Marriage does not have all its perfection until it receives its sacramental consecration. More precisely: its unity is incomplete, when compared to the supernatural unity of Christ and of the Church; but, it must be added, only when compared to this unity. We realize then, that marriages which have in no way received the consecration of this unity, that is to say, marriages contracted between pagans, can be dissolved at the conversion of one of the partners, if it is necessary in order that this partner may be able to lead freely his Christian life in the unity of the Church. It is the *Casus Apostoli*. And we realize also that this case is the only one and that other, even most serious, motives, urgent personal reasons or even reasons of State, cannot prevail against a bond so natural and so sacred, from the moment its formation is consummated.

What we have just been enumerating are the essential claims, the natural law of human love. This natural law, now that our bodies have become members of Christ and that our race has been elevated by grace, becomes more urgent and more rigorous. There is question of respecting in ourselves, no longer merely humanity, but Divinity, and of keeping ourselves pure through respect for the Word that has become flesh.

But, even without this elevation to the supernatural state, even if God had in no way revealed to us His will, this law would have been enjoined on us by our nature itself and by God who created our nature. To infringe it would have been evil in itself, intrinsically evil.

Alongside this law which admits neither exemption, nor excuse, nor lightness of matter, there are other prescriptions, less rigorous, against which one can sin without falling gravely.

They are necessitated by the prudence which the concupiscence within us postulates. We add a few words about them.

Because of the close union which exists, in these matters, between certain excitations and evil desires, it happens that some actions, without being in themselves provocative of evil, do arouse the passions. To seek for such actions: readings, spectacles, company, imaginations, etc., with the purpose of bringing on the evil in itself, is, of course, grave.

But, often, the attitude of the will is undecided. One allows himself to go along with an ambiguous emotion, with a disturbing excitation, poorly defined, unwholesome, but not appearing clearly as "evil." To act in this way, to do these actions without proportionate reason, is an imprudence and culpable, gravely or lightly, according to the danger run.

Such imprudences often constitute a lack of sincerity with oneself and a culpable and affected effort to obscure the conscience.

Qui facit veritatem, venit ad lucem. Limpidity and clearness are necessary in these matters. Nothing is so unhealthy, absurd, exhausting for the heart and harmful to psychological health, as the vague desire consented to of a satisfaction which one pretends to refuse. The integral and rigorous observation of all the requirements of purity is the only one which can be easy: it is the only one which corresponds truly to the nature of man and of love. Anything else is walking on a slippery slope, trickery by which one warps one's most intimate sentiments, a source of weakness and of softness, of fatigue and of neurasthenia.

These requirements of purity are hard. But let no one be cruel enough to beat down any of them.

There is question of one of the foundations which support the entire moral edifice: of respect for humanity in what is most essential to it. "Turn not against itself that love which is the source of humanity and which is one of the most powerful energies of your personality"; the Sixth Commandment says nothing else.

It is hard to be a rational animal and to direct one's body by one's soul even to the depths of one's being, even to the point where the will engages itself in the organism. A man must labor and bleed in order to purify and to spiritualise slowly those shadowy regions where the past of our species and of ourselves has allowed too many evil roots to sink in.

But our dignity as men and as Christians, the dignity of our bodies, thinking reeds, of our bodies become by Baptism temples of God, briefly, our moral value, both natural and supernatural, is worth the cost.

For this long and dolorous effort, a rigorous stimulant is necessary. This stimulant is the natural law, which we have just been studying.

Please, let no one blunt this indispensable needle; let no one be guilty of that insult to humanity, of that theft, which the lowering of its principles to the level of its weaknesses would be. To break in the soul the spring which makes it rise, is to make it poor of what is best in it: of that which ought to make it better.

Indulgence for persons, yes. We cannot see into the souls

of other men, we cannot judge the real gravity of falls of which we know only the outside.

Indulgence especially—and veneration—for the souls of good will who carry on without ever despairing an obstinate struggle against difficulties ever reborn. It is by their combats that, little by little, in human love, the angel takes empire over the beast. Let them only never be discouraged; let them not tire of taking up arms again and again! God alone knows whether it is their falls or their resistance that most truly characterises their moral attitude. We can and we should dare to say, it seems to us: in cases like this, it is the good which triumphs over the evil: for, after all, the good proceeds from moral factors: the grace of God and human courage: while the evil is the effect of weakness and, in large part, of certain psychological determinants, of habits and of temperament. This does not mean, of course, that the falls are not culpable, and that one can retire from the struggle; it means, on the contrary, that the very intensity and loyalty of the struggle can warrant a presumption against the gravity of the faults—and that, against faults perhaps grave and very rarely, if ever, exempt from culpability, it is of obligation to struggle ardently.

The principle is always the same: in pity for human weakness we must make starkly clear the requirements of the natural law. They are perfectly adapted to our resources and to our needs.

But, in the name of God! let our fight be made without fear, without anguish or panic. The foundation of Chastity is not terror, but respect and love.

Fright is like connivance: it contains an admission of weakness and it is a manner of thinking of these things. But it is their total exclusion which we must try to secure;

we must not think at all of what we cannot do: interior complicities too easily awaken. In these matters, it has been said, it is by flight that one carries off the victory. True certainly, but there is flight and flight, and to flee by dreaming of the temptation, were it to curse it, is to entertain it by preoccupying oneself with it. Flight, here, is diversion; it is the counter-attack; it is the clear reaction, but calm, even joyous; it is absorbing oneself as totally as possible in something else; it is the effort to make for one's self a disposition of soul altogether opposed, devoted, generous, optimistic, charitable. But once more: to have all its energies, chastity must have all its stature: to be practised easily, it must be practised totally.

II

After this eulogy of marriage and of love, we may now show that one can renounce both the one and the other without descending to a lower plane, but, on the contrary, in order to rise to higher level.

It is a dogma. The Council of Trent has defined it: "If anyone declares that the conjugal state ought to be preferred to the state of virginity or of celibacy, and that it is not better and more blessed (*melius ac beatius*) to remain in virginity and celibacy than to be joined in marriage, let him be anathema." [4]

It is important to place this Conciliar Canon clearly in evidence at the beginning of this section.

There remains the theological labor of rendering the truth which it teaches as intelligible as possible.

We may begin with a truism: it is not because it makes us renounce what is good in marriage, that continence is

[4] Denz. 980.

good. One would have to be totally lacking in Christian sense and unaware even of the true notion of things, to place the excellence of chastity, as Schopenhauer does, in a drowsiness of the "will to live." Apathy and indifference do not have, of themselves, the decided force which is essential to virtue.

If chastity were only that, if it were only a restriction, it would be a diminution; more precisely: if chastity were not of charity, it would be sterility.

It is charity which gives to perfect chastity its adequate reason for being and its total explanation.

So it would seem proper to begin this part of our study by a eulogy of charity, as we opened the first part by a eulogy of conjugal love.

However, we shall not do so, especially since we have treated of this virtue in a preceding study.

In the state of pure nature, as we would have known God only in the mirror of creatures, we would not have been able to love Him efficaciously except through them. As a general rule, it would have been in our opinion at least, in the conjugal life that we would have loved God in His creatures in the most ardent way and in the way best suited to our nature. It is in that life that we would have found most of the stimulants to generosity and to forgetfulness of self. This love, like the other activities of man, would have been measured by the natural being of man. But, it is in marriage that the being of man, in the natural state, would have been realised at the maximum. It is then in marriage that we would, ordinarily, have loved God at the maximum. Celibacy, in spite of the advantages which it offers for intellectual contemplation and for the practice of good works, would often have lacked stimulants human enough to be very efficacious. It would then have constituted in principle an exception, praiseworthy indeed, but it could not have been the object of a counsel universally proposed.

But, in the supernatural state, God does not remain inaccessible; He Himself places Himself within the range of our love by charity; man, through charity, can love God, not according to the measure of his human forces merely, but with a divine ardor.

The conclusion is evident. The exercise of charity, once it is rendered possible for us, takes precedence over all else, and we can do no better than renounce all other loves to vow ourselves more completely to her.

Human love was beautiful, certainly. It becomes even more beautiful when, in Christian marriage, charity perfects it. But pure charity, the life consecrated entirely to divine love, is more beautiful still.

The married man, as Saint Paul says so well, *divisus est*. He is pulled about in different directions; concupiscence still rules him strongly, and all the energies which human love places in action in so absorbing a manner, even when they are rightly ordered and are holy, are easily distracted from a movement which could have gone towards God much more directly and much more strongly.

This does not mean, of course, that marriage renders the perfect exercise of charity impossible: the example of too many saints shows the contrary. It only renders it, of itself, more difficult. So, as a general rule, for Christian perfection chastity is of counsel.

He who practices it, by suppressing what would have divided or encumbered the movement of his soul, renders his will more one, more simple and so more energetic. Loving with a unique love the one thing necessary, he should succeed, through the attitude which he assumes, not merely in lessening concupiscence more and more, but also in mortifying in himself the lower appetites, or rather, in spiritualising them, by absorbing them progressively into a supernatural tendency.

So a man arrives at the government of himself; or rather, according to the Scriptures, so the Kingdom of God is established in souls. Men become like the angels: *erunt sicut angeli Dei;* they become like to their Father in heaven: *prima virginum Trinitas.*

And, as a result, men will be only the more "human." For Chastity, the most divine of loves, is also the most human. We cannot, as Christians, love God with a love which we would refuse to our brothers, because men and God are inseparable in Christ.

In Christ. Still and always He. Everywhere, in Christianity, Christ is the explanation of the life which He gives to His own and of the virtues which He demands of them. Is it not proper that He who is the first principle in the line of supernatural being, should be the first principle also in the line of the intelligibility of the supernatural, that is to say in Theology?

In Christ, humanity has received, with an elevation of being, an achievement of unity. There is no longer, in the sight of God, that is to say, in the substance of things, any separation between Jews and Gentiles, between Greeks and barbarians, between men and women; a unity of grace has taken up our entire race in a unique and divine life, and all of us together, in Christ, form only one, one only body, one only living being and, as the Scripture says, one only Christ all in all.

This unity is, indeed, entirely supernatural; but God who established it to divinise our nature, has adapted it perfectly to our nature.

So marriage, inasmuch as the fecund unity of our race is sketched out in it, is no longer more than a figure of this supernatural unity. *Sacramentum hoc magnum est, ego autem dico in Christo et in Ecclesia.* It was the act of the species; behold, it has now become, as such, a sign and a symbol of grace. In itself, in the case of baptised persons it includes a relation to and requires a union with a thing which surpasses it absolutely; without which it would have been complete, but which it cannot, by essence, do without from the moment when it is offered to it—we mean the unity which binds Christ to the Church.

So the divine Goodness has lifted it up from its own level: it was the cause of man; the divine goodness has made it also a cause of grace, and has changed into charity the love which constituted it.

But, what we must now emphasize is that, because of this elevation marriage maintains its grandeur, inasmuch as it is unity and inasmuch as it is love, through a unity and a love which surpass it. It holds then, within itself something which ought to suggest doing more than marriage can and yet along the same line: along the line of love towards humanity.

Conjugal love is, by necessity of its natural law, very limited in its object. It is also, as a general rule, very much hampered by concupiscence in its intensity.

The exclusive love of Christ, but of the whole Christ God and man, Head and members, Saviour and faithful, is infinitely more one, more detached from the stupefying effects of self-seeking; it is then more energetic in its movement. It is besides totally universal in its object.

On the other hand, that which differentiates these two loves and which constitutes the excellence beyond comparison of the second, renders the two hardly compatible.

It remains then to choose. It remains, if one wishes to love humanity to the greatest possible extent, to renounce marriage, at least in the majority of cases. And behold perfect chastity counselled by love, and by love for humanity.

But, it must be repeated again, if one renounces marriage, it is not because he dreads the sacrifices and devotedness which it requires. It is, on the contrary, because of the services and the labors which it prevents.

He who vows Chastity does not extinguish human tenderness in himself. He will love, but differently, with a love freed to the maximum of covetousness, disengaged from personal seeking and from sensualist calculations. He will love, but with a love ardent and large; with a love which, to be always ready to serve all men, renounces even the sweetest and the most sacred of bonds from the moment that they prevent him from living for all in a Catholic devotion. Considering in man, not the rational animal which he is by nature, but what God has made him by grace, he will see in his neighbor the child of God, the member of Christ, the member of the same body. And he will see him as, at the same time, very close to himself, *proximus,* and very exalted. His love will be very respectful, worshipful almost, very human and divine at the same time, chaste love.

And chastity, love stronger than love, will give fathers and mothers to those who no longer have them. It will surround with solicitude and with tenderness the miseries of the sick and the decrepitude of the aged.

It will cause young Christian men and women, in a passionate unrest about the lot of their brothers, to go off to suffer and to die in tropical forests or the ice of the Pole, following the Good Shepherd in the search for souls.

It will dream of giving itself even unto death and, jealous of being indissoluble like conjugal love, it will take away from itself by vow the right of taking itself back.

Through it the poor will have perpetual servants; the tiny little ones and adolescents will have educators vowed to their formation; the mass of humanity: Christians, sinners, pagans, all will possess intercessors whom they will be able to use and to abuse, and whose austerities, whose cold nights of prayer, whose sufferings, labors and life will be theirs, will be for them.

When chastity and conjugal love are compared, the more desperately human love is chastity.

Does it not tend even to absorb the other? Will the day never come when it will be given to all to understand "the word which all, now, do not understand," the *expedit non nubere?* Is our race destined for so magnificent an end? Will our holy history have the most splendid, and, from the supernatural point of view, the most intelligible of coronations? God alone knows. God alone is good enough, patient enough too, and especially, strong enough, to bring about such miracles.

In the meantime, the word of God, like a ferment, makes the dough rise and the Church repeats to successive generations the divine proposition of a love more intense, more divine and more human, that is to say, more Christian.

More Christian, yes. Let us return to the word one last time, for it is the last word.

Perfect chastity, like all the perfect virtues, is, essentially, an attitude which Christ inspires in His members and of which the last explanation is in Him. It expresses a manner of being human but divinely, a manner of being a child of God, of which He alone is the source, who is the only Son and the unique Man-God.

The perfect virtues are mysterious like the Christian life of which they are the most adequate expression.

One alone can make them understood, as far as supernatural things can be understood here below; He who alone is able to inspire them. To know how good Christian chastity is, one must have received from Christ the love which comes from Him and which justifies it. *Si quis amat, novit quid haec vox clamet.*

It is the strength, the joy and the glory of those who have vowed their entire lives to Christ, that is to say, to God and to men, that they are, like Christ, consecrated, body and soul. They are given, they are handed over, and it is their state to be able to wear themselves out in serving all their brothers all their days. They follow the Lamb whithersoever He goeth, to pain, to redemption, and to God.

To redemption: it must not be forgotten that the Christian life comes forth perpetually from death. To live it intensely, to spread it widely, it is necessary to follow a way which is a way of mortification and of death. If marriage is holy, it is because it also is a sacrifice: the sacrifice of pure individualism and of pure egoism. But, in the genus sacrifice, there is something better, evidently; there is a more total forgetfulness of everything which is delight and sweetness.

It is Chastity which realises this more complete sacrifice.

That aspect of things is extremely important: that aspect of mortification, of abnegation, which is essential in Christianity. We do not insist on it further however, because we wish, in these pages, to show what expansion, what life, what higher life is implied in it. And is it not by meditating on this higher life—in Him who communicated it and at what a cost!—that one will most generously dedicate himself to all that it demands of labor and of struggle against self?

It is only too true that, in man, even in regenerate man, concupiscence endures and pushes him towards sin.[5] It must be combated by entering into the dolorous battle which Christ has won in plenitude and which, from this plenitude, must be won in the members of Christ.

But, precisely, and it is on this point that we wish to insist, chastity is a union with the sacrifice of Jesus Christ, and this sacrifice was for Christ the supreme victory and supreme love: it was then that He finally communicated Himself to humanity to take up humanity in Himself and to vivify it through union with Him.

Such is, in Christ, chastity and the death which it implies. It is life, it gives birth. Its offspring are born to the life divine. But it is all humanity which it causes to be reborn. The renunciation which it requires is total, but its purpose is to effect, in the totality of Christ, the total resurrection.

No life supports its man as that life does.

It must be taken as it is.

Things conserve themselves and grow through the causes which have engendered them. As charity is chastity's reason for being, it is also its strength and safeguard.

Against morbid introspection, against enervating melancholy, against preoccupations about well-being or pleasure, in brief, against all the relaxations of soul which prepare falls, the great remedy is charity, that is to say, the ardent love of God, especially where He exists for us, in the

[5] Denz. 792.

Eucharist, in our souls, and in the duties of our state—and the ardent love of our neighbor.

No little tendernesses ridiculous and limited; but towards all a wideawake solicitude and the appetite to serve: nothing breaks the egocentric movement of concupiscence like the generous explosion of charity.

Prudence, yes, certainly; mortification, sincerity with oneself, yes; all this is indispensable. But true prudence consists in replacing what one wishes to suppress; nothing mortifies the evil like the application of its contrary, and the freest tactic is the offensive.

It is one and the same love, one and the same charity which constitutes the grandeur of marriage, which necessitates the rigorous requirements of purity, which suggests, as a means of perfection, perfect chastity—and which gives men strength and joy enough to rule their conduct in accordance with these principles and these precepts.

All is linked up in the Christian moral teaching.

Everything in it is essentially positive; we have been able to see that. In all that concerns the Sixth Commandment, there is question only of respecting human dignity, which God has made great and which Christ has made still greater.

Christianity in its entirety is before all else positive and it is love of the good. The perfect Christian life, and the counsels of perfection more even than the precepts, are not in the first place renunciations, but preferences. *Finis legis est charitas.*

That is why the practice of chastity which is enjoined on every man during the long years which precede marriage, is so useful for marriage itself; one might almost say: so necessary. It teaches a man to possess himself in order to be able sincerely to give himself, not to have an inconstant soul, to have the strength to be answerable for the word which he will pledge on the day when he will promise to have only one love.

That is why, even in marriage, a certain reserve and a real mortification are necessary. On condition of being joyously consented to by both parties, they are too conformed to human nature and to the economy of the supernatural, not to be, in conjugal love, a principle of energy and duration.

That is why finally the practice of the counsels is an excellent preparation for those who are to form Christians to the observance of the precepts. The vow of chastity, especially, in teaching them what charity is as a stimulant of life, has this advantage among others, that it gives to the ensemble of the faithful, in matters which concern purity, educators who are suited to it.

So are we led back to the thoughts by which we began this study. The state of chastity has a social and ecclesiastical bearing.

It is a concrete protest against the exaggerated search for pleasure, against all the sacrilegious distortions which seek to make of love a mere personal satisfaction. It is destined to recall to men the grandeur of marriage, of marriage which God has made so holy that the Church dares to seal it by giving to the spouses the Bread of Angels.

But let those who practice it, practice it as it is: as a state of Charity greater and higher, because it is more detached. So will they be able to inspire in those entrusted to their care a very beautiful idea of marriage and of love, because they will have one finer still.

CHAPTER XI

Authority, Obedience

A multitude not reduced to unity is confusion; unity not dependent on the multitude is tyranny.

Pascal, Pensées, éd. Brunschvigg, No. 871

THE problem of authority and the problem of obedience have their place in Politics as they have in Moral Science, and their position is more sharply defined in our day than ever before. But, if they have a prominent place in public life, it is because they are especially important in the interior life, in consciences.

So it is there especially that they should be studied.

In these pages, we desire to see how it is the very foundation of the life of each individual which demands authority and obedience, and how, in consequence, far from being a hindrance to personal life, they are the condition for its full unfolding. Only so do they show themselves in their true light and with all their charm.

The first two studies, this and the following one, will inquire into the matter from the point of view of natural moral teaching, without excluding supernatural considerations, of course, since it is at them that we wish to arrive. They will seek out the reasons why the very nature of man demands authority and obedience, and what sort of authority and obedience it demands. The third study will consider the question from the supernatural point of view, and it will put to itself the question: what is the reason for the existence of religious obedience and what is the spirit in which it should be practiced. The two first studies, to tell the truth, do not of themselves enter into the subject matter of the present volume, but they are the introduction to the third, which has a prominent place in it, and, in fact, the three form only one complete study.

We shall begin by examining what authority is, and what is its necessity and its function.

THE PRINCIPLE OF AUTHORITY

First the principle.

The principle of all reality, of all Moral Science and of all Politics, is God.

Created by Him, existing in our entirety and always only through Him, we should not will except through Him. Dependence in relation to the Being through whom everything exists is our manner of existing. God is then the supreme norm of good and of evil, the regulator of liberties and the first authority.

THE NATURAL LAW

Let us come now to civil and political authority, the only one of which there will be question in these pages.

We are dealing here with natural law, that is to say, God directs us in this matter, not by positive revelation but through our nature.

Our nature is not merely the ensemble of our essential constituents; it is also the indication of the mode of conduct which is suitable to us. In making us men, God says to us equivalently, by the very being which He confers on us, that He wishes to see us act like men. As the winged seeds of the maple have in their structure the reason for the spirals which they trace in falling, so our nature bears, in its very construction, if we may so put it, the law of its procedures.

This law which our nature is for us by God's design, is the natural law. This law is more adapted to us than any other, since it forms one body with our substance; it is more inevitable, since we carry it with us; it is sacred and obligatory above all others, since it comes to us in our being and through our being from the Infinite Being.

SOCIETY

But Civil Society is imposed on us by the natural law.

God has made us social animals. He has fashioned us in such a way that we do not enter into life except through a society: the family; in such a way also that we cannot lead fully our intellectual and moral life, or even our animal life, except with the aid of our fellows. What would we be without that which we hold from the generations which have preceded us and from our contemporaries?

Hence, the law dictated to us by our nature and by the God who made it, is that we should integrate ourselves into the society of men.

But what is the society of men?

The reply cannot present any difficulty: it is the totality of the human race.

However, humanity is too imperfect and too far removed as yet from the formation which it can attain to unify itself perfectly. A well-constituted society which groups all men does not exist in fact. Is it even possible? States are the only things of this kind which exist. These are then the actual expression of the social aspect of human nature.

They impose themselves on our will through the very thing which makes us sociable, that is to say, through our nature and so by command of God.

The veritable and clear-seeing love of humanity renders obligatory the service and the love of country, that is to say, patriotism. On the other hand, true patriotism, the reasonable love of country, should include love for humanity in general, and, consequently, in a certain measure, the love of other countries.

Those who, under pretext of preaching love for humanity in general, attack patriotism, sin then against the very love which they owe to humanity. And on the other hand, those who, through an exaggerated love for their country, come to despise or to regard with indifference or hostility neighboring nations, go counter to the reasonable love of their own country. This exaggerated and exclusive patriotism, often called nationalism, is only an egoism, national egoism; it is vile and dangerous like all egoisms. It is, in the international order, the principle of war and the origin of ruin; it is, in each State, the principle of divisions, of social and regional antagonisms, of rebellions and of sabotage of the public interest; briefly, the cause of collapse; so true is it that the will does not go counter to its natural law without going counter to itself.

CIVIL AUTHORITY

But there is no society without unity, and there is no unity in society without authority. In consequence, civil authority is imposed on us by the natural law which imposes society on us. That is what we are going to explain.

Society is nothing other than a union of men. It includes then essentially a unity and a multiplicity: the multiplicity is the members, the crowd of associated persons; the unity is the co-operation of all towards a single end by the same means; society is the combination of the two, the unity of the multiplicity.

This unity is not, by itself, a concrete reality in flesh and blood. It is only an element of the complete whole which an assembly of men is; it is, as the Scholastics say, its form, or, as the moderns say, it is its "soul," the "collective soul." Its rôle in society is comparable to that of the vital principle in a plant; it is the principle of union, of co-operation, of concord; it supposes, in order to exist, the elements of which it is the bond, and it resides, not in itself, but in the associates as associates.

But it cannot reside only there. As long as it consists only in a spiritual union between wills, it remains imperceptible, and, in practice, it is useless. To unite men efficaciously, the unity must be visible and tangible; and to maintain cohesion, it must be incarnated in a stable and strong organism, capable of expressing and of imposing on all the collective good, unity.

A society of flesh and blood men, whose cohesion was not maintained by a flesh and blood unity, would be scarcely more united than a flight of real birds enclosed in a spiritual cage.

There are in every society as many elements of discord as there are members, for each one comes into it with the obtuse and obstinate narrowness of his own egoism. Conflicts, misunderstandings, universal carelessness will soon cause complete disintegration, if a very concrete institution, one or many men, and well armed too, does not take in hand the cause of unity.[1]

Especially is this true in the case of States, those complex societies whose organism is at once so immense and so

[1] St. Thomas, S.T. I^{a}, Qu. XCVI, art. 4.c.

delicate and whose stability is so necessary and yet so vulnerable. The existence of such an institution is a matter of life and death.

This institution is the government; its right is authority; its function is to incarnate the unity of the group, and so to defend this group inasmuch as it is one, against itself as multiple.

Authority is here revealed exactly as it is: as imposed on us, not by arbitrary decree, but by the very Providence which created us and in the very act by which we were created. Required by the nature of society, which, itself, is required by our nature as God made it, authority, we can say, is imposed on us by God through our nature; *omnis auctoritas Deo.*

There is no need of invoking a primitive social contract or a positive consent of the subjects to justify its empire. Those are superficial views. The requirement of authority is more profound in us than our acts are: it rises from the root of our acts: from our nature; it comes from an even more remote source: from God who is the principle of our nature and of our being.

Because of this divine origin, because of the intermediary, our nature, through which they are imposed on us, authority, and hence, obedience, are not merely entirely adapted to our being; they are required by it. We caricature them by comparing them to yokes and to iron collars falling heavily from above and crushing liberty. They are an aid, a light, a force demanded by our conscience and by our being, which was made to be incomplete without them.

THE ESSENCE OF AUTHORITY

Authority in general can be defined: a right to command in conscience. Political authority, in particular, is a right—

and a duty—to impose on the consciences of the citizens the common good. It must then, in order to be authority, express to us what our consciences ought to express to us, and our consciences inasmuch as we are social beings, that is to say, it must express the general interest.

The chief does not then act according to his essence except by proclaiming, not his own good pleasure, but the collective good. That he should so arrange things as to find his advantage in national prosperity, is excellent. But before all else, let him empty himself of himself and forget his private interests in order to become a public person and in order to lend his voice and his fist to unity. It is his essential function.

Certainly, in a society of men, purely spiritual forces do not suffice to maintain order. Just as the human soul is not separated from the body, the right of commanding in conscience cannot endure without the right of physical constraint—it is imperative under pain of death for society. The suppression of prisons would be Utopia and a crime against the natural law and against the individual, just as the radical and immediate suppression of all armed forces would be an assault, not merely on the security of the country, but on international peace. The means of coercion are required by our nature.

But our nature wishes that they be in the background. The soul takes precedence over the body; in the moral conduct of men, moral forces have a right to the first place; the less frequently the means of constraint are required, the better for all concerned. Otherwise, disorder will be installed under the pretext of defending order.

THE WILL TO OBEY

To re-enforce authority, the first essential is to strengthen its grip on the consciences of men through the education of their consciences. If an increase in physical constraints is not accompanied, in the subjects, by a growth in the will to obey, it can provoke only a disturbance of equilibrium—and collapse.

The true problems in Moral Science, and hence also in Politics, are moral: they are posited and are resolved primarily in the conscience. To better the political régime, the will to obey must be formed.

And since the will, by nature, is made to obey, to develop it along its own line ought to suffice to render it more voluntarily dependent on legitimate authority. Obedience to authority is then a condition *sine qua non,* not solely of public order, but also of the intense exercise of personal will and of personal liberty.

Let no one ever say then that the restoration of authority requires the curtailment of liberty: this would be to declare that there is a radical opposition between the two, such that nothing can be given to the one which is not taken from the other.

Such a principle is properly the revolutionary principle: it makes the State rest on an essential antagonism: internal struggles will be only the expression of the profound hostility which was at its base.

But it is a lying principle. Authority is that by which society exists, and hence, that by which the social being, and the liberty of this social being, are possible. Liberty then, as it grows, and if it grows properly, cannot help contributing to the increase of authority.

THE FORM OF GOVERNMENT

The nature of society requires the existence of authority; but it does not determine in a necessary manner the form which this authority should assume; many political régimes are possible in Moral Science. All that can be said is that, given the nature of society, every form of government, in order to incarnate the social unity, ought to constitute *unity,* and the unity of the people, of the *multiplicity*. A type of government which existed without unity, or which did not incarnate the unity of the people, of the multiplicity, would not be a veritable authority.

In the first place, authority without unity is not authority. Power cannot reside in the amorphous multitude of individuals. Pure demagogy, anarchy, is not a political régime. Is it even a possibility? Universal suffrage conceived—or rather caricatured—as the simple voice of the multitude, as the sum of the egoistic views of individuals, cannot be the sovereign authority in a State: it is not even a semblance of authority.

On the other hand, power which would be only unity, which would have no relation to the multitude of subjects, would not be the unity of a multiplicity. Unity, yes; unity of multiplicity, no. It cannot be authority. Absolute despotism does not constitute a political régime.

These two extremes—unity without anything more, pure multiplicity—show the two excesses which authority ought to avoid in order to remain authority.

If we now ask ourselves what is the perfect government, the answer is not hard. The best government is the one which offers as much unity as possible; but this unity is not any unity at all: it must be a unity which is as far as possible the unity of the multiplicity, the unity of the nation.

The ideal evidently would be that it should be fully one, entirely concentrated in the hands of only one man, of an immortal man, with the purpose of securing the common good. *Unitas plurium debet esse ab uno*. And at the same time, to be truly the unity of the mass, he ought to hold the entire mass within himself, to identify himself entirely with it: to be truly the unity of the people, he ought to be the people itself, the people inasmuch as it is one.

Utopian ideal, evidently. A man cannot be present to the interior of others to unify them in his unity. There is only the Man-God, Our Lord Jesus Christ who, in the order of grace, contains in Himself, in a certain manner, all the faithful, as members of His Mystical Body. Besides, in this Body, that is to say in the Church, the unity and the authority are of another order, and are perfect in a way different from that found in Civil Society. But of this supernatural society and of this supernatural unity we shall treat in another study: we are here considering only Civil Society. In this we cannot discover a unity at once perfectly one and perfectly united to the crowd. We must then conclude that the perfect authority and the perfect government, like the perfect man, do not exist.

Is this to say that we must put aside all reflections about the ideal government? On the contrary, we must think about it, not to attain it, but to tend towards it. The best government will be the one which will approach the closest to perfection, which will combine the maximum of unity and the maximum of union with the people. Men have elaborated many of these combinations. From royalty under all its forms to the republic under all its modalities, the types of government which have existed and those of which no one has yet dreamed are indefinite in number. All are good if they are adapted to peoples and to circumstances, and if they express in the best possible way the unity of the nation.

FORMATION OF THE GOVERNMENT

In any given people the determination of the type of government and of the subject of authority depends on a great number of factors.

The process is not the same in States as it is in the Church, where God Himself has revealed the mode of government and, up to a certain point, the subject of authority. In Civil Society God does not guide men by direct revelation but by their reason and by a multitude of secondary causes.

These causes are all the agencies which, in collaboration with the free activity of men, concur at the same time in the formation of societies and in the establishment of authority in these societies. Authority and society are born together. They must be: they are too united for one to be produced without the other. Can a union exist without that which constitutes its unity, or can this unity be effected without the union of which it is the expression?

Civil authority is fashioned by the same causes that mould human groupings. These causes are as diverse and as numerous as they can possibly be. Of the physical and geographical phenomena, a landslide, a flood, a fertile plain, a river, a chain of mountains, strongly influence the constitution of primitive societies, and, through these, the societies which prolong them. Psychological causes, like the resemblance of language, of character, of history, the community of traditions, of education and of race, are operative too, and in different manners bring men together. To these must be added the treaties, the free agreements, between private individuals and between societies and the action of the more outstanding personalities. All these causes and many others work actively on the birth and the transformation of societies. It may be questioned if there is a single law of nature which cannot and which, in fact, does not intervene, were it only remotely and to an infinitesimal degree, in this complex fact of the genesis of human groupings.

These same causes preside at the birth of authority. The most fortuitous events, like a happy choice of the right site for a cabin, the presence of a tribe at the fork of a river, or of a family on a hill easy to defend, the long life of a series of able individuals in the same line of descent, in a word, all the causes which act on men, that is to say, all the laws of nature, while they form human groupings, at the same time indicate for them their centre and fix the subject of their unity. From the combination of all these innumerable, often imponderable, generally unsuspected actions, society is born, and with it, its unity and authority.

God alone knows all the factors which have acted on the formation of peoples and of empires and of nations; for on Him alone they all depend. Very few of them depend on men. What can we do about it, if a well-spring is in a certain place and forms a centre, if a certain desert is a natural frontier, if a certain man died too young to become the chief? All this depends on laws of whose existence we are scarcely aware and whose action we can with difficulty discover. Man assists, often unaware, ignorant, powerless, at the labor which brings forth States.

Besides, the people will never be the unique agent of their formation; they will never dispose absolutely of themselves; no régime can be exactly what a nation desires; no system of election will perfectly express the will of the society. Man's effort is to this extent in vain; he will never act alone in the constitution of States; his action is linked to the action of nature: willingly or unwillingly, he will suffer the counter-blows of cosmic events.

Man has an influence certainly, and sometimes rather a strong influence on the beginnings or on the destinies of Civil Society and he should compel himself to be ever more active in these matters and especially to improve the character of his action. That is his responsibility, and each one according to his powers will be answerable for his action.

But the great artisan, in these matters, is not man; it is God. It is God who, through man and through natural forces, outlines the political map of peoples when He plans the geography of the globe.

HOW AUTHORITY GROWS

All that authority needs in order to grow, is to operate according to its nature, that is to say, to serve the common good.

In the case of the head of government, let the individual be in some sort absorbed and let him disappear in his function. This virile and courageous self-effacement will confer on him a prestige and a force which no military might can give: it will secure for him a moral grandeur and a moral superiority. Becoming, in an intense and visible manner, a public person, he will lift himself up, by his very service, above narrow individualisms, above individuals. His voice will have a more majestic ring than other voices: it will be the great voice of the nation, it will be the voice of our social nature, the voice of God Himself who imposes society on us. It will therefore be also the voice of the moral conscience of the citizens. Its decisions, then, will be strong, much stronger than the good-pleasures of any

Roi-Soleil, strong with the social claims of all our being, strong with the will of God.

The true grandeur of the head of government is not his own. He is only a "representative" of God, representative of the obligatory unity of the State. In this sense, civil authority is representative, essentially representative. Not that there should necessarily be representatives in the actual sense of the word and a parliament, but because the very nature of authority is to be a function, the function which serves to express to the group the unity of the group.

To serve, yes. Authority is a service, but a magnificent service. It consists, not in flattering individual caprices, but in making the nation do what its nature and its conscience require of it. It will use force, if necessary, and vigorously; but always with a sovereign respect, because its purpose will not be to lower others before itself, but to establish in them the reign of their conscience and of their God.

Then too, even when the head of government resists misguided opinion and when he forces the nation to hard and necessary sacrifices, there will be nothing of the despot about him. He merely serves, but as a courageous and loyal servant.

The duty of the nation is not to protest, but to follow. And it will follow, for it will see clearly that the chief, in spite of his severity, or rather, through his severity, does not pretend to compel performance simply of what he wishes, but of what the nation itself truly wishes, inasmuch as it is a nation, and not a conflict of egoisms.

In visibly "serving" the common good, the chief gives an example of obedience in the way proper to him, and besides, he makes clearly apparent to the eyes of all what it is that justifies and requires obedience: the common good demanded by nature and by God. So does he show authority as it is, as an enforcement of obedience.

FORMATION OF CHIEFS

Chiefs are not then formed by developing individualism and independence. Too zealous censure of the established régime is a dangerous school of politics: it risks teaching insubordination rather than respect for authority, which is treated as in *anima vili.*

It is some help, but really very little, for one who aspires to be chief, to have a clear head, an inflexible character and powerful muscles. These form a well-built individual, but they are not enough to give us the man in whose words a people can hear and follow the voice of its own conscience.

To command is a public function. A man prepares for it by freeing himself—at least a little—from narrow egoism, from too selfish preoccupations and from the conceit which often accompany them. He who does not so fear the responsibilities of power that he trembles at the thought of them, is so little prepared to govern that he is ignorant even of what authority is.

When the soul has thus been purified, it must be still further refined, so that it will be able to understand the interests of others, to shudder at the sorrows of the nation and to thrill to the veritable aspirations of the mass.

He who does not love does not understand and acts very little. In the formation of a chief, the first essential is to frame a will ardently devoted to the common good, capable of sacrificing its time, its labors and its popularity for the great interests of all.

Reflection on these matters always leads back to the same point. Forgetfulness of self, abnegation, and love of the neighbor—in other words, humility and charity, those two great virtues of the Gospel, are, in chiefs as well as in subjects, the foundation of the Christian city. Nothing is as necessary as they are to those who take, as they should, with respect, with anguish, the crushing burden of directing those whom God has made their equals and whom Christ has made their brothers and His own.

"Sweet and humble of heart," "to love one another," "to desire, not to be ministered unto, but to serve," these words of the Saviour are at the same time the program of true authority and the chart of truly moral obedience. Even for the political life of men, the Master, the unique Master is Christ, the King of Kings.

In the first place, the formation of consciences; in the first place, virtue; in the first place, charity especially.

COUNTERFEITS OF AUTHORITY

It has been said: *Divide et impera.* The formula has seemed wise. It is only absurd or criminal. *Divide et impera* is a simple contradiction. *Imperare,* in the sense of governing, means essentially to unite: authority expresses the unity of the group; by suppressing unity it destroys itself. Authority lends reality to the collective soul: by annihilating the collective soul, it kills itself.

The formula *Divide et impera* becomes coherent only by giving another meaning to *imperare*. *Imperare* can mean to force oneself on others as the strongest, to compel them to do one's own will, however different their interest or their aspirations may be. Evidently, to command in this way, the crowd must be prevented from organising and from uniting. Then, yes: *Divide et impera.* Keep the people divided, nourish rivalries and misunderstandings; otherwise, if it unites, if it becomes aware of its interest and of its strength, it will rise up against you.

The formula has become coherent in our day, but it is

criminal. The concept of authority to which it gives expression is contrary to the natural law. Authority holds its power from its function, and this function is to unify. The people obey, because authority expresses their collective good and their general interests. If authority makes use of its eminent place to cause division and to destroy the unity of the people, that is to say, the nation as a nation, it goes, by an abuse of force and an abuse of confidence, contrary to its very essence. And if revolt occurs, it will itself have caused it by ceasing to be authority.

This concept (contrary to the natural law) of authority, enters in part into some notions of authority which we are going to examine—not, we repeat, for the sake of erudition or of polemics, but to make our point of view precise, by comparison with others.

There is first "property-authority." It may appear convenient to consider authority as similar to the holding of private property. Authority, one will then say, is like a situation, a place, a privileged place, in society—a place empty of itself. This sort of arm-chair, this unoccupied good, becomes the property of the first occupant capable of filling it.

This comparison between authority and private property is useful for explaining certain points of law. But every comparison limps. Authority in fact—like society, like man—is not susceptible of appropriation in the strict sense of the word. One never has the right to make use of it according to his fancy like a commodity. It is not of private domain, but of public order; a function, a social function, it does not appear in its true light unless it is considered, not as an individual possession, but as a thing of society, as a reality *sui generis*.

More specious is the concept of "egoism-authority." Here the supreme power is considered, no longer as private property, but as the exploit of an egoism which is, however, still private. This concept might be explained in the following way: authority is constituted on the day when an individual finds that he is strong enough and skilful enough to force the others to work for his advantage; on that day, authority is born of the egoism of this man and rests between his hands. It is perpetuated there, as long as he has a whip strong enough and a head clear enough to constrain the others to serve him. Besides, in the long run, experience teaches the servants that being forced to work is an advantage for them, and the master takes into account the fact that it is to his interest to keep his men well-nourished. Everyone—how beautiful it all is—is satisfied with exploitation, including the exploited.

Little by little, from this still defective society, a more perfect régime emerges: monarchy for example. This would be, essentially, the coincidence between the egoism of an individual—the king—and the common good, the strength and wealth of the nation. This coincidence would even make the monarchical régime the best régime.

This history of authority, whether it is actually proposed by anyone or not, is an insult to authority; not because it is totally false, but because it is lamentably incomplete, and because it cheapens the rôle of authority. Authority is essentially a public thing, and its majesty consists in the fact that it formulates, not the good of an individual, but the good of all. In comparing it to an egoism like the others, one despoils it of its veritable prestige.

There is perpetual competition, declared or latent, between each egoism and the other egoisms. Because of its narrowness, an individual interest is opposed to the others, it is a principle of conflict. The same thing will be true of the interest of the monarch in the State. If it is an egoism like the others, it will enter into conflict with all the others. His advantage will be to re-enforce his own power, while weakening the conscious cohesion of the nation. At least until he realizes that his true interest is to constitute the unity of the people and to serve as centre, as expression of this unity. That would be perfect: but then his power would cease to be an egoism and become a function.

As long as power is represented as an egoism, it opposes the other egoisms which the nation contains. It opposes also the egoisms which, according to this way of looking at things, other nations are. When all nations are regarded as princely egoisms, they are considered as being virtually always in competition.

With interior dissensions and exterior hostilities, menacing rivalries are on every hand in the domain of egoism. In presenting order in terms of egoism, one formulates only disorder.

In another order of ideas, a third concept of authority might be proposed, which we shall here call "influence-authority." This concept would consist in thinking that authority is only a certain prestige. There are, incontestably, men endowed with the gift of commanding and who, naturally, act as chiefs and are followed.

This innate superiority, quite certainly, is a precious gift in the man who has the duty of leading others. But by itself alone it does not constitute authority any more than the gesture of an orator establishes the logical value of his discourse. It is a force; it can be used well or badly. One who would utilise it to exalt himself while reducing others to subjection, would be only an ignoble exploiter of the weaknesses of others. The force which could have sustained society, raised it up, trained it, he uses to burden society with his full weight.

This is plain: there are ways of conceiving authority which, if they are not completed, are ways of denying it. The same thing is true in other matters. In what concerns the right of private property, for example, there are owners who, without their being in the least aware of it, are its great adversaries: they are the rich egoists and monopolists who, neglecting their social duties, make this right appear, contrarily to its essence, as an obstacle to the common good. In the same way, there are zealots for public order who are promoters of trouble: they are the men who present this order as a veritable disorder, as a simple privilege of certain individuals.

On the one hand and the other, those who act in this way can give themselves the air of defending principles; they often defend only personal advantage or acquired position; in any case, as far as principles are concerned, they bring them into disrepute. Not only do they take away from them what gave them their strength by constituting their transcendence, but also, in making of them the ramparts of their interests, they compel them to descend to the level of conflicts.

Authority, since that is what we are interested in, finds its force in something which is exactly the contrary of a privilege, that is to say, in a service, and the service of the multitude, but of this multitude inasmuch as it is one. In the Christian city, writes Saint Augustine, each one wishes only to serve all the others in charity: the chiefs by their solicitudes and the subjects by their submission, *in hac serviunt invicem in charitate, et praepositi consulendo, et subditi obtemperando.*[2]

[2] De Civitate Dei, XIV, 28, P.L., XLI, 436.

CHAPTER XII

The Obedience of Children and of Citizens

OBEDIENCE, to be moral, should perfect the will. But nothing is as essential to the will as willing is. Obedience then to be moral, should not merely cause the will to choose correctly, but also and especially, it should cause it to choose strongly.

But, from one point of view at least, obedience consists in a restriction of the act of willing: it means yielding a place, and the best place, in this act to the will of another. We are thinking here of the obedience which the natural law requires and of obedience to men. To obey, we know well enough, is essentially to place the will of another at the origin of our decisions, and to will, not what we ourselves decide, not what we wish of ourselves, but what is imposed on us by this other. So considered, obedience is an act of will which restrains itself.

But, it cannot be anything like that if, as we have said, obedience is a perfecting. On the contrary, the restriction which it implies, if it is real, must be only partial and must be compensated for by an increase.

Hence, from the point of view at which we are placing ourselves, to justify obedience and its restriction, we must inquire whether our act of willing demands an increase, and an increase which is obedience with its apparent renunciations.

So put, the problem is carried to the will itself. We must examine the nature of the will in order to discover in it the manner of willing and of obeying which is imposed on it.

It is, as we know, in the nature of things that moral philosophy seeks the norm of our duties. In the natural order, in fact, our nature is the only manifestation which God makes to us of His will and of our obligations. The manner of being which He imposes on us is, at the same time, an order which He intimates to us. Since our nature comes from God, the insufficiencies and the requirements of our nature come from God also, and they make us aware of His requirements. Inevitable as they are for us, inasmuch as they are the very voice of our being, they are absolute, obligatory, moral in a word, inasmuch as they emanate, like our being and in our being, from God.

But, to return from these reflections to obedience, we ask ourselves what its place is in this natural morality. If our duty is assigned to us by our nature and measured by the forces of our will, what reason can we have for directing ourselves by or for leaning on the will of another? No one is held except to what is possible to him. And who cannot, by himself alone, accomplish what is possible to him?

However, the answer is, "No one can." The thing may seem paradoxical, but it is certain. No man, by himself alone, can do either all that is possible to him or all his duty. This does not mean that the natural law of man does not correspond exactly to the nature of man. It means that no man, by himself alone, possesses the complete human nature. And in fact every man, during the long years of infancy, remains incomplete as an individual. Every man, also, during all his life, remains incomplete from the social point of view. There is a double insufficiency placed in us by our nature itself, which prevents us from acting as we ought by ourselves alone. There is then also a double requirement to lean on and to rule ourselves by the wills of others, if we are to act properly. This double requirement, which forms a unit with our being, comes to us, like our being, from God, and it is a duty for us, a duty which God decrees for us by our being, to accept it, it and the dependence which it places in us. All this, we repeat, comes from God, *omnis auctoritas a Deo.*

THE OBEDIENCE OF CHILDREN

A. *The reason for its existence.*

Let us consider first the case of children—and the family obedience which is imposed on them.

"The child," it has been said, "is not a man; he is becoming one." Paradox or truism, the formula expresses in every case a very exact truth: the child is a being incompletely realised and he should continue to be born for a long time. He is then made to receive perpetual complements from outside himself. Also, his little stomach itself is in a perpetual state of appetition, because there is an entire body to construct and materials are needed. His intelligence too is all curiosity and docility: there is an entire *tabula rasa* to be filled in. The child feels that he is indigent of knowledge and incapable of acquiring it personally; he is then made, by nature, to believe his parents and to accept from their knowledge what is lacking to his own. The same thing is true of his will. Psychologically speaking, it is all receptivity, flexibility, in need of leaning on a stronger will. The child perceives that he is weak, inconstant, feeble even in his obstinacy, and that he lacks solidity in his decisions, as he lacks it in his cartilage. To obey is natural and instinctive to him, so much so that we remark his little revolts and are astonished at them, as we would be astonished at finding in an adult the submission of a child. This psychological disposition discloses the nature of things. The being of the child is, for the child, a demand for growth, and for growth not merely in body but also in the faculties of the soul and in the will. It is then, for the child, a requirement, and a requirement which, like his nature, comes to him from God, and which claims for him, in the name of God, what is necessary to his growth, that is, to lean on and to rule himself by the will of another, to obey.

No more than he is made to grow alone, is a child made to will alone. Family authority is as necessary for him as food is. His maximum of voluntary expansion is attained in the warm atmosphere of the fireside; in the educative influence of paternal authority; his being itself requires obedience as it requires growth: to obey, for him, is to grow.

B. *Its end.*

As is very evident, this situation is not intended to last indefinitely. There comes a time when it no longer has any reason for existing; the child has become a man; he can, in his turn, be the father of a family and even serve as support for his aged parents. He sees as clearly, he wishes as strongly as they—more strongly even: there is no longer any reason why he should obey them.

So the moralists are in accord in declaring that, at the period of majority, obedience ceases to be a duty; the parents retain only their influence, a superior position as natural counsellors—and a perpetual right to respect, to love and to assistance.

C. *Its crisis.*

The moment of transition is the difficult one. For there is a transition. It is only in the Code that majority begins abruptly at twenty-one years. In reality, much before that age, the child becomes little by little capable of governing himself alone, and, even after that age, he remains thoughtless and destitute of experience.

Also it is only by a juridical fiction that the strict authority of the parents, total up to majority, becomes nul the following day. In reality, and in order to be adapted to the natural law which constitutes their value, authority and obedience ought to be adapted to the development of the child and to grow less in the measure that he grows. Their rôle is to prepare for their suppression, by education.

Then too, it is a psychological error in the father of a family to wish to retain, total and unchanged to the very end, the power over his young folks which he exercised when they were little tots. If he succeeds in the effort, it will only be by prolonging to that extent the childhood of his sons and by thwarting that education which is the reason for the existence of obedience.

There is error and egoism in this abuse of force. The father is the strongest: he holds the purse, he can even appeal to the courts. But, in requiring from his grown boys a docility which no longer has any reason for existence, he demands more than his right and he sets in motion terrible reactions. We know what the young people become at the university on the day when this embarrassing guardianship disappears. They are not alone in their responsibility for their indecencies. The fathers of families ought to understand and we should tell them: they compromise the future by clinging to the past. The worst fault in education is neglecting to teach the children to walk alone, because, finally, they will have to walk alone anyhow.

In the measure in which the child is capable of it, the paternal authority ought to prepare for the day when, inevitably, it will disappear. In the measure in which the child is capable of it, the submission which is demanded of him should be justified. For the tiny tots the justification consists entirely in the tenderness of the parents and in their devotion. Those who replace the parents, masters and educators, will justify their authority by their abnegation and their goodness. The child, all sentiment and all imagination, does not as yet claim any other justification. But that he must have; his nature as a human being requires it, and, without something paternal, the discipline of the college or of the house, not being conformed to the nature of things, cannot give a moral formation: it trains and it debases without educating.

When the children grow up, their developing intelligence claims a reasonable and reasoned obedience. It is certainly not necessary, before they are entirely developed, to discuss matters with them on a basis of equality. They are still bound to obey even without understanding. But preparation must be made for the moment, which comes so quickly, when they will be men. It will be necessary then at times, and more and more frequently, to explain to them the reason why obedience is required, and so to enable them to bring up their own children later on.

By so doing, authority does not abdicate its position; it merely refuses to be a kind of violence opposed to the nature of things; and, in acting conformably to its essence, it augments both its moral value and its hold on the child. He will never take it for a strait-jacket, if it grows with him as he grows, if it makes him grow. And his first care, on the day of his final formation, will not be to shake off the yoke, but to make use of the support for a long time to come.

Parents, by bringing up their children properly, that is

to say, by dealing with them as they actually are, will so completely win their confidence, that they will be able to continue to "bring them up" for a long time.

Let us conclude: obedience, because it is a virtue, is educative; the submission which it demands "lifts up."

THE OBEDIENCE OF CITIZENS

A. *The reason for its existence.*

In virtue of his social being, man is incomplete without society. There are numerous goods which he cannot acquire, numerous acts of willing which he cannot accomplish except in union with the organized ensemble of his fellows. Man is no more made to will alone than he is made to live alone.

But, as we have already explained, a society of men cannot exist or be prolonged without a visible, firmly established organism. The very formation of a society too, since it terminates in the setting-up of a unified moral being, establishes necessarily a co-ordination of members, an ensemble of attachments about a central point. Towards this point flow, by the very nature of things, as towards the heart or the head, the various items of information about the collective life, and it alone is competent to express the needs of the ensemble. To it then, to this organism of unity, it belongs to give the formulas for social co-operation, that is to say, the laws; and the individual wills, since they are made to co-operate, to will together, are made to obey it.

Civil laws, for the conscience of citizens as citizens, correspond to a void and to an appeal, just as paternal orders do for the conscience of the child as a child. It is impossible for this conscience, through lack of sufficient information and of prestige, to know, to pursue and to cause others to pursue unanimously the common good, and nevertheless, inasmuch as by nature it forms a part of a society, it must proclaim and must command this good—behold the void. It is then essential for it to try to get some voice to proclaim it efficaciously in its place—behold the appeal.

So, when authority promulgates the law, it does nothing else but state what the conscience was already proclaiming, but in blank merely, in indigence, in effort. So its word, in virtue of what the conscience is, is in principle, the voice of the conscience and the voice of God who made the conscience.

When then we say that laws oblige in conscience, we do not mean that they penetrate into it by breaking in, but that they come forth from it by a sort of making explicit; that they come forth from it, assuredly, as a formula imposed from the exterior, but also as a revelation demanded by the interior.

The primary force of civil authority is not constraint exercised from without, otherwise it would be one of those violent things which do not endure; it imposes duties in virtue of the natural law, and the constraint which it exercises, and without which it would not even exist, is in the very first place a moral constraint, that is to say, conformed to the nature of the will.

Of course, man is not an immaterial will, and the right to constrain inherent in authority should have, like man, a corporal aspect. Police and prisons are necessary; and they will be necessary as long as man remains material and imperfect, that is to say, always. It would be Utopia and a crime to suppress physical coercion. But it would be folly to see in it the principal force of authority. The essential thing in moral science is the interior.

Obedience is not terror nor passive inertia. It is the free acceptance of a duty in conscience.

This does not mean, of course, that authority is not

legitimate until it has been, in fact, consented to by the people, nor that obedience is dependent upon a sort of agreement, of a social contract entered into by the nation and its chief. Obedience, like society, like authority, comes from the nature of things; it has no use for our manipulations. God imposes it on us as he orders us to be men, and the creation of the supreme power is no more our affair than the creation of our nature is.

But, precisely because they are imposed by our nature and by God, authority and obedience are necessarily conformed to our nature. The study of our being is enough to let us know that it *ought* to "consent to" authority, and that it ought to obey; and it would also suffice to establish that a power is directing us in a direction clearly and continually opposed to our nature, to establish by this sign that it is no longer authority and that it is no longer the representative of God. *Injusta lex non est lex.*

B. *Its purpose.*

In the State, as in the family, the rôle and the reason for the existence of authority is to raise up.

An authority careful exclusively of holding itself aloof and of prolonging the minority of individuals and of peoples would bring itself into disrepute and would present to the nation false credentials for its right to command.

This does not mean, evidently, that authority ought to throw off all prestige: it requires prestige to be effective and to give better service.

But this means that its principal prestige should be the evidence of its character as collective unity and as organic function. Obedience does not in any way demand an act of faith in the personal excellence of those in power, as if they were made of more precious matter. But it ought to aspire to being an actuation—individual in the case of family obedience, social in the case which occupies us, of civic obedience—of the private will, and an actuation obligatorily demanded by this private will. Its function is to infuse into the citizen the spirit of the ensemble, preoccupation with the whole, briefly, a mentality similar to that of the governors.

It is then a ruling soul which it forms in inferiors, by its own virtue and by the force of things.

Let us explain. Obedience does not consist in installing oneself as master and in arrogating power to oneself. It tends, not to suppress the distinctions between governors and governed, but to diminish the distances between them. The process is not the same, in fact, in the State as in the family. In the family, the child will one day become as developed, as much a man as his father, and obedience, in him, will no longer have any reason for existing. In civil society, on the contrary, the citizens, taken individually, however informed we may suppose them to be about the social necessities, will never become, by identity, the organism which incarnates the collective unity: the multiplicity, as multiplicity, cannot be its own unity. Between governors and governed, the distinction can vary in modality and in degree, but it is indestructible. What ought to diminish between the two is separation. In order that the society may be one, in order that the authority may be strong, in order that the obedience may be legitimately proud, it is necessary that obedience, as it forms more and more the social and national spirit, permit the subjects to do, in submitting to the laws, nothing but their own will—not their egoist or individual will, but their educated will of social beings, persuaded of their social exigencies and of their social obligations and rendered concerned about the conditions of their union.

C. *Its crisis.*

There are moments, in the life of peoples as in that of individuals, when obedience becomes more difficult. These are the moments of crisis and of transition. In the life of the individual, this moment, we have seen, is the one in which, as majority is approaching, he can normally continue to support only an authority which is being transformed into influence. In the life of peoples, these are all the epochs when, as the social soul is forming more rapidly, the need of an authority more in contact with the aspirations of the unity which it incarnates makes itself more clearly felt.

The peoples live, in fact, and it must even be stated, saving surly pessimism, that they are approaching—oh! very slowly, and through many vicissitudes—the adult state. The repeated experience of the reverses of individualism train the social sense little by little, and the increasing multiplicity of the means of communication forms and makes explicit, in the long run, a group mentality, a collective soul.

Under pain of becoming scanty and awkward and of ripping like an old garment of infancy on the body of an adolescent, obedience ought to adapt itself to the age of nations as well as to that of individuals. A mode of government, perfect yesterday, can be no longer supportable today, because the past is a gain for the present, not a vice. Also, to remark it in passing, a sliding, in one direction or the other, of a political constitution is not necessarily an alarming index of instability. The whole thing is to see if it comes from a lack of solidity, or from a possibility of flexibility and of adaptation to the changing conditions of the national life.

Formidable forces are working on humanity: vital forces, intellectual forces, moral forces. As it approaches more and more closely to its majority—which is, however, inaccessible, as we have seen—humanity requires more and more clearly to tend towards its end in a conscious and deliberate manner. In epochs of more intense fermentation, these claims become more living and more pressing. Society realises, inevitably, that it has changed, and that the obedience which is suited to its stage—the only one, therefore, which is suited to its natural law—is no longer the candid submission of a child. It wishes to follow the common good in a more deliberate, more personal, and, hence, more moral and better way, and nothing is more just than this claim.

A power so ill-informed as not to take account of these realities can succeed assuredly in blocking, for some years, the course of the torrent. But the torrent will not halt forever, and if, on the day when it leaps the dikes, its rush is the more furious, will it be its fault?

The essential rôle of power is to conduct, not to stop, and the rôle of obedience is to co-operate with the educative function of authority. That is not too much co-operation between the two for the crossing of the dangerous pass in times of crises. Each will make its own contribution, but the end, on the one side and on the other, will be the same: the formation, especially the moral formation, of the ensemble of citizens to the social and political point of view. There is the tranquillity of order—there veritable social peace is found.

CONCLUSION

Such is obedience when we consider it in the very thing which renders it obligatory in us, and which also justifies it. It is not properly a passivity set up in the will, but, on the contrary, the reception of an "educative" activity; far from being a yoke which crushes, it is the very increase of our moral being, inasmuch as this ought to come from outside ourselves. God, who imposes it through our nature, has made it conformed to our nature and capable of realizing our nature.

These conclusions are not valid except for obedience considered in the natural state. In the supernatural state, everything is better still.

CHAPTER XIII

Religious Obedience

THE SUPERNATURAL ORDER

The elevation of humanity to the supernatural state, as it has established on the earth a new manner of being, has at the same time established a new manner of willing and of obeying.

The true reality here below is no longer the diversity of nationalities and of social conditions; it is Christ one in all. God, by a new creation, gives a new life, and this life, since it is His own, can come only from Him. So too the prolongation of this life and the increases which it demands, can come only from Him.

The Father is always at work here below building up the Body of His Son. From the first beginnings of time until the end of the ages, He follows, through all history, one unique design: to give to the Only-Begotten the plenitude of His Body and to the Incarnation its last and mystical prolongations.

Whatever does not contribute to this unique work is nothingness and waste. Whatever does not descend from the Head to its members is useless for life.

It is all over then with our pretended self-sufficiency. How shall we still find wherewith to glorify ourselves in ourselves? As members, we do not exist, except "in prolongation," and the source of all supernatural activity, of all salutary thought, of every decision truly good, is in Him in whom all has been given to us—in order that He may be, in all things, first.

OBEDIENCE IN THE SUPERNATURAL ORDER

Operari sequitur esse. The act of willing, in the supernatural order, ought to be modeled on the supernatural life from which it emanates: that life is received; the act then ought also to be received. In order properly to express our manner of being, it ought to come to us from without, from Christ. This means that it does not develop except in dependence and that it is, essentially, obedience.

And, in fact, what are we concerned with in the state of grace? Simply with placing acts humanly good, conformed to Rational Ethics? God forbid! Once we are become, in name and in fact, sons of God in His only Son, we ought to be perfect as our heavenly Father is perfect. No other model is worthy of our elevation. As a child is the living definition of his father, as—with due proportion—the Word is the image and the expression of the substance of God, so should we be holy as the Lord is holy. The sentiments which it is right for us to feel should be the reproduction of those which the Saviour felt, and our charity ought to be the image of his. As the natural law requires that a man live like a man, the law of grace requires that a Christian live in Christ.

Infinite requirement, in some sort, it must be agreed, and unrealisable by our energies.

How shall we know, dull rational animals, *quae placita sunt ei?* How, if no one tells us? And how shall our unsteady will succeed in walking as Jesus Christ has walked? How, if it remains alone?

It must either fall back powerless, or unite itself to a superior will, one that is stronger, capable of divine things —to the will of the Man-God. Without the light of Christ to direct our intelligence, without the force of Christ to sustain our wills, we are the most pitiable of creatures.

And this is readily understood. Members as we are of Christ, our being, as we have said, is "in prolongation" of our chief, as the body is in continuation, in λπήρωμα, of the head. Our willing then, and our knowing, are also "in prolongation." Their full realisation, their activity, their orientation—their power too, their omnipotence almost—are possible only "in prolongation," and not in independence. First principle and prime mover in the supernatural order, Christ ought to be, in His own, the origin of all things, and the most perfect, the most personal acts of willing, will be those which, in themselves, come the most completely from him.

It should be carefully considered, this attitude of "those of Christ." Οἱ τοῦ Χριστοῦ, those of Christ, those whose supernatural being is in Jesus before being in themselves, are not, thank God, complete wholes. No division in Christ! The branch lives by the opening through which it drinks the sap of the root; the member lives by its insertion in the body; we, Christians, live and act by our bond, by our implantation in Christ.

Our act of willing is no more a complete whole than our grace is: it does not have its beginning in itself; it lives by the blood which it draws from a divine heart, from a heart which beats more ardently than ours, and whether we live, decide, or act, *Christi sumus,* all our being is of Christ.

This incompletion of our individual willing, this vital attachment, this practice of taking our direction and our strength from a divine will, is as essential to us as respiration.

And it is obedience.

Obedience is the supernatural manner of acting.

PERFECT OBEDIENCE

The more intense the supernatural life becomes, the more perfect obedience will wish to be. Obedience has then its degrees, as the fervor of the Christian life has.

There is first the minimum degree of obedience, required of all Christians: all, in order to be saved, must obey the Commandments of Christ and of the Church. It is a defined dogma: "Christ has been given to us not merely as a Redeemer in whom we may have confidence, but also as a legislator whom we must obey." The Council of Trent has inserted this definition in the midst of its canons on justification and grace.[1] And, in fact, the relations between grace and obedience are close. The obligation of obeying Christ and those who continue Him is only the expression, in the matter of our conduct, of that dependence on the Saviour which places sanctifying grace in the very substance of our soul and of our will. This same necessity is also only the expression, in terms of asceticism, of what the Conciliar definitions say about actual grace in terms of doctrine. All these points of our religion are connected, and all formulate, from different points of view, the relation to Christ which makes us Christians. The supernatural act of willing ought to be attached to Christ, such is the general truth; and the applications follow: it should be attached to Christ, and by an elevation of its substance: so we have sanctifying grace—and by the help of excitation, of illumination, of aid: so we have actual grace—and by the decision, in our

[1] Denz. 831.

free will, to be ruled in our acts by Christ and by those who represent Him. And that is obedience. We do not sin against obedience without sinning against grace.

But if one wishes to live his Christian life with more intensity, three things will be necessary: that he be animated by a more elevated habitual grace, that he be sustained by more powerful actual helps, and that he practice a more complete obedience. There is then, corresponding to the perfect life, which is of counsel, a perfect obedience, which is of counsel also.

Let us explain this perfect obedience. Strictly obligatory obedience is far from covering all our conduct. Even when the Precepts of the Church and of Christ are added to the Commandments of God and the Natural Law, there remain many, and relatively important actions, about which nothing is ordained. Shall we perform them as we like? Or shall we not try to be directed by Christ in these also?

For those who seek Christian perfection, the answer is not doubtful. In our plans of conduct, as long as they are only the discovery of our reason, there is a presumption of insufficiency. To act perfectly as Christians, we must, in all our acts and in an assured manner, follow, not our own mind, but the "mind of Christ." To act in all things as the children of God, we must always and in certitude, be led by the Spirit of adoption.

The aspiration of the will of a Christian then, inevitably tends towards a kind of life in which all its actions will present themselves, in a clear manner, as ruled by God. *Voluntas parendi cupida.*

This direction, saving perpetual miracles, cannot be an interior leading of grace, just as, to follow it, simple docility to grace does not suffice. Man's soul is not silent enough nor docile enough to hear always clearly the prudent whispers of the divine invitations; there is too much disturbance in his heart for all the supernatural indices to be distinctly perceived there. Perpetual lightning flashes, perpetual tumults, do not suit our psychology nor the tranquillity of the divine plan. God, who has assumed our nature, who sanctifies our nature, does not wish to make it crack under reiterated and abrupt interventions of His grace. All the rest of the redeeming plan teaches us that God directs man by human ways; He has saved him by a man: the Man-God; He continues to lead him by men: the ecclesiastical magisterium.

If there is a means of knowing always the will of God and of uniting ourselves always to His activity, it is probably a human voice which will tell us of it. That, at least, is what we should expect from the manner in which God has fashioned our psychology and also from the manner in which He has disposed the economy of salvation.

There is then what may be called a postulate of Christian perfection: that is, there is something which those who wish to be totally "of Christ" inevitably desire: a state of life in which Christ, by men (i.e. by the means most adapted to us—and to Him, we might add)—may say to us always what He desires of us.

To this interior fact an exterior fact corresponds. The Church has approved the religious state and religious obedience. She allows, she recommends, that men should make a vow, under conditions which she determines, to obey other men. These superiors, she herself appoints, she herself controls them, she herself forms and instructs them by the rules which she approves and which she alone imposes, by the supervision which she exercises, by the appeals which she authorizes and which at times she even enjoins.

But the Church is nothing other than the authentic Body of Christ. He who hears Her, hears Him, and Her approbation is, in all reality, that of the Saviour.

This approbation is not a purely juridical phenomenon nor an accidental directive to be added to the ecclesiastical precepts. It is a reply to an appeal. Christ has heard the language of our will, the aspiration to obey, to obey always and entirely, which is, in His members inasmuch as they are His members, the very act of willing. *Et fiat tibi sicut vis.*

Or rather, no. Our will has not spoken first. The first, in all, is Christ. It is He who, making for Himself members among the nations, wishes to unite them to His work and to employ them very actively where His mysterious operation proceeds most energetically. It is He who, having decided to unite them fully for the edification of His Body and to do His works through them, gives them the inspiration to be members and to act as members,—*sicut baculus in manu senis,* or rather, *sicut membrum in corpore Christi.*

Author and finisher of our good desires as of everything else, it is He who has made perfect obedience for Christians and Christians for perfect obedience, in order that, He in us and we in Him, we may be all-powerful in Him who makes us strong.

OTHER JUSTIFICATIONS OF OBEDIENCE

Obedience, being an attitude essential to the Christian life, justifies itself by its suitability to all the aspects of the Christian life.

If it is true to say that the perfect Christian life is a holocaust, total Obedience will justify itself by the complete sacrifice which it constitutes. The obedient man keeps nothing for himself: he gives with his will all his acts, and, with all his acts, all his goods. He becomes perfectly Christian by delivering Himself entirely to Christ.

And if the Christian life is a consecration, it can be said to the glory of Obedience, that this is the total consecration: it empties man entirely of himself in order to fill him with the divine will.

And if the Christian life, coming from Calvary and from the death of Christ, is a mortification, we can say that it requires total obedience for its maximum of intensity. By obedience, in fact, man deprives himself of his dearest good, and no effort, no victory over himself, is more complete than this abnegation of willing.

But mortification, as is entirely evident, can be, in any life, only a secondary aspect, because it is transitory. Christian mortification—and the Christian life—is, before all else, a vivification. And this vivification also, to attain its fulness, demands obedience. Obedience, in fact, is the incorporation of our will in the work and in the will of Christ. He who obeys does not lose his will, he finds it again, in Christ, animated with new energies, supported by the Immovable, pressed on by the Irresistible.

The Christian life consists, before all else, in receiving. Its most characteristic act—its Sacrament—is Holy Communion. Communion is our supernatural sacramental food and without it our supernatural life would quickly grow faint. Like our life in general, our will, in the supernatural order, has need of nourishment, and its nourishment is, as was that of Christ, to do the will of the Father, *meus cibus est ut faciam voluntatem Patris,* to obey. Perpetual obedience is, in a mystical, not sacramental, fashion, our daily bread. Through it, under the cover of actions which are ordinary, but commanded in the name of Christ, the very will of God takes possession more and more of ours and transforms us unto His image from day to day by the Spirit of the Lord.

Christianity, let us say it again, was announced by the angels of the Nativity as a peace, the peace of Christ descending here below. From this point of view too, total obedience is perfectly Christian. Nothing expresses the peace of the Saviour like the cloisters where men obey. To obey is pacifying, to obey removes the difficulties and the hesitations of willing, to obey gives the serene assurance that one wishes with God and that one will then never be confounded.

But to conclude these justifications, we must energetically assure ourselves that the peace of Christ, the peace of Obedience, has no element of drowsiness or of renunciation of willing. It is a caricature of the religious life to represent it as a sweet Nirvana in which, before its time, the silent tranquillity of graveyards reigns.

It was not by sleeping that Christ obeyed His Father; it is not by holding back that one unites himself to the will of the Saviour, the universal salvific will. The Christian life is activity; it is ardent, generous, obstinately solicitous about the salvation of one's brothers and about the glory of God. Obedience, which is the perfection of the Christian life, is the height of this activity, since it is communion with the operation of God and of Christ. It is Obedience which must make the missionaries and the Little Sisters of the Poor; it is Obedience which attaches the religious, soldiers of Jesus Christ, to their life of charity and toil.

CONSEQUENCES

To obey then is to love; to obey then is to unite oneself; to obey then is to realise oneself fully; to obey then is to act. The attitude, as you see, is complex and rich in its simplicity. We shall examine some aspects of it, in order to understand it better.

To obey is to will more strongly than one's own will can, because it is to will with God. If men, marching shoulder to shoulder, become bold at the contact with their fellows, what will be the courage of the will when it realises that God Himself is its light and its force? It wishes, and God wishes with it and in it. What can the entire creation do to arrest the Creator? A man can go on with spirit: heaven and earth pass and give way, but not God. Intrepidity, joy in work, confidence go along of themselves when one co-operates with God, the All-Mighty. So the truly obedient men are not little timid fellows, malleable and deformable at will, but bulky and determined characters. Francis Xavier, a type of obedient man, is the perfect image of these conquerors whom nothing disconcerts and who go across the earth like a plough-share.

To obey is not to accept orders passively, but to make our own the indications of conduct given us. The thing ought to be clearly expressed, because it is a characteristic of true obedience. To obey is essentially to unite one's voluntary activity to the activity of God and of Christ, indicated by human intermediaries. To obey is then to act: how could one be in communion with the Pure Act in a state of inertia? The truly obedient man does not receive orders with indifference, but with love, because he loves and because he seeks with ardor the will of God. And this not merely in the case of each separate order, but with regard to the ensemble of orders as well; it is the general direction of Christian activities which interests him: he must be about the things of his Father in all his entirety. That is to say, that one cannot, if one wishes to obey well, be unconcerned about the seasonableness of the commands which one receives, or indifferent about the general direction of the group, leaving this to superiors. All our human nature, its spontaneity, intelligence, practical spirit, all ought to be sanctified and utilised in our co-operation with the work of Christ and in Obedience. Obedience is not intended to suppress and to numb all this, but to animate it with a new life and hence to animate it with new energies. Through Obedience then we must inform superiors, or appeal even, when orders apparently ill-advised are given. It is not for nothing that the Church has established the right of appeal and that the rules of religious Institutes provide for representations to be made by inferiors. These are not concessions to human weakness. They are a mark of the respect which the work of God has for human nature, because this work is essentially a work of exaltation and of respect. God, who wishes us in our entirety, does not begin by mutilating, but by purifying. God, who wishes us to be active, asks us then to unfold ourselves and all our initiative in His service and in dependence on His grace. Our appeals, our requests, our objections even, if the object is worth the trouble of course, are a part of the co-operation which He asks of us and an element of Obedience. One can then, one ought to make them, and to struggle at times against an order, but in a spirit of submission, and in the purest possible desire to see the will of God accomplished. An Obedience which does not re-act can be a sign of coldness in the service of God, and perfection can require that one should not leave to Superiors the second-last word.

But Obedience must always have the last word. For the last foundation of obedience is confidence in Christ who assists His Church, and this act of faith cannot be confounded. Where there is no question of sin, and when due representation has been made, it is better, in every case, to obey. And we must obey without after-thought and without regret consented to, silencing interior recriminations. God has spoken, He must have the last word.

It is a question of principles, not of persons. Superiors are not either infallible, or inspired, or even, necessarily at least, very intelligent, or very virtuous. Saint Ignatius, who was well up on Obedience, considers without difficulty and with perfect serenity the case of a superior altogether beneath his task. He concludes that nothing in obedience is changed by that—any more than, to use a comparison imperfect in other respects, the real presence is diminished by the bad quality of the flour used for the hosts.

It can then happen, and it does happen, that orders of superiors, considered according to sound human prudence, are harmful to the perfection of the inferior and to the good of the apostolate. These errors can be totally excusable, for every man can deceive himself, and a good superior more than any other, for, making decisions more often, he runs by that very fact and by duty, more risks of mistakes. The errors can even be culpable, either in the superior himself, or in major superiors who have put an incapable man in authority. In this case, and in proportion to the importance of the interests at stake and to the evidence of error, the duty of inferiors is to notify still higher superiors and to do all in their power to bring about a better direction. But once all the representations have been made, there is nothing left but to obey, and with all one's heart. It is not superiors or men whom we have sworn to obey, but Christ. The moment has come to bear witness that we keep our word and that we believe in God. The Lord is powerful enough and wise enough to make all turn out for our greater good. Such is the great principle and the definitive truth on obedience: we have delivered ourselves to the management of Christ in the manner which He approves. Useless to know any more about it: He will not fail us, and in proportion to our faith and to our love, He will well know how to arrange things so that we shall not come, through obedience, to loving Him less, for having wished, according to His own plan, to love him more.

This is the last and the most beautiful word on Obedience. For those who obey truly, seeking sincerely the will of Christ in all—there is no longer anything but the will of Christ. Their efforts, their representations even, their submission, all this is union with the will of the Saviour, Who saves the world.

To obey, in Christ, is then a kind of dignity. If religious obedience brought in only human considerations, it would quickly become meanness and arrogance in both inferiors and superiors. But when one thinks of Him Whom alone one obeys, one sees that Obedience is an act of worship and that it has no explanation except in one presence. Between superiors and inferiors, at the moment of obedience, Jesus Christ at once rises in some sort, for faith. It is He Who speaks by the superior, it is He Who inserts Himself into the will of the inferior; each can then look upon the other with the same veneration in the Lord: they are leveled, each one in his own manner, in the same love of Christ, Who by men communicates Himself to men in order to render them all like to Him.

So, in the faithful, in the Body of Christ, the Incarnation is going on mystically.

The Incarnation was accomplished in Mary, for us, at a word of obedience: *Fiat mihi secundum verbum tuum.* And the Word was made flesh.

The Incarnation is prolonged in us, through Mary and

through the Church, in the same manner: through Obedience. The rôle of humanity is to accept, to co-operate; it is to unite its action to the will of God and to the work of God, to grace and to the sacraments.

Pater Noster, fiat voluntas tua. The prayer of the Lord, the one which expresses authentically the attitude of the children of adoption, is the prayer of Obedience. And Obedience, as the prayer continues, makes the earth become like heaven and engages the will of God in ours. So do we receive our daily bread; so the divine life is fed and developed in us: he who does the will of God dwells in eternity, and he who observes the Commandments receives in himself the divine Persons, who come to make in him their habitation.

Fiat. The word of Obedience is that of the Annunciation and of the Incarnation, that of the Agony and of the Redemption, that of the supernatural life and of the adoptive filiation.

Fiat, may the will of God be done.

But, to repeat it for the last time, this fiat is not a simple passive abandon to the will of God. "May the will of God be done," yes . . . and let me do it. The will of God is to be loved and served with all our heart, with all our soul, and with all our strength. He wishes all our will without complaints, or thefts, without attenuation or enfeeblement. In order to divinise it in its entirety, He wishes all of it, with all the freshness of its initiative, with all the strain of its effort, with all the hardness of its perseverance. We do not obey except in willing strongly.

Like Poverty and Chastity, Obedience appears, at first sight, pure renunciation.

In fact, it is. The Christian life was born of a sacrifice,

that of the Cross; it is born perpetually of a sacrifice, that of the Mass. The road which is pre-eminently the road of Christian perfection should be a road of sacrifice.

There can be no question, in consequence, of denying or of diminishing the mortifying and the painful elements in these virtues. Christ became for us obedient even unto death; it is unto death also that, for Him and in Him, we must become obedient. Sin is, in the first place, a disobedience to God: to extirpate it from ourselves, we must make obedience enter in, and as deeply as possible.

Obedience is then abnegation and struggle, and, by this title, it is good.

But, precisely because it is good, this abnegation is only the reverse side of an exaltation.

That is what we wished to show in these pages. Obedience, like all the Christian virtues is, in the very first place, a union with God in Christ. It can, at first sight, seem a pure diminution: that is only an outside, which strikes the senses, but which hides the essential. In its depths, it is growth; it is assimilation by the life eternal.

The death which it implies is a death which ends in a resurrection: Christians, as they are crucified with Christ, are, with Him, risen from the dead.

If then one does not obey well except in willing strongly, one does not will strongly, with a force which has all its supernatural energy, except in obeying. So only does one wish entirely as a child of God and as a member, *commembrum,* of all humanity, in Him Who is the Man-God.

Let Christians then, each one according to his state, obey, but as Christians, that is to say, let them will, but with a will which has inflowed into them through their Chief.

Let them be Christians. The formula, here as everywhere

in Moral Science sums up all, in bringing all to the maximum. Let them be Christians, and they will be men as their nature requires them to be, with the perfection which the Word made man has brought into humanity, and they will be like to their Father in heaven, with all the realism which has become possible in this Man, Christ Jesus, who is the Son consubstantial to the Father.

Remarks and Bibliography

It will be readily observed that there are not many notes and references in this book, scarcely more in fact than in the articles which they produce. We wish to point out however, for the benefit of those readers who may be disappointed at not finding more, that our reason is that we have already given an abundance of them in a previous book: Le Corps Mystique du Christ, Études de théologie historique (Museum Lessianum, section théologique, XXVIII et XXIX) 2 vol., 2e édit., Bruxelles, 1936.

In fact, it is especially while making applications to conduct that Scripture and Tradition have spoken about incorporation in Christ. What they have said on this topic is arranged according to subject-matter in the alphabetical table which closes the second of the volumes to which we have just referred. These references are repeated here only rarely; where they do occur, they are indicated by the abbreviation: le Corps mystique, table alphabétique.

(Translator's Note: The above references are given in full in "The Whole Christ," by Emile Mersch, S.J., translated by John R. Kelly, S.J., The Bruce Publishing Company, Milwaukee.)

The studies numbered I, V, VI, VIII, IX, X, XII, XIII correspond to articles which appeared in the Nouvelle Revue Théologique, t. LVI, 1929, pp. 50, 90, 207; t. LVIII, 1931, p. 5; it., p. 97; t. LXII, 1935, p. 225; t. LIX, 1932, p. 97; t. LV, 1928, p. 5; t. LIV, 1927, p. 36; it., p. 54. The fourth study corresponds to an article which appeared in the Revue d'ascetique et de mystique, t. X, 1929, p. 337. The seventh study is taken from a work which appeared in the Participation active des fidèles au culte (Cours et conférences des semaines liturgiques, XI, p. 95, Louvain, 1933). The eleventh study borrows its material from two articles, one of which appeared in the Nouvelle Revue Théologique, t. LIII, 1926, p. 81, the other in the Cité chrétienne, t. I, 1927, p. 393.

The bibliography does not aim at completeness. In the volumes dedicated to the historical theology of the Mystical Body as many references as possible were given. In a book on Morality it would be foolish to attempt to present a bibliography even moderately complete. Those who wished could find the important books listed in works like the Dictionnaire de théologie catholique, de Vacant-Mangenot-Amann; in the Lexikon für Theologie und Kirche, in the bibliographical information of the Vie Spirituelle, Juvisy, of the Revue d'ascétique et de mystique, Toulouse (see especially the Bibliography), of the Zeitschrift für Aszese und Mystik, Innsbruck (consult the Bücher und Aufsätze), in works like those of F. X. Mutz, Christliche Aszetik, 6e éd., Paderborn, 1923, of O. Zimmermann, Lehrbuch der Aszetik, 2nd éd., Fribourg, 1932. Further help will be found in the directions given by J. De Ghellinck, Lectures spirituelles dans les écrits des Pères, Paris, 1935; A. Cayré, A. A., Précis de patrologie, Paris, 1927, 1930; P. Pourrat, la Spiritualité chrétienne, 4 volumes, Paris, 1918-1928; A. Tanquerey, Précis de théologie ascétique et mystique, Paris, 1923, etc.

We mention here only a few works which have a particular interest from the precise point of view taken in these pages.

F. Juergensmeier, *der Mystische Leib Christi als Grundprinzip der Aszetik. Aufbau des religiösen Lebens und Strebens auf dem Corpus Christi mysticum,* 6e éd., Paderborn, 1936. (*The Mystical Body of Christ as the Basic Principle of Religious Life,* London, 1939.)

E. Mura, *le Corps mystique du Christ, sa nature et sa vie divine d'après saint Paul et la théologie, synthèse de théologie dogmatique, ascétique et mystique,* 2 vol., 2e éd., Paris, 1936-1937 (see t. II pp. 188, ss.).

P. Glorieux, *Corps mystique et apostolat,* Paris, 1935 (see especially pp. 81-108 et 45-70).

J. Anger, *la Doctrine du corps mystique de Jésus-Christ,* 4e éd., Paris, 1934 (see pp. 386-428, et 130, ss., 276, ss.).

J. Duperray, *le Christ dans la vie chrétienne d'après saint Paul,* 4e éd., Paris, 1928.

G. Staffelbach, *die Vereinigung mit Christus als Prinzip der Moral bei Paulus* (*Freiburger theologische Studien,* XXXIV), Fribourg, 1932 (bibliographie méthodique).

E. Drinkwelder, O. S. B., *Vollendung in Christus,* Paderborn, 1934 (see pp. 167, ss.).

F. Tillmann, *die Katholische Sittenlehre, die Idee der Nachfolge*

Christi (*Handbuch der katholischen Sittenlehre,* III), Dusseldorf, 1934.

P. PRAT, S. J., *la Théologie de saint Paul,* 2 vol., Paris, t. I, 18e éd., 1930; t. II, 16e éd., 1929 (see especially t. II, pp. 375, ss.). (*The Theology of St. Paul,* London, 1926.)

CUTHBERT, O. S. F. C., *In Christ, a brief Exposition of the Christian Life,* London, 1933.

N. CABASILAS, *la Vie en Jésus-Christ,* trad. S. BROUSSALEUX, Amay-sur-Meuse, s. d.

P. DE BÉRULLE, *Œuvres,* published by F. BOURGOING, 2e éd., Paris, 1657 (see especially pp. 492-734).

C. DE CONDREN, *Recueil de quelques discours et lettres,* Paris, 1643.

J.-J. OLIER, *Œuvres complètes,* published by MIGNE, Paris, 1856.

ID., *Lettres,* published by E. LEVESQUE, 2 vol., Paris, 1935.

H. RAMIÈRE, *l'Apostolat de la Prière,* new edition, Paris, 1861.

ID., *le Cœur de Jésus et la divinisation du chrétien,* Toulouse, 1891.

C. GAY (Mgr.), *la Vie et les vertus chrétiennes,* Paris, 1874.

D.-J. MERCIER (Cardinal), *A mes séminaristes,* 12e ed., Bruxelles, 1913.

ID., *Retraite pastorale,* Bruxelles, 1910.

ID., *la Vie intérieure,* Bruxelles, 1918.

C. MARMION, O. S. B., *le Christ dans ses mystères, conférences spirituelles liturgiques,* 5e éd., Maredsous, 1919. (*Christ In His Mysteries,* St. Louis, 1923.)

ID., *le Christ vie de l'âme, conférences spirituelles,* 12e éd., Maredsous, 1921. (*Christ, The Life of the Soul,* St. Louis, 1935.)

ID., *le Christ idéal du moine, conférences spirituelles sur la vie monastique et religieuse,* 2e éd., Maredsous, 1922. (Christ, the Ideal of the Monk, St. Louis, 1926.)

ID., *Sponsa Verbi, la vierge consacrée au Christ, conférences spirituelles,* 20e éd., Maredsous, 1924. (*Sponsa Verbi, the Virgin Consecrated to Christ,* St. Louis, 1925.)

P. CHARLES, S. J., *la Prière de toutes les heures* (*Museum Lessianum,* section ascétique et mystique, I, VIII, XI), 3 vol. Bruges, 1922-1924. (*Prayer For All Times,* 3 vols. New York, 1925-30.)

A. VONIER, O. S. B., *Christianus,* New York, 1933.

ID., *l'Esprit chrétien,* trad. J. REYMOND, Avignon, 1922.

ID., *la Nouvelle et éternelle Alliance,* trad. L. LAYNÉ, Saint-Brieux, 1932. (The New and Eternal Covenant, London.)

ID., *la Victoire du Christ,* trad. ID., Paris, 1936. (*The Victory of Christ,* New York, 1934.)

R. PLUS, S. J., *Vivre avec Dieu,* Toulouse, 1921. (*Living With God,* London, 1934.)

ID., *Dieu en nous,* Toulouse, 1919. (*God Within Us,* New York, 1935.)

ID., *la Dévotion au Père,* Toulouse, 1929.

ID., *Dans le Christ Jésus,* Toulouse, 1923. (*In Christ Jesus,* London, 1937.)

ID., *le Christ dans nos frères,* Toulouse, 1924. (*Christ In His Brethren,* London, 1937.)

A. RADEMACHER, *das Neue Leben in Christus,* Steyl, 1927.

C. MARTINDALE, S. J., *the Wounds in Christ's Mystical Body,* New York, 1935.

M. GESCHWIND, C. J. et M., *Vivre du Christ,* Paris, 1934.

J. CHARTON, S. M., *Pour vivre le Christ,* Paris, 1925.

ID., *l'Ame transformée au Christ,* Paris, 1934.

J. GRIMAL, S. M., *"C'est le Christ qui vit en moi,"* Lyon, 1936.

D. JORET, O. P., *l'Action de Jésus en chacun de nous,* in *Vie spirituelle,* t. XII, 1925, p. 521.

ID., *l'Ascension de Jésus dans le cœur des siens, Ibid.,* p. 325.

A. TANQUEREY, *le Verbe incarné, source de vie surnaturelle, synthèse doctrinale et pratique, Ibid.,* t. XII, 1926, pp. 377 et 520.

P. VON CHASTONAY, *der Mystische Leib Christi und die Aszese,* in the *Zeitschrift für Aszese und Mystik,* t. XI, 1935, p. 235.

P. L. SCHEITMUELLER, O. F. M., *die Praktische Folgerungen aus der Idee des Corpus Christi mysticum,* in *Seelsorge,* t. XII, 1934, p. 435.

A. MEUNIER, *la Norme de la moralité,* in the *Revue ecclésiastique de Liège,* t. XXVI, 1934-35, p. 43.

D. H. LORD, S. J., *Our Part in the Mystical Body,* St. Louis, 1935.

L. GIRARD, S. M., *La spiritualité du Nouveau Testament et la "petite voie" de l'enfance spirituelle* in the *Études et documents thérésiens,* t. V, 1936, pp. 13, 81, 111.

J. L. JANSEN, C. SS. R., *de Leer van Christus' mystiek lichaam toegepast op de liturgie,* in the *Nederlandsche katholieke stemmen,* t. XXXV, 1935, pp. 111, 144.

F. MUGNIER, *le Sacerdoce du Christ, du prêtre et du chrétien,* in *Christus,* t. IX, 1934, pp. 110, 213, 319.

R. GARRIGOU-LAGRANGE, *le Sacerdoce du Christ,* in *Vie spirituelle,* t. XXXVII, 1933, p. 5.

H. BLEIENSTEIN, *der Heilige Priester,* in the *Zeitschrift für Aszese und Mystik,* t. VIII, 1933, p. 193.

W. STOCKUMS, *das Friestertum,* Fribourg, 1934.

La Participation active des fidèles au culte (*Cours et conférences des semaines liturgiques,* XI), Louvain, 1933.

J. HOHNJEC, *De sacerdotio actionis catholicae,* in *Bogoslovni vestnik,* t. XIII, 1933, p. 32.

E. NIEBECKER, *das Allgemein Priestertum der Glaubigen,* Paderborn, 1936.

B. CAPELLE, *le Chrétien offert avec le Christ,* in *Questions liturgigues et paroissiales,* t. XIX, 1934, p. 299, t. XX, 1935, p. 3.

E. ROLAND, *la Messe, principe d'unité spirituelle* in *Christus,* t. IX, 1934, p. 320.

E. LEROUX, *la Communion eucharistique,* in the *Revue ecclésiastique de Liège,* t. XXVI, 1934-1935, p. 73.

V. HERIS, *Les Fidèles et la messe,* in *Vie spirituelle,* t. XLVII, 1936, p. 113.

J. B. UMBERG, *Gemeinschaftsgebet und Liturgie,* in the *Zeitschrift für Aszese und Mystik,* t. III, 1923, p. 240.

R. PIERRET, *la Prière liturgique,* in *Vie spirituelle,* t. XXXIII, 1932, p. 141.

H. DE CANDOLE, *the Sacraments and the Church. A Study of the Corporate Nature of Christianity,* London, 1935.

A. VAN HOVE, *Kerk, mystiek lichaam van Christus en Katholieke actie,* dans *Ons Geloof,* t. XXII, 1935, p. 49.

P. DABIN, S. J., *l'Apostolat laïque* (*Bibliothèque catholique des sciences religieuses,* XXXIX), 2e éd., Paris, s. d. (voir pp. 202, ss.).

P. GLORIEUX, *l'Action catholique et l'enseignement dogmatique,* dans la *Vie intellectuelle,* t. XXVIII, 1934, pp. 357, 381.

S. TROMP, S. J., *De corpore Christi mystico et actione catholica ad mentem sancti Johannis Chrysostomi,* Rome, 1933.

ID., *Actio catholica in corpore Christi,* Rome, 1936.

H. Hendley, *the Mystical Body of Christ* (*Catholic Truth Society of Ireland*), Dublin, 1934.

P. Mesnard, *l'Action catholique dans la famille,* in *Vie intellectuelle,* t. xxix, 1934, pp. 180, 357.

M. Zundel, *l'Esprit des vœux,* in *Vie spirituelle,* t. xxxvii, 1933, p. 29.

P. Claeys-Bouuaert, *le Principe surnaturel de l'obéissance,* in the *Revue d'ascétique et de mystique,* t. i, 1920, p. 50.